Continuum Studies in Contemporary North American Fiction

Series Editor: Sarah Graham, Lecturer in American Literature, University of Leicester, UK

This series offers up-to-date guides to the recent work of major contemporary North American authors. Written by leading scholars in the field, each book presents a range of original interpretations of three key texts published since 1990, showing how the same novel may be interpreted in a number of different ways. These informative, accessible volumes will appeal to advanced undergraduate and postgraduate students, facilitating discussion and supporting close analysis of the most important contemporary American and Canadian fiction.

Titles in the Series include:

Bret Easton Ellis: American Psycho, Glamorama, Lunar Park
Edited by Naomi Mandel

Cormac McCarthy: All the Pretty Horses, No Country for Old Men, The Road
Edited by Sara Spurgeon

Don DeLillo: Mao II, Underworld, Falling Man
Edited by Stacey Olster

Margaret Atwood: The Robber Bride, The Blind Assassin, Oryx and Crake
Edited by J. Brooks Bouson

Philip Roth: American Pastoral, The Human Stain, The Plot Against America
Edited by Debra Shostak

Toni Morrison: Paradise, Love, A Mercy
Edited by Lucille P. Fultz

LOUISE ERDRICH

Tracks, The Last Report on
the Miracles at Little No Horse,
The Plague of Doves

Edited by Deborah L. Madsen

continuum

Continuum International Publishing Group

The Tower Building
11 York Road
London SE1 7NX

80 Maiden Lane
Suite 704
New York, NY 10038

www.continuumbooks.com

British Library Cataloguing-in-Publication Data
A catalogue record for this book is available from the British Library.

ISBN: 978-1-4411-00979 (paperback)
ISBN: 978-1-4411-10459 (hardcover)

Library of Congress Cataloging-in-Publication Data
A catalog record for this book is available from the Library of Congress.

Typeset by Newgen Imaging Systems Pvt Ltd, Chennai, India
Printed and bound in India

Contents

Series Editor's Introduction

Each study in this series presents ten original essays by recognized subject specialists on the recent fiction of a significant author working in the United States or Canada. The aim of the series is to consider important novels published since 1990 either by established writers or by emerging talents. By setting 1990 as its general boundary, the series indicates its commitment to engaging with genuinely contemporary work, with the result that the series is often able to present the first detailed critical assessment of certain texts.

In respect of authors who have already been recognized as essential to the canon of North American fiction, the series provides experts in their work with the opportunity to consider their latest novels in the dual context of the contemporary era and as part of a long career. For authors who have emerged more recently, the series offers critics the chance to assess the work that has brought authors to prominence, exploring novels that have garnered acclaim both because of their individual merits and because they are exemplary in their creative engagement with a complex period.

Including both American and Canadian authors in the term 'North American' is in no sense reductive: studies of Canadian writers in this series do not treat them as effectively American, and assessment of all the chosen authors in terms of their national and regional identity, as well as their race and ethnicity, gender and sexuality, religion and political affiliation is essential in developing an understanding of each author's particular contribution to the representation of contemporary North American society.

The studies in this series make outstanding new contributions to the analysis of current fiction by presenting critical essays chosen for their originality, insight and skill. Each volume begins with a substantial introduction to the author by the study's editor, which establishes the context for the chapters that will follow through a discussion of essential elements such as the writer's career, characteristic narrative strategies, themes and preoccupations, making clear the author's importance and the significance of the novels chosen for discussion. The studies are all comprised of three parts, each one presenting three original essays on three key recent works by the author, and every part is introduced by the volume's editor, explaining how the chapters to follow engage with the fiction and respond to existing interpretations. Each individual chapter takes a critical approach that may develop existing perceptions or challenge them, but always expands the ways in which the author's work may be read by offering a fresh approach.

It is a principle of the series that all the studies are written in a style that will be engaging and clear however complex the subject, with the aim of fostering further debate about the work of writers who all exemplify what is most exciting and valuable in contemporary North American fiction.

Sarah Graham

CHAPTER 1

Louise Erdrich: The Aesthetics of *Mino Bimaadiziwin*

Deborah L. Madsen

The author of thirteen novels, four volumes of poetry, a short story collection, two books of non-fiction, five children's books and a textbook on writing, Louise Erdrich is one of the most prolific, most read and most acclaimed contemporary North American writers, though she is often specified as an ethnic Native American writer. She has been the recipient of a Guggenheim Fellowship, and in 2000 she was honored with a Lifetime Achievement Award from the Native Writers Circle of the Americas. In 2009 she received an Honorary Doctorate from Dartmouth College, her *alma mater*. Among the writing honors she has received is the Pushcart Prize for poetry and the 1984 National Book Critics Circle Award for her first novel, *Love Medicine*; the short story 'Fleur' was awarded the 1987 O. Henry Prize; *The Last Report on the Miracles at Little No Horse* was a finalist for the 2001 National Book Award; and she received the 2006 Scott O'Dell Award for Historical Fiction for the young adult novel, *The Game of Silence*. *The Plague of Doves* was a finalist for the 2008 Pulitzer Prize and won the Anisfield-Wolf Book Prize, an award that honors works that enhance understanding of cultural diversity and racism. With the exception of this latter award, the formal recognition of Erdrich's work signifies the wider place she holds in the canon of contemporary American literature. Indeed, in interviews she has commented upon the labeling of her work as that of an ethnic Native

American writer. In a 1986 conversation with Hertha Wong, she remarked:

> I think of any label as being both true and a product of a kind of chauvinistic society because obviously white male writers are not labeled 'white male writers'. However, I suppose that they're useful in some ways. I could as well be 'woman writer' or whatever label one wants to use. But I really don't like labels. While it is certainly true that a good part of my background . . . and a lot of themes are Native American, I prefer to simply be a writer. Although I like to be known as having been from Turtle Mountain Chippewa and from North Dakota. It's nice to have that known and to be proud of it for people back home. (Chavkin and Feyl Chavkin, 31)

However, the quality of Erdrich's work as that of a Native American should not be under-emphasized. Her characters, geographical settings, themes, imagery, plots and stories draw heavily from her Native inheritance. Erdrich is, as she remarks above, a member of the Chippewa tribe. Chippewa is the legal US term that describes the 'Ojibwe' (alternatively spelled 'Ojibway' or 'Ojibwa') people, who form a large part of the Anishinaabe tribal group. 'Anishinaabe' is the term used by members of the group to identify themselves; the chapters in this book refer to Erdrich's tribal affiliation using these various terms. As I will suggest below, Erdrich's core theme is the Ojibwe concept of the 'good life' – *mino bimaadiziwin* – even though opportunities for living well, with courage, generosity and kindness are limited for her characters, many of whom are of mixed native and European descent, who live under conditions of colonization and within a history of physical and cultural genocide.

Erdrich and Native Place

Karen Louise Erdrich was born on 7 June 1954 in Little Falls, Minnesota, and is an enrolled member of the Turtle Mountain band of Chippewa Indians. Her parents, Ralph and Rita Erdrich, both taught at the Bureau of Indian Affairs boarding school, Wahpeton Indian School, and encouraged the creativity of all their seven children; Heid and Lise Erdrich are also accomplished creative writers. Erdrich is of mixed native and European descent: her father is German American and her mother Chippewa and French. She grew up in Wahpeton, North Dakota, remaining there until 1972 when she went to Dartmouth College in New Hampshire to study in the then-new Native American Studies program. In her commencement address to the Dartmouth graduating class of 2009, Erdrich recalls:

The morning I was to leave for Dartmouth, from my home in Wahpeton, North Dakota, which I'd hardly ever left, I was so afraid that I almost did not go. I applied in the first place because my mother, a strong Turtle Mountain Chippewa woman, had seen a picture of the winter carnival ice sculpture in a National Geographic Magazine, and noted Dartmouth's historic commitment to educating American Indians. We didn't think about co-education, or what it would mean to be so far from home. I'd never been on a plane. (Web)

Her experience at Dartmouth enters into Erdrich's writing in various ways, and from her junior year her writing began to attract awards. Dartmouth figures most prominently in the novel, *The Crown of Columbus* (1991), that she co-wrote with her former husband Michael Dorris. This mystery-thriller begins with the heroine Vivian Twostar working late in the Dartmouth library when she accidentally discovers what she believes is the lost diary of Christopher Columbus, the 'treasure map' that the characters hope will lead to the eponymous crown. One of the several jobs at which Erdrich worked while a student at Dartmouth was at the old reference library microfilm desk. The collaboration between Dorris and Erdrich represented by this novel began at Dartmouth; Dorris had also arrived in 1972 to head the new Native American Studies program. Their correspondence continued after Erdrich's graduation; she returned to Dartmouth in 1979 as writer-in-residence after completing an MA in Creative Writing at Johns Hopkins University. They married in 1981, and, in interviews, describe how their collaboration shaped every word they each wrote. While they published under the pseudonym 'Milou North', the travel memoir, *Route Two*, and *The Crown of Columbus* are the only books to bear both authorial names. The non-fiction book *The Blue Jay's Dance* (1995) provides insight into Erdrich's life as a writer and mother during her time in Cornish, New Hampshire with Dorris. This memoir is in part a writer's diary and also a domestic or maternal autobiography, but the overarching theme is the relationship Erdrich enjoys with the natural environment of the region surrounding the remote farmhouse she shares with her family. The landscape of New Hampshire also features in *The Painted Drum* (2005) as the place where a collection of artifacts from a North Dakota Ojibwe reservation has been found as part of an estate. This novel brings together the two primary places in which Erdrich has lived, though in a 1993 interview, conducted while she was still living in New Hampshire, she confesses, 'I've never stopped missing and loving the Great Plains although for the last eighteen years I've been east or west of their definition' (Chavkin 242).

The Crown of Columbus and *The Blue Jay's Dance* are rather exceptional in the choice of geographical settings because most of Erdrich's fiction is set in North Dakota, on an Indian reservation and the surrounding white towns of Argus, Hoopdance and Pluto, and the city of Fargo. Minneapolis, where Erdrich now lives and runs an independent bookstore, Birchbark Books, also features in her fiction. The beginnings of Erdrich's extended series of North Dakota novels are to be found in the short story 'The World's Greatest Fisherman', which was written in only a few days over Christmas 1981. In a 1985 issue of *Dartmouth Alumni Magazine*, Erdrich and Dorris recount how Dorris's aunt had read of a call for entries for the Nelson Algren Award for short fiction and sent them the notice only 12 days before the deadline. Despite the demands of holiday house guests and their children, Erdrich describes shutting herself in the kitchen and writing almost non-stop for two days, pausing to show drafts to Dorris, who, having injured his back, was lying supine on the sitting room floor. The story won, bringing Erdrich to national attention and causing her to become aware of the commonalities among 'The World's Greatest Fisherman' and stories she had published earlier, notably 'The Red Convertible' and 'Scales' (Chavkin and Chavkin 13–14). These stories formed the core of her first novel, *Love Medicine*, which was the recipient of numerous awards and launched her reputation both nationally and internationally. *Love Medicine* was re-released in 1993 in a revised edition that added the following chapters: 'The Island', 'Resurrection', 'The Tomahawk Factory' and 'Lyman's Luck'. These new chapters served to integrate the novel more closely into her expanding series of interconnected narratives, especially *The Bingo Palace*, which was published in the following year, 1994.

The use of a common fictional geography that becomes more detailed and complex with each new novel introduced a significant innovation into Native American literature. While place and relationships with the land are important themes in Native American writing, the writer most akin to Erdrich in this respect is William Faulkner, and many critics have commented on the similarity between the two. Like Faulkner's Yoknapatawpha County, Erdrich's use of geography is fictionalized and cannot be related directly to real locations identifiable on maps. Indeed, only in *The Last Report on the Miracles at Little No Horse* (2001), the seventh novel in the series, is the reservation named as the eponymous Little No Horse. As Peter Beidler and Gay Barton have shown, the geographical spaces depicted in Erdrich's North Dakota novels are represented in deliberately misleading ways to discourage the eager reader from making too-simple identifications with real places.

If we consider Erdrich's North Dakota novels in their publication sequence, and in terms of her use of time and space, what emerges is a sense of the sprawling and immensely complex network of historical and geographical relationships she has created. Erdrich's fictional North Dakota landscape is first established in *Love Medicine*, a narrative encompassing the years 1898 to 1984, which is set primarily on an unnamed Ojibwe reservation. The novel that followed, *The Beet Queen* (1986), surprised some reviewers by shifting the main setting to the off-reservation town of Argus to focus less on indigenous characters than on the German settler community in the period from 1932 to 1972, though the character of Fleur Pillager links the two narratives. Fleur is also the link to *Tracks* (1988), which returns to the reservation with some incidents set in Argus from 1912 to 1924. *The Bingo Palace* (1994), as Peter Beidler and Gay Barton point out, is set during an indeterminate year in the late twentieth century (perhaps the late 1980s or early 1990s), but the time frame of the novel is complicated by the use of memories and flashbacks (29); still, the setting is primarily the reservation where the story addresses, in part, the contentious contemporary issue of gambling on Native reservations. Fargo, North Dakota is the primary setting of *Tales of Burning Love* (1996), with scenes set in Argus and on the reservation. In this novel the initial circumstances for Sister Leopolda's beatification, which is developed in *The Last Report on the Miracles at Little No Horse* (2001), are established; the novel is set in the mid-1990s but with recollections that take us back to the 1960s. *The Antelope Wife* (1998) is set in contemporary Minneapolis but includes accounts of eight generations of characters whose stories are told from the present-time year of 1945. *The Last Report on the Miracles at Little No Horse* finally names the North Dakota reservation as Little No Horse and offers a story explaining its unusual name. Following Agnes De Witt's departure from Fargo, all of the primary action takes place at Little No Horse, though the novel returns to the broad historical sweep of earlier novels (here from 1910 to 1997). *The Master Butchers Singing Club* (2003) returns to the immigrant characters, Pete and Fritzie Kozka, introduced in *The Beet Queen* as living in Argus, and explores the inter-war years in Europe and the US. *Four Souls* (2004) continues Fleur's story from her departure from the reservation in 1919 (explained in *Tracks*) and follows her to Minneapolis where she seeks revenge for the loss of her Pillager land. The novel ends with her return in 1933 and thus moves between Minneapolis and the reservation. The circumstances of Fleur's birth are revealed in *The Painted Drum*, which is linked by the characters of John Jewett Tatro and his grandfather, who was an Indian agent on the reservation, to *Four Souls*, *The Bingo Palace* and *Tracks*. When the older Tatro leaves the reservation, he takes with him looted Ojibwe artifacts, thus bringing together North Dakota and New Hampshire settings; Faye's effort to return the drum to its rightful owners brings the action into the early twenty-first century. *The Plague of Doves* (2008) is linked to the previous novels not through characters but through place: the town of Pluto that is the primary setting was once part of tribal lands but now lies just outside the reservation boundary. Through this sequence of novels, Erdrich has used her central geographical focus on North Dakota to create a complex skein of connections in time and space.

Indigenous Historical Contexts

Underlying Erdrich's concern with place and specifically with the indigenous lands that, historically, have become reservation lands, is awareness of the profound connections among land, family and *mino bimaadiziwin*, or the living of a good life. In her 2009 Dartmouth commencement address, she tells of working in the Baker Memorial Library in proximity to the mural The Epic of American Civilization by José Clemente Orozco. She offers a celebration of the knowledge that has been acquired by the graduating class:

> With this knowledge you have the makings of *mino bimaadiz-iwin*, in Ojibwe, the good life. Knowledge with Courage. Knowledge with Fortitude. Knowledge with Generosity and Kindness.
>
> This is *mino bimaadiziwin*.
>
> This concept of *mino bimaadiziwin* resonates with the message of Orozco's ferocious skeletons. It says knowledge without compassion is dead knowledge. Beware of knowledge without love.
>
> Now I don't mean romantic love – Harlequin Romance Love – I don't write those books. It is the kind of love you have: devotion to the world. (Web)

One of the major points of conflict between indigenous and Western worldviews – and a source of internal strife both for reservation families and communities – is the nature of the human relationship with the natural environment or 'devotion to the world'. In *The Last Report on the Miracles at Little No Horse*, Sister Hildegarde describes the colonizing view of the conflict over land, referring to tribal attitudes as doomed: 'They'll lose all the land, of course, being unused to the owning of land. Incredibly, it makes no sense to them. They avow, in their own peculiar way, that the earth is only on loan' (72). But the narrator expresses the view that is authorized and legitimated by the narrative itself: 'Into this complex situation walked Father Damien, with only the vaguest notion of how the ownership of land related to the soul' (76). He comes to understand, through the troubles of his parishioners, that the health of the soul – and of the body both individual and collective – depends upon a relationship with the natural environment that is the land, based upon the values of *mino bimaadiziwin*: essentially, courage, responsibility, respect, honesty and generosity. The core concern of Erdrich's writing is the problem of pursuing the way to the good life in the wake of colonialism.

The question that tears apart the reservation families, especially in Erdrich's early fiction – the Kashpaws, the Lamartines, the Pillagers and the Morrisseys – is how to respond to white encroachment upon tribal lands; how to deal with the land frauds, the broken treaties and the assault on tribal culture by the interests of the Catholic Church, on the one hand, and the commercial exploitation of reservation resources, on the other. The story of Fleur Pillager, which is one of the strongest threads linking the North Dakota novels (she is featured in *Love Medicine, The Beet Queen, Tracks, The Bingo Palace, Four Souls* and *The Painted Drum*) is a case in point. Fleur loses her claim to Pillager lands as a result of the economic demands made by the corrupt Indian agent, demands which force Margaret Kashpaw to choose between paying the taxes on Pillager or Kashpaw land. Thus, the action by the corrupt representative of the US government fractures family relationships and, with them, alliances within the tribal community. Bernadette Morrissey's role as secretary to the Indian agent raises suspicions that Morrissey lands will be immune from confiscation and this intensifies inter-tribal hostilities. Fleur's land is then violently cleared of timber by the Turcot Lumber Company and part of that timber is used to build the mansion in Minneapolis of John Mauser, the owner of the company. So Fleur leaves the reservation to pursue her revenge against Mauser, placing her daughter Lulu in a government boarding school. Thus, the original trauma of land loss and family severance is passed on to the following generation: Arwun (John James Mauser II), the dysfunctional child born from Fleur's marriage to Mauser, and Lulu, who endures the assault on tribal cultural identity that was the project of US Indian boarding schools.

Among the historical traumas experienced by Native American communities in the wake of colonization was the assimilative program of residential or boarding schools. One of Erdrich's early poems is 'Indian Boarding School: The Runaways', the subject of which is the efforts of children to cross the long distances that separate them from home. Boarding schools were deliberately placed far from reservations in order to prevent parental access to children and to discourage the children from running away. The poem describes the harsh sanctions meted out to returned runaways: corporal punishment and humiliating punitive tasks like scrubbing pavements – a humiliation recalled by

Lulu Nanapush after she tried to run back to the reservation. In contrast to Lulu's experience, Nector Kashpaw is taken away to school but benefits from his Western education so that upon his return to the reservation he becomes part of the tribal government and eventually chairman. He is able to travel to Washington to negotiate on behalf of the tribe, though his partially assimilated condition does create problems in his personal life. His brother Eli, however, is hidden by his mother, Margaret Rushes Bear, who refuses to surrender both her sons to US government schooling, and Eli is therefore raised according to traditional lifeways. In *The Painted Drum*, Fleur's half-sister is said to have survived the Carlisle Indian School, which was established in Pennsylvania in 1879 as the first Native boarding school. The superintendent of Carlisle, Richard Pratt, is famous for his motto 'Kill the Indian and save the man'. By this he means that by removing Native children from all tribal influences and assimilating them completely into US culture, their 'humanity' could be protected from the presumed 'savagery' of indigenous lifeways. The strategies used to pursue this goal included brutal punishment for speaking tribal languages, the adoption of Western styles of dress and food and complete severance of relationships with family and clan groups. Children in schools such as Carlisle were required to perform hard manual labor to produce their own food, clothing and other necessities for the running of the school. This was the result of chronic underfunding of the schools, which also produced overcrowding and the periodic outbreak of devastating diseases such as tuberculosis. In *The Plague of Doves*, Evelina refers in passing to the 'Haskell Princess', evoking the Haskell Institute (now the Haskell Indian Nations University) which opened in 1884 in Lawrence, Kansas as the United States Indian Industrial Training School. The fictional Haskell Princess is said to have died of tuberculosis, as did thousands of children who were living in cramped conditions that encouraged the spread of the disease. Haskell, like Carlisle and other Indian boarding schools, was an 'Industrial Training School' where children were educated to take up low-skilled positions in US society rather than to achieve full assimilation. Indeed, the children received only basic formal instruction, spending much of their time in manual labor. Bruce Trigger and Wilcomb Washburn report that between 1880 and 1895 the US Office of Indian Affairs opened 20 off-reservation residential schools and reservation day schools (199).

As in her referencing of Indian boarding schools, Erdrich frequently alludes to actual events in the history of US–Indian relations, for example, the lynching that is central to *The Plague of Doves*; the US Cavalry offensives against Sioux villages upon which scenes in *The Antelope Wife* may be modeled (Beidler and Barton 40); the White Earth timber scandal in *Tracks*; references to the Wounded Knee Massacre in *The Master Butchers Singing Club*; and, in that novel and *The Plague of Doves*, the *métis* rebel Louis Riel. These references make specific allusion to a general history of violent dispossession, physical and cultural genocide and the continuing disenfranchisement of Native Americans that is an important context for Erdrich's fiction. Over the course of her three novels for young adults, *The Birchbark House* (1999), *The Game of Silence* (2005) *and The Porcupine Year* (2008), Erdrich recounts the story of the young Ojibwe girl Omakayas and her family as they encounter the *chimookomanag*, or white settlers, for the first time. They find themselves dispossessed of both their traditional lands, as they are pressured to move west, and also the traditional lifeways that the land supported. Living on an island in Lake Superior, they build birchbark cabins surrounded by gardens in the summer, spend the autumn in ricing camps on the lake shore and, at the onset of winter, move to cedar log cabins near the town of LaPointe. These historical novels, set in the mid-nineteenth century, represent, through the particular case of Omakayas, many of the historical experiences of Native Americans generally.

Depopulation as the result of warfare and massacres, and disease – especially smallpox, measles and tuberculosis – reduced the Native population from an estimated 50 to 100 million (Stannard 151) at the end of the fifteenth century to approximately 2 million today (Utter 17, 23). It should be noted, however, that the Native American population is one of the fastest growing 'ethnic' groups in the contemporary United States. From the immediate post-contact period of the late 1400s, the effect of missionary activity has been a sustained loss of traditional religions. It was in 1978, with the passage of the American Indian Religious Freedom Act, that Native peoples were finally able to practice their tribal religions free of persecution. After the American War of Independence, the era of treaty-making began; this was a necessity because although Britain had ceded its colonial holdings to the United States, agreement had not been sought from the indigenous peoples living on those lands. However, the breaking or abrogation of those treaties has resulted in the systematic loss of tribal lands to white settlers. The appropriation of land for US settlement accelerated during the Removal era, following congressional passage of the Indian Removal Act in 1830. Entire tribal communities were forcibly relocated to lands west of the Mississippi River: the Cherokee in the Trail of Tears of the 1830s, the 1862 removal of Dakota and Lakota and the 1864 Navajo Long Walk are among the best-known of these deportations. Native opposition to the taking of their lands dates from first contact. But conflict with the United States intensified during the Removal era (the Creek War of 1813–14, the Black Hawk War of 1831–2, the Seminole Wars of 1817–18,

1835–42 and 1855–8) and particularly after the Civil War when a highly militarized US government turned its attention to the Plains Indians of the West. The so-called Indian Wars included the 1864 Sand Creek Massacre, the Modoc War of 1872–3, the Red River Indian War of 1874–5, the 1876 Battle of the Little Big Horn, the Nez Percé War of 1877 and the 1890 Massacre at Wounded Knee. The slaughter of bison to the point of extinction during the 1880s supported the war effort by depriving tribes of food and material for clothing, housing and utensils. However, the single most devastating strategy for the appropriation of Native lands was the Dawes Act or General Allotment Act of 1887. By this act Congress authorized the division of reservation land into individual allotments to be given to qualified individuals. In order to qualify, tribal members had to submit to the test of blood quantum, proving that they were 'Indian', before receiving an allotment. This restriction, together with the small parcels of land that were allotted, resulted in a land 'surplus' that was sold to white settlers. Trigger and Washburn state, 'When a final accounting was made in the 1930s, government officials estimated that the Dawes Act had brought about the loss of over 90,000,000 acres . . . of Indian-owned land' (210).

The Indian Reorganization Act of 1934 ended the practice of allotment and also instituted a series of measures that recognized the sovereign status of tribal nations. This policy was reversed in the two decades following the late 1940s through the actions of Congress and the Senate Subcommittee on Indian Affairs, ushering in the 'Termination' period which lasted until the early 1960s. During this period, the Bureau of Indian Affairs (BIA) assembled a list of tribes with whom the federal government could sever treaty relations, remove the sovereign status of tribes and 'terminate' the federal recognition of tribal status along with guaranteed treaty rights and payments and protection of reservation lands. The Menominee and Klamath were 'terminated' in this fashion, but the poverty and social problems that ensued inspired vigorous opposition among other tribes marked for termination and an eventual abandonment of the policy. Federal efforts to force Native assimilation through the BIA continued in the mid-twentieth century with the Indian Relocation Act (1956) which encouraged Native people to leave reservations and move to government-designated urban centers – such as Minneapolis, Chicago, Los Angeles, Denver, Dallas, San Francisco, Oklahoma City and Cleveland – by promising vocational training and resettlement assistance.

The legacy of this history in the contemporary United States is poverty-stricken reservations with very high levels of unemployment resulting in increased violence, alcoholism, family dysfunction, substance misuse, poor schooling and government dependence. This dependence was encouraged by US policies that empowered the federal government to act as 'trustee' to the Native holders of allotted lands, particularly with regard to the financial proceeds from the exploitation of their resources, specifically, coal, timber, grazing, and gas and oil leases. The recently settled *Cobell versus Salazar* case drew public attention to more than one hundred years of mismanagement and theft of Native Trust money managed by the BIA. Under the terms of allotment, the federal government was responsible for providing regular accounting of trust funds and payment of those funds to trustees. The plaintiffs requested $40 billion in restitution and in 2008 were awarded $455.6 million; the 2009 result of the appeal against this decision resulted in a settlement that comprised a $1.412 billion Accounting/ Trust Administration Fund, a $2 billion Trust Land Consolidation Fund and an Indian Education Scholarship Fund of up to $60 million. However, Congress has yet to requisition the funds to enact this settlement. Widespread tribal poverty is also responsible for the increasing use of reservations for the disposal of commercial and toxic waste materials as a source of scarce revenue.[1] This history of colonial oppression, dispossession and cultural assault forms the wider context to Erdrich's work and is taken up in various ways in the chapters that follow.

Ojibwe Contexts

The genocidal history of US–Native relations is the source of what Anishinaabe writer and scholar Gerald Vizenor refers to as 'tragic wisdom' (*Postindian* 38): Native knowledge of the duplicity of Western languages, the damaging impact of stereotypes (such as the noble or doomed Indian) and the destructive nature of Western colonial views of the land. According to Vizenor, this history does not necessarily make tragic victims of Native people but can be generative of positive knowledge, especially the knowledge born of what he calls 'survivance'. Survivance is more than simple physical survival and resistance; it is the continuation through time of a tribal view of the world. Survivance is a way of seeing the world and is also an understanding of what the world is and of what it is composed (Vizenor 'Survivance'). Erdrich's exploration of the possibilities for *mino bimaadiziwin,* or the living of a good life, in the contemporary United States is strongly informed by the concept of Native survivance.

This survivance worldview is perhaps nowhere more evident than in her use of Ojibwe ontology: an understanding of the world in which different forms of creation are co-existent and valued equally. This can be seen, for example, in her treatment of human–animal interactions; in *The Antelope Wife* some incidents are narrated by dogs, characters have animal ancestry and Blue Prairie Woman marries a stag. Most surprisingly – and disturbingly from a Western ontological perspective – the incidents in which a soldier suckles a baby are echoed by Blue Prairie Woman suckling a puppy. In an Ojibwe ontology, there is no hierarchical separation of human and non-human creation but rather the two are continuous with one another and so are of the same ontological status. This extends to inanimate objects like the eponymous drum that saves the children in *The Painted Drum*, as well as Shamengwa's violin and also the stones that are sentient in *The Plague of Doves*. Sentient stones carry a particular cultural resonance in Ojibwe mythology because the brother of the tribal trickster figure, Nanaabozho, is a stone. The epigraph to *The Last Report on the Miracles at Little No Horse*, attributed to Nanapush, makes the claim that every part of creation is a 'relation' and is in relationship with every other part: '*In saying the word nindinawemaganidok, or my relatives, we speak of everything that has existed in time, the known and the unknown, the unseen, the obvious, all that lived before or is living now in the worlds above and below*' (n.p. italics in original). Thus, the representation of a world in which all elements of creation are related to each other is a survivance strategy, a powerful assertion that despite centuries of colonial violence and tribal loss, Ojibwe culture still flourishes.

Erdrich uses several Ojibwe cultural figures, including Nanaabozho the trickster, the evil Gambler and the *windigo*. In some stories the Gambler and the *windigo* are the same character. The trickster appears in Ojibwe origins stories, such as the earthdiver myth in which the world is created anew as Turtle Island following a flood, as well as a range of contemporary narratives. The trickster is a joker, a character who deflates and exposes the pretensions of others but who sometimes is humiliated himself by his foolish actions. However, he is primarily a creative character. In Erdrich's fiction, memory, language and storytelling traditions all contribute to the personal and historical recollections that structure the characters' distinctive identities and worldviews. The word represents both knowledge and experience (survivance and tragic wisdom), and so language becomes the medium of re-creation, shaping the new from the old. In this respect, all of Erdrich's very diverse narrators could be said to perform the trickster's world-making function. Even more, it could be argued that the author who creates these often unreliable narratives is herself the supreme trickster in her fictional world. In contrast to Nanaabozho, the Gambler and the *windigo* are world-destroyers; the Gambler tempts his victims to venture their lives in a game of chance and, when they lose, he turns them over to the *windigo*, a cannibalistic monster that possesses considerable spiritual power. In a number of stories, Nanaabozho takes on the Gambler and defeats him through his cunning and quick wit.

Erdrich interweaves tribal Ojibwe cultural elements with the history of US–Native relations in her negotiation of the complexities of contemporary *mino bimaadiziwin*. In other words, her core theme is the challenge of self-definition within the context of Native American history and pressures applied by such institutions as tribe, family, Church, police and the BIA. In Erdrich's fiction the past merges with the present within the context of continuing traditions as her characters seek modern identities through the interplay of past and present social realities. A vexed aspect of identity construction is the question of home and belonging within the context of dispossession. Characters experience a conflict between the desire to leave and a longing for home, a conflict related to their concern with tribal origins, on the one hand, and their marginality or otherness in the 'whitestream' (as John Gamber terms the 'mainstream' in his chapter), on the other. Within this context, the importance of family cannot be overestimated. Family relationships are at the heart of tribal and kinship structures despite the fact that families are displaced and broken as the consequence of poverty, alcoholism, promiscuity and illegitimacy, violence and self-hatred that is directed towards children and spouses. The historical violence done to tribal unity is represented through broken and dysfunctional families. Violence is now domestic; hunting is now done by the police. But family reveals how enmeshed are the personal and the political in Native American life.

The stories of these families and the individuals who comprise them are most often told by unreliable first-person narrators who speak from inside the community. No authority or central narrative consciousness is invoked to order the characters' lives; rather, the multi-vocality of Erdrich's fiction resists the notion that truth and authority can exist as fixed absolutes. In this way, and by refusing to judge her characters, Erdrich's narratives incorporate and interweave both personal and also historical/political factors. This polyphonic storytelling technique supports Erdrich's cyclical style of narration. Each novel tells of characters who already exist in Erdrich's larger fictional world; they are not invented new for each story. As a consequence, the reader is encouraged to think of the characters as possessing a reality or ontology that is independent of particular narratives. The novels give voice to a plurality of characters, each telling parts of the larger story from different points of view. The dominant voice, however, is that of the community. Erdrich's storytelling is concerned with the community as it deals with the problems and issues that occur. This focus upon the tribal community, past and present, supports Erdrich's aesthetics of survivance, as does her cyclical use of time, which resists Western linear or chronological time. From an Ojibwe perspective the past is integrated into the present where it continues to live and to shape the living of contemporary lives. Thus both her temporal and spatial settings are predominantly tribal. In a 1985 interview with Laura Coltelli, together with Michael Dorris, she explained the conscious decision to locate her novels within a tribal community where the outside world (such as Washington DC, which Nector as tribal chairman visits on tribal business) is neither very present nor very relevant to the lives of the characters (Chavkin 24). The fictional world is encompassed by the community and the primary interest of the narratives is focused upon how the community deals with itself and its members, and their search for a way to live an Ojibwe 'good life'.

Conclusion

Erdrich sees herself as primarily a storyteller and, in interviews, has described her early experiences of listening to relatives tell stories, especially her paternal grandfather, Patrick Gourneau, who was the tribal chair of the Turtle Mountain Reservation while she was growing up. 'Sitting around listening to our family tell stories has been a more important influence on our work than literary influences in some ways', she tells Hertha Wong. 'These you absorb as a child when your senses are most open, when your mind is forming. That really happened, I know, in our family' (Chavkin 38). The tribal influences upon Erdrich's writing include her narrative techniques as well as her core themes. She brings into contemporary North American fiction the enduring indigenous presence of a tribal culture that endures through survivance and flourishes through *mino bimaadiziwin*.

PART I

Tracks

Introduction

Tracks is Louise Erdrich's third published novel and, in some respects, her most important. A. Lavonne Ruoff has described how a manuscript version of the novel not only preceded publication of *Love Medicine* in 1984 but differs significantly from the published text of *Tracks*. Ruoff explains how sections of the manuscript were rewritten for inclusion in the revised edition of *Love Medicine* ('Afterword' 183) and she recalls Erdrich's description of *Tracks*, in a 1993 interview with Allan Chavkin and Nancy Feyl Chavkin, as 'the first manuscript I finished, but I have since divided up and re-used pieces of that manuscript elsewhere. It has become the old junked car in the yard front, continually raided for parts. It is the form of all else, still a tangle' (238). Erdrich suggests that the original manuscript of *Tracks* is foundational to all of her writings that have followed. Rather than a 'tangle', however, Erdrich's third novel is technically constructed in a simpler manner with the use of only two narrators (Nanapush and Pauline) in place of the polyphonic style of *Love Medicine*. While the narrative is structured more simply, *Tracks* remains a complex exploration of the psychological, emotional, social and cultural impacts of ongoing US settler colonization upon members of a Native American community, complicated further by Erdrich's use of unreliable narrators who are deeply involved in the situations that the narrative describes.

Colonialism provides the wider context for each of the three chapters in this part. Allan Chavkin and Nancy Feyl Chavkin address the inter-generational transmission of self-destructive behaviors in the wake of colonization through the analysis of the family. Using family systems theory, they show how Erdrich's characters are shaped by their family environments, while those families are in turn responsive to wider socio-cultural pressures. Trauma as an inter-generational experience arising from centuries of genocidal colonial policies offers Connie Jacobs a context in which Erdrich's characterization takes on new meaning. Jacobs draws on recent theories of psychological and cultural trauma to account for Erdrich's creation of her unlikable and alienating narrator/protagonist Pauline Puyat. Taking an even wider view of the history of loss that continues to disrupt Native communities, families and individuals, David Stirrup addresses Erdrich's discursive engagement with the US legal system and specifically the devastating consequences of the 1887 General Allotment Act for Native reservation communities that lost immense tracts of land and, together with the land, traditional lifeways that depend upon relationships with the natural environment. A 'between worlds' condition marks the construction of Erdrich's characters – mixed-blood and Native characters, Pauline and Fleur, alike – and these chapters illuminate the multifaceted ways in which colonialism as history, as law, as genocide and as cultural devastation has created this condition.

In 'A Bowen Family Systems Reading of *Tracks*', Allan Chavkin and Nancy Feyl Chavkin use the theories developed by American psychiatrist Murray Bowen to analyse the problematic character and narrator, Pauline Puyat. As Chavkin and Feyl Chavkin note, 'Erdrich's genius in *Tracks* is that she not only enables the reader to enter a psychotic mind and see its distorted thought process but also that she reveals how Pauline's interaction with various family systems contributes to her psychological deterioration.' A key insight from family systems theory is that the emotional dynamics producing dysfunctional behaviors are not recognized by the individuals who act them out. Thus the psychopathology of Pauline is invisible to herself but is unconsciously expressed in the rhetorical terms of her narrative as she recounts her experience of the various families to which she belongs: the Puyats, the Morrisseys, the family of Fleur and Nanapush and also the community of sisters governed by the Mother Superior of the convent. Although Pauline presents her history as a story of spiritual growth – what Chavkin and Feyl Chavkin describe as 'Pauline's odyssey from shy mixed-blood fifteen-year-old girl with an inferiority complex to her new self-conception of herself as saintly twenty-one-year-old white nun empowered by God to convert the sinful Indians' – what she says does not mesh with what she does. Family systems theory allows analysis of Pauline's behavior as an accelerating pathological downward spiral. In the culminating episode of Pauline's transformation, she sets out to Matchimanito Lake to defeat the mysterious creature or *manitou* said to live in its depths, but in fact murders Napoleon Morrissey, the father of her child. In Pauline's rationalized retelling of the event, Satan took on Napoleon's form while she was strangling him with her rosary, but Pauline's behavior is exposed as a paranoid delusion by the recognition that she is preparing herself emotionally for her move to the new 'family' of the convent. Pauline repudiates her old life and her old self by entering the convent as Sister Leopolda but she marks that transformation by dumping Napoleon's corpse near Fleur's shack in the firm knowledge that his family will assume Fleur killed him. Thus Pauline commits an act that ensures the feud she started will continue despite her absence.

In the family systems theory upon which Chavkin and Feyl Chavkin draw, the family is particularly important as an interpersonal nexus where stress and anxiety are controlled. On the levels of community, family and individual, all the characters in *Tracks* are subject to extraordinary stress as they deal with the effects of white incursions into Native land and culture. The specific effects of increasing white dominance over Native lives are represented in the narrative as the epidemics of infectious disease, famine and the destruction of the traditional woodland environment by logging companies. Connie Jacobs, in 'Trauma Theory and *Tracks*', also takes the character of Pauline as the starting point for her discussion of the effects of dislocation, removal and oppression wrought by colonialism. Where Allan Chavkin and Nancy Feyl Chavkin address the dynamics of dysfunctional families through this character, Jacobs looks to the effects of inter-generational trauma upon families and their individual members. As Pauline Puyat and later as Sister Leopolda, this character recurs throughout Erdrich's North Dakota cycle of novels: as a minor but important character in *Love Medicine*, *The Beet Queen* and *Tales of Burning Love*; as a narrator/protagonist in *Tracks*; and as the object of the eponymous 'report' in *The Last Report on the Miracles at Little No Horse*. In Jacobs's analysis, Pauline emerges as a victim of the unresolved historical trauma impacting Native American communities. The complexities of remembering and forgetting a painful history of colonization are woven through the two narrative viewpoints – Nanapush's and Pauline's respectively – that structure Erdrich's novel. Pauline 'acts out' her violent traumatic legacy through her compulsive self-mortifications and violent actions. But her actions belie her words; Jacobs points out that in order to sustain her delusional reinterpretation of herself and her history, Pauline 'must continually forget, distort, and disavow'.

Both Jacobs and David Stirrup explore the intense pressures exerted by colonization on individuals and their inter-family relations. The loss of much of the tribal land-base is one of several interconnecting

conditions of historical trauma. It is also the result of deliberate US policies of removal, assimilation and termination designed to end tribal
sovereignty and open land to white settlers. Stirrup counts *Tracks*
among those Native literary texts that work as testimony, witnessing the
impact of US legal decisions on Native peoples. Allotment, the appropriation of tribal property rights and the abrogation of treaty rights are
the most prominent of those decisions. Rather than focus upon the
theme of dispossession as such, Stirrup shows how, through her exploration of the historical fact of Native land loss, Erdrich engages issues of
tribal rights and sovereignty. In the 1993 interview cited above, Erdrich
claims that 'Everyone should be politically and socially committed in
personal life, but not in art. Political art is polemic and boring' (241).
However, as the chapters in this part show, Erdrich's art is politically and
socially engaged, in complex and artfully nuanced ways.

CHAPTER 2

A Bowen Family Systems Reading of *Tracks*

Allan Chavkin and Nancy Feyl Chavkin

Introduction

Using Murray Bowen's family systems theory, we will suggest a way of reading Louise Erdrich's *Tracks* that will demystify the bizarre behavior of Pauline, one of the two narrators and the most puzzling character of the novel. Bowen's theory reveals how individuals are shaped by their family systems. One of the key assumptions behind the theory is that interactions of family members are not random or incidental in many cases but governed by concealed structural patterns of which family members typically are unaware. In the first part of the chapter we will provide an overview of Bowen family systems theory and explain in some detail three of Bowen's concepts that are essential for understanding *Tracks*; in the second part we will employ these concepts to analyse Pauline's perplexing character. Erdrich's genius in *Tracks* is that she not only enables the reader to enter a psychotic mind and see its distorted thought process but also that she reveals how Pauline's interaction with various family systems contributes to her psychological deterioration.

Part I: Bowen Family Systems Theory

I.i. Murray Bowen, Pioneer in Family Systems Theory

American psychiatrist Murray Bowen (1913–1990) is regarded as the founder of family systems theory, which assumes that the family unit is the primary source of emotional experience. Prior to Bowen's family systems theory, psychologists studying human behavior primarily focused on the individual. Murray Bowen's contribution of family systems theory extended the study of the individual to include the context of the family and society (Prochaska and Norcross 373).

After his medical training, Bowen served as a doctor in the army during World War II. He had planned to become a heart surgeon when he returned from the military, but his experiences during World War II, especially his witnessing 'the impact of stress on human functioning' led to his decision to become a psychiatrist (Titelman, *Triangles* 4). From 1946 to 1954 Bowen worked with schizophrenic patients at the Menninger Foundation in Topeka, Kansas, where he became intrigued with 'how the family played a part in the development of psychiatric disorders' (Titelman, *Triangles* 5). After Menninger, Bowen moved to the National Institute of Mental Health in 1954. In 1959, as a clinical professor in the Department of Psychiatry, Bowen began extensive work with families at Georgetown University Medical Center, and in 1975 founded the Georgetown Family Center where he was director until his death. During these years at Georgetown University, he did detailed multigenerational research on families, formulated his family systems theory, and stressed the usefulness of constructing 'genograms', diagrams that typically presented information on three generations of the family, including some key emotional relationships. Such diagrams provided a visual mapping that could allow one, in some cases, to see patterns and relationships in a family that might not otherwise be evident. He also used diagrams to illustrate the dynamic emotional interactions in triangles and other relationships.

An outgrowth of psychoanalytic thinking, Bowen family systems theory 'offers the most comprehensive view of human behavior and problems of any approach to family therapy' (Nichols 84). John Knapp and Kenneth Womack have argued that it is the most useful of psychological theories with which to examine the family in literary works.

I.ii. An Overview of Bowen Family Systems Theory

Bowen presents eight important concepts as the core of his theory; they are the nuclear family emotional system, differentiation of self, triangles, emotional cutoff, family projection process, multigenerational transmission process, sibling position and societal emotional process. We will use three of these concepts for the purposes of examining *Tracks*. The other five concepts are not relevant for exploration of this novel, and therefore we will not discuss them in this chapter. Differentiation, emotional cutoff and triangles will provide the keys that will unlock the mystery of Pauline's perplexing and at times grotesque behavior and reveal the nature of the psychopathology that shapes the plot of *Tracks*.

Arguing that his theory is based on biology, Bowen suggests that the family's operating system is a consequence of billions of years of evolution. He describes the family as 'an emotional unit' or 'an emotional field'. In their book, *Family Evaluation*, Kerr and Bowen explain:

> The emotionally determined functioning of the family members generates a family emotional 'atmosphere' or 'field' that, in turn, influences the emotional functioning of each person. It is analogous to the gravitational field of the solar system, where each planet and the sun, by virtue of their mass, contribute gravity to the field and are, in turn, regulated by the field they each help create. One cannot 'see' gravity, nor can one 'see' the emotional field. The presence of gravity and the emotional field can be inferred, however, by the predictable ways planets and people behave in reaction to one another. (55)

Behavior of family members within the emotional field often results in predictable patterns of behavior; the actions of one member of the family reverberate throughout the family and result in reciprocal reactions by other members of the family. The family system, whose primary function is the management of anxiety, typically has enormous influence on members of the system. In other words, the individual's behavior should be understood within its social context, that is, within the family system. In *Tracks* Pauline's behavior needs to be seen as shaped by her involvement with her family of origin and the other families that she is part of, including Bernadette Morrissey's family, Fleur's family and, finally, 'the family' of the convent on the reservation.

I.iii. Differentiation

Differentiation of self is the cornerstone of Bowen's theory. He stresses the need for the individual to 'differentiate' or maintain independence from his family even while remaining within its emotional field. He argues that the emotional system is regulated by the need for individuality and the need for togetherness, two opposing 'life forces' that have their foundation in biology. The life force of togetherness pressures the individual to conform to the demands of others, while the life force of individuality urges the individual to follow his own desires and beliefs. The two variables of differentiation and anxiety determine human functioning. Bowen distinguishes between two kinds of anxiety. Acute anxiety is a response to a specific threat and is time limited, while chronic anxiety, which is not time limited, is a response to imagined threats and apprehension of what might occur and 'often strains or exceeds people's ability to adapt to it' (Kerr and Bowen 113). The lower the level of differentiation of the individual and the less emotionally separated the individual is from the family, the more chronic anxiety the individual experiences.

Differentiation is a 'process through which the human individual develops from being symbiotically attached to the mother, in the context of the parental unit, to being an emotionally separate self in relation to family and others' (Titelman, *Emotional Cutoff* 20). Differentiation is not an absolute quality but a matter of degree; there is a spectrum ranging from high levels of differentiation where one responds with the aid of intellectual processes and is able to 'maintain a degree of objectivity and emotional distance' to low levels where one responds primarily in an emotionally reactive way and suffers from intense chronic anxiety (Becvar and Becvar 141). Individuals with low levels of differentiation tend to be conformist in their thinking, unreflectively rigid in their attitudes and excessively dependent on others for their emotional security and sense of well-being; they 'fuse' with their family and relate in an automatic way to others according to past emotional patterns.

Bowen's term 'fusion' refers to the confused intermingling of thinking and feeling where feeling completely engulfs thinking and the individual becomes emotionally reactive to events and people; it also refers to the absence of boundaries between people, as in symbiotic relationships (Prochaska and Norcross 174). Those with low levels of differentiation depend excessively on the approval of other family members and will often attempt to pressure others and will submit to pressure in order to achieve the 'groupthink' that dominates families where there is an 'emotional oneness or emotional stuck-togetherness between family members' (Titelman, *Emotional Cutoff* 21). One of the consequences of fusion is the exertion of pressure within the family to remain loyal to the emotional core of the family, especially to the parents. The more threatened the family feels, the greater the pressure is put on other family members to fuse with the family, creating what Bowen calls an 'undifferentiated family ego mass'. When one member of a family experiences stress, it can easily spread to other members, much like a highly contagious disease. The more anxiety individuals within the family feel, the more they look for the relief associated with the emotional unity of the stuck-together family ego mass. Such a situation is harmful and produces a false sense of security in which individuals can develop emotional illness as a consequence of their failure to differentiate themselves from their families.

Bowen uses the terms 'pseudo-self' and 'solid self' to help explain the distinctions that he sees between well and less differentiated people.

The pseudo-self or pretend self is highly susceptible to emotional pressure and will 'lend' (i.e., sacrifice self) in order to achieve the togetherness demanded by the family. The principles and beliefs of the pseudo-self are quickly changed to enhance one's image with others or to unthinkingly oppose others (Kerr and Bowen 103). Always capable of being molded and highly susceptible to anxiety, the pseudo-self engages in groupthink and succumbs to the pressure to conform.

In contrast, the solid self can withstand groupthink and can cope well with anxiety. The 'solid self is made up of firmly held convictions and beliefs which are formed slowly and can be changed *only from within self*' but at the same time is flexible in coping with difficulties (Kerr and Bowen 105). The solid self resists coercion and responds to events not in an emotionally reactive way as the pseudo-self does but in a calm reflective manner. By relying on intellectual processes instead of reacting emotionally, the solid self is able to avoid emotional entanglements that people with low levels of differentiation create.

I.iv. Emotional cutoff
While one response to chronic anxiety is fusion or 'emotional stuck togetherness' among family members, another way a family member might respond is by emotional cutoff. Emotional cutoff (sometimes referred to just as cutoff) is the consequence of discomfort that an individual feels as a result of chronic anxiety prompted by excessively close association with other family members or individuals outside the family. Originally Bowen used the concept of emotional cutoff to refer to the separation of a child from his or her parents as a consequence of an 'unresolved attachment' (i.e., parent–child fusion), but later the term came to be used to explain 'many variations of emotional distancing that occur among individuals both within and outside their family systems' (Titelman, *Emotional Cutoff* 23).

In any case, when a relationship becomes too intense and anxiety too great, the individual might respond to this 'unresolved attachment' by separating himself from the source of anxiety. In some cases this involves the infamous 'geographic cure' in which the individual puts great physical distance between himself and the source of his anxiety, whether that source is certain family members or other individuals outside the family, and cuts off or limits contact. In other cases the individual might remain in close physical proximity to the person or people who are the source of anxiety but again will severely restrict contact.

Bowen observes that emotional cutoff does not solve the problem that prompted it. In the short run, emotional cutoff can enable one to control or ward off acute anxiety 'but at the same time it can augment chronic anxiety and impede its resolution in the long run' (Titelman,

Emotional Cutoff 23). Individuals employing cutoff often resort to blaming parents and others for their problems instead of accepting responsibility; suffering from emotional illness, they tend to act impulsively and immaturely in relationships. When relationships become problematical, they resort to emotional cutoff and run away from them.

I.v. Triangles

In addition to emotional cutoff and fusion, another way that people cope with tension is through triangles. When there is tension between two people (sometimes called a dyad in family systems terminology), such as a husband and wife, a third person is often triangled in to absorb the excess anxiety. As Roberta Gilbert explains, triangles can develop if anxiety 'is up even a little' (50). Triangles can function in diverse and complex ways, some of which are positive, as, for example, when a triangle functions to reduce acute anxiety and help the family function better, but triangles can be problematical (Becvar and Becvar 141).

In some situations triangles can destabilize the family system because of secrets, misconceptions and the conflict that they create. In some cases when a triangle forms, two people are insiders and one person is the outsider who would like to replace one of the insiders and, as Prochaska and Norcross explain, there can be some intense jockeying for position: 'The favored position is to be a member of the close twosome rather than the odd one out. When tension mounts in the outsider, the predictable move is to try to form a twosome with one of the original members of the twosome, leaving the other one an outsider' (374). A triangle that originally formed to reduce anxiety in the dyad may in fact intensify anxiety and conflict, especially when one or more of the individuals of this triangle possess low levels of differentiation. If a triangle forms with three individuals of high levels of differentiation and low levels of anxiety, the triangle usually will not significantly disturb the functioning of the family. On the other hand, if the triangle is constituted of one or more individuals with low levels of differentiation and high levels of anxiety, the triangle often becomes rigid and conflictive and typically will interfere with the functioning of the family. A conflictive triangle occurs in *Tracks* with devastating consequences. The triangle of Fleur, Eli and Pauline leads to an interlocking triangle when, with the aid of Pauline's scheming, 14-year-old virginal Sophie Morrissey is triangled in and has sexual relations with Eli, resulting in an emotional earthquake with damage to the two family systems.

Bowen states that the triangle is 'the basic building block of any emotional system, whether it is in the family or any other group' (Bowen

373). The presence of triangles and their impact on the family system depends largely on levels of differentiation of family members and the amount of chronic anxiety in the system. Peter Titelman explains: 'Insofar as all humans are not fully differentiated, they live with some degree of chronic anxiety. . . . The lower the levels of differentiation and the higher the levels of chronic anxiety, the greater the presence of triangling, and the more likely that rigid triangles develop in a family. Conversely, the higher the levels of differentiation and the lower the levels of chronic anxiety, less triangling occurs, and less rigid triangles develop' (*Triangles* 36). The problem of triangles becomes more complicated when a fourth person is triangled into the original triangle. Bowen explains that this interlocking triangle has developed because anxiety is unable to be contained in the original triangle and thus overflows into a new triangle (Kerr and Bowen 140). Bowen and his followers make clear that in some situations triangles can play an enormous role in fomenting conflict in families and relationship systems, as happens in *Tracks*.

Part II: Using Bowen Family Systems Theory to Understand Pauline

The two narrators of *Tracks* are similar in their hope that their audience will accept their interpretation of the events that they narrate. Nanapush's audience is clear; he is telling his story to Fleur's daughter in the hope that she will forgive her mother for abandoning her when she was a child if she understands what happened in the past. He is also trying to persuade her not to marry into the Morrissey family; again he hopes that if she understands the cause of the feud between her family and the Morrissey clan, she will remain loyal to her family and not marry a Morrissey. In contrast, Pauline's audience and her intention with her narrative are not as clear as Nanapush's, but a careful reading of the text reveals that she, too, is not simply telling a story for its own sake but narrating her 'history' with the assumption that her audience will be persuaded by her interpretation of the events and accept her self-evaluation. Pauline unconsciously feels the need to defend her past behavior, which has been destructive and even murderous on occasion. She presents her history as one of spiritual growth, the story of how she metamorphosed from shy Pauline to the bold Saint Leopolda. Bowen family systems theory enables the reader to understand what actually happened. As a person with a very low level of 'differentiation of self' who suffers from chronic anxiety that leads to emotional illness, she engages in 'cutoff', abandoning her family of origin to search for a new family with which to 'fuse'. Using Bowen family systems theory and current research on psychopathology, we will focus on Pauline's enigmatic narrative in order to reveal that Pauline lacks self-knowledge and often does not understand the implications of what she says. The image that Pauline has of herself and her interpretation of events are belied by her behavior.

Pauline's behavior is a consequence of her psychopathology and her problematical relationships within several family systems; her psychopathology helps shape those family systems, and those family systems affect her psychopathology. We will trace Pauline's odyssey from shy mixed-blood 15-year-old girl with an inferiority complex to her new self-conception of herself as saintly 21-year-old white nun empowered by God to convert the sinful Indians. Although Pauline would have the reader believe this odyssey should be seen as a miraculous one in which a saint is born, we will show that this odyssey can best be interpreted as a downward spiral of psychological deterioration culminating in a dissociative episode in which Pauline has completely estranged herself from her adoptive and actual families and has only a tenuous connection with the real world.

II.i. Pauline's Emotional Cutoff and Her Move from the Reservation to Argus

Although Pauline is not aware of it, the beginning of her narrative reveals that she is unhappy with herself and the family in which she was born. Her description of herself suggests that she has an inferiority complex; in fact, she describes herself as 'a skinny big-nosed girl with staring eyes' (16). Her inferiority complex seems largely a consequence of her mixed blood. Remarks that she makes suggest that she wishes that she could be all white like her 'pure Canadian' grandfather and that she wishes she was born into another family, a pure white family. She refuses to speak the Native language and learn Native skills and, believing that she 'was made for better', she convinces her father to allow her to leave the reservation and work in his sister's butcher shop in Argus (14).

Although it is not clear how conscious Pauline is of what she is doing, she is engaging in emotional cutoff. She desires to leave the reservation in order to separate herself geographically and emotionally from her family of origin. One can assume, too, that she does not have real affection for her Argus relatives, for later she tells Bernadette Morrissey that they mistreated her; with this convenient lie, Pauline gains Bernadette's sympathy, and it does suggest that Pauline sees her relatives in Argus as part of the family that she wants to abandon. She lives with them at this time only as a convenient way of obtaining her father's permission to leave her family of origin on the reservation. It is worth noting that when Pauline hears about the consumption epidemic on the reservation while she is living in Argus, she expends very little effort to discover whether her parents and sisters have perished or if they have been able to travel north to escape the illness. She does have dreams of her sisters and mother dead in trees, and one wonders if these dreams might be best interpreted as wish fulfillment instead of the dread of the death of family members, for she reveals no real concern for their fate at this time, and even later she does not try to discover what happened to them. In any case, whether they actually die or not is no great matter to Pauline, for she acts as if they no longer exist.

One of the contradictions that one finds in Pauline's character is that while she is unhappy with the Indian blood in her family, she becomes infatuated with Fleur Pillager when she becomes her fellow worker in the butcher shop. At this time Pauline is ambivalent about this issue of Indian blood, and she is also ambivalent about Fleur even though she seems completely infatuated with her, becoming her shadow. Erdrich has suggested in an interview with us that Pauline is 'afraid of Fleur, as many women who allow themselves to be controlled are threatened by women who do as they please' (Chavkin and Chavkin 224). In any case, Pauline is unaware of all the reasons for her love-hate feelings for Fleur. Apparently the timid Pauline, invisible to the men at the shop, simultaneously admires and resents Fleur for her independence, self-confidence and physical attractiveness. Later in the novel there is evidence that Pauline is sexually attracted to Fleur even if Pauline is unable to acknowledge that feeling. When Fleur is raped by the men at the butcher shop, Pauline observes voyeuristically and does nothing to help her. The next morning when the rapists go into the meat locker as protection against the tornado, Pauline locks the door. Only one man survives, her aunt's live-in companion Dutch James, and as a consequence of his incarceration in the meat locker he loses various body parts from severe frostbite. Pauline's narrative does reveal a perverse preoccupation with death and hints that she enjoys having the power of life and death over others.

After nightmares about her three victims, including her aunt's companion Dutch James, she leaves Argus to return to the reservation. Eventually Bernadette Morrissey invites her to become part of her family, which includes her brother Napoleon, her son Clarence and her two daughters, Sophie and Philomena. Pauline assists Bernadette, who helps the dying and later prepares the corpses for burial. Although Pauline has become part of the Morrissey family, for the next two years she continually visits Fleur's family, who treat her as if she were one of the family.

II.ii. Interlocking Triangles and the Destabilizing of Families

Because of the consumption epidemic, famine and the danger of losing their land to the lumber companies, many people living on the reservation are under great stress. Bowen explains that triangles often form in families under great stress, and one does see this phenomenon in *Tracks*, especially in Fleur's family. In Bowen's theory the triangle is a complex phenomenon that functions in diverse ways, but in some situations triangles can have a pernicious impact upon the family system. Although Fleur's family and Bernadette's family treat Pauline generously, Pauline's behavior does not suggest she appreciates their treatment of her. Her

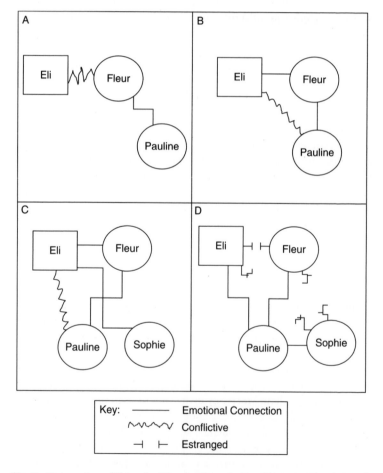

Fig. 1. Progression of Triangles That Leads to the Feud between Fleur's Family and the Morrissey Family

involvement with the two families destabilizes them by fomenting conflicts among family members. In Figure 1 we can see the progression of the most important triangles that occur in *Tracks* which permanently alter the relationship between Fleur's family and the Morrissey family. In Diagram A, tension develops between Eli and Fleur, and Pauline is triangled in to absorb the tension. In Diagram B, tension shifts from Fleur and Eli to Pauline and Eli. As Pauline's narrative implies, she becomes sexually attracted to Eli, makes a flirtatious pass at him, is rejected, and decides to get revenge for the rejection by bewitching him and the 14-year-old virginal Sophie Morrissey so that Eli will seduce Sophie and then Pauline can reveal the scandalous behavior of this sexual liaison to both families. Diagram C presents the creation of an interlocking triangle when Sophie is triangled in after Pauline's scheming. Soon after Eli and Sophie have sexual relations, Pauline reveals to both families the sexual transgression that has recently occurred, and the families are appalled. Fleur casts a spell on Sophie and banishes Eli, who moves in with Nanapush. Diagram D presents the consequences of the sexual escapade and its aftermath. While Pauline still maintains a relationship with the others in the triangle, relations among Eli, Fleur and Sophie are estranged.

Pauline's informing the families of the sexual liaison between Eli and Sophie has terrible repercussions. The relationship between Eli and Fleur nearly ends, and the Morrissey family is in great turmoil. The most important consequence of this sexual escapade is the animosity that develops between the two families, which leads to violence, retaliation and a permanent feud.

II.iii. Pauline's Ambivalent Attitude towards Fleur

After a long period of separation, Fleur forgives Eli for his infidelity, and they are reconciled. Pauline continues to visit the family as before. Pauline's sexual attraction for Fleur becomes clear to the reader, if not to Pauline herself. Having become fanatically religious, thereby sublimating unacceptable sexual feelings into socially acceptable religious fervor, Pauline continues to visit Fleur's home, supposedly to reveal her religious purity to the pagan Indians. To demonstrate her holy zeal, Pauline punishes herself in a variety of ways, including not bathing and not changing her clothes, which stink. On one of her visits, Pauline does not resist when Fleur strips her naked and washes her. Pauline has taken a vow not to touch herself, but she does allow Fleur to wash her, even as Pauline warns herself 'not to experience any pleasure' (154). The warning to herself is in vain, for the experience of Fleur washing her makes her abandon 'my Lord and all His rules and special requirements' (154). Pauline's description of being washed is erotic. Pauline goes into a pre-orgasmic swoon, and she lets 'the water course over me and let the hands [of Fleur] on my hips, my throat, my back, my breasts . . . break me down' (154–5).

Fleur acts solicitously in this washing scene, and one would think that Pauline would be grateful. In fact, Pauline's actions do not show any gratitude towards Fleur and other members of either Fleur's family or the Morrissey family. Immediately after the scene in which Fleur washes Pauline, a desperate Fleur needs Pauline's help as she tries to avoid a miscarriage. Usually Pauline is competent, but in this crisis she is so surprisingly inept that a furious Fleur reveals her outrage by throwing a knife at her, and later when Margaret returns home, she spits at Pauline to show her contempt for her complete failure to help Fleur. Later Pauline herself attempts to expiate her guilt for her dismal failure to help Fleur by deliberately mutilating her hands by scraping them raw. Pauline's behavior when Fleur miscarries is not an anomaly, however. One sees a pattern throughout her narrative in which her behavior reveals hostility towards Fleur. It becomes especially apparent later in the novel during a traditional healing ceremony that Nanapush has arranged for Fleur, who is having difficulty coping with a profound depression that is partially a consequence of her miscarriage. Believing she has supernatural powers, Pauline interrupts the healing ceremony by bringing it to a premature conclusion when, in her attempt 'to prove Christ's ways' (190) to those involved in this pagan custom, she suddenly plunges her hands into boiling water and then shrieks, jumps up and crashes the tent in which the ceremony is taking place.

II.iv. Pauline's Defense Mechanisms and Her Borderline Personality Disorder

Pauline continually acts in such a way as to alienate members of Fleur's family and the Morrissey family. Her interaction with them reveals the defense mechanisms of splitting and projective identification that the unconscious mind uses in an attempt to shield itself. Pauline sees people as either completely good or completely bad, saints or sinners, and she associates white blood with the good and Indian blood with the bad. In denial and unable to recognize her self-hatred, she comes to view herself as 'wholly white' while seeing members of the Morrissey family and Fleur's family as sinners because of their Indian blood (137). Unable to acknowledge her own Indian blood and the disturbing aspects of her own character, such as her hostility towards others, she believes without any doubt that Fleur and other family members possess these disturbing aspects – that is to say, Pauline projects what she is unable to recognize in her own personality onto the others, which eventually causes them to react in an unfriendly manner towards

Pauline, thereby confirming in Pauline's mind what she has projected upon them.

Though she cannot consciously acknowledge it, Pauline has an 'underlying dread' of being bad. This feeling, Jerold Maxmen observes, is central to individuals with borderline personality disorder (572). Such individuals typically 'disown this badness by projecting it onto others ("projective identification"), act out to escape feeling this "badness," employ reaction formation . . . or may behave self-destructively' (572). Maxmen's description accurately describes Pauline, who acts out, engages in self-mutilation on a number of occasions and meets the diagnostic criteria for this personality disorder. Individuals suffering from borderline personality disorder reveal 'a pervasive pattern of instability of interpersonal relationships', unstable identity and impulsivity that begins by early adulthood. In fact, in her narrative Pauline provides unmistakable evidence of at least five of the nine criteria for this personality disorder that are necessary for an authoritative diagnosis. Pauline meets the diagnostic criteria of items 2, 3, 5, 8 and 9 of borderline personality disorder in the *Diagnostic and Statistical Manual of Mental Disorders*, the standard work for the classification of mental illness:

1. frantic efforts to avoid real or imagined abandonment. **Note:** Do not include suicidal or self-mutilating behavior covered in Criterion 5.
2. a pattern of unstable and intense interpersonal relationships characterized by alternating between extremes of idealization and devaluation.
3. identity disturbance: markedly and persistently unstable self-image or sense of self.
4. impulsivity in at least two areas that are potentially self-damaging (e.g., spending, sex, substance abuse, reckless driving, binge eating). **Note:** Do not include suicidal or self-mutilating behavior covered in Criterion 5.
5. recurrent suicidal behavior, gestures, or threats, or self-mutilating behavior.
6. affective instability due to a marked reactivity of mood (e.g., intense episodic dysphoria, irritability, or anxiety usually lasting a few hours and only rarely more than a few days).
7. chronic feelings of emptiness.
8. inappropriate, intense anger or difficulty controlling anger (e.g., frequent displays of temper, constant anger, recurrent physical fights).
9. transient, stress-related paranoid ideation or severe dissociative symptoms. (710)

II.v. Pauline's Final Emotional Cutoff and Her New Identity

The severity of Pauline's borderline personality disorder becomes clear to the reader if not to Pauline near the end of her narrative when she decides that she will repudiate her old life and join a new 'family', the convent on the reservation. Before actually becoming a nun and cutting herself off completely from her past, she decides that she will make one final visit to Matchimanito Lake to do battle for Christ and destroy Lucifer, whom she believes has assumed the form of the lake creature. After this last visit, Pauline makes clear that she will isolate herself completely from the two Indian families that she has been part of; once again her low level of differentiation and chronic anxiety will result in total emotional cutoff. While for a period of time she was enamored of an idealized Fleur, now she completely devalues her and the others, as once again she employs primitive defense mechanisms, denial and splitting to protect her fragile identity. Fleur and the others are worthy only of her contempt: 'They could starve and fornicate . . . worship the bones of animals or the brown liquor in a jar' (196). When she goes out onto the lake in a stolen boat and observes Fleur and the others on the shore, she sees them as the 'kingdom of the damned', including even her own abandoned daughter, Marie, whom she refers to as 'the bastard girl' (198).

Pauline's perception of reality, which at various times in the past had been inaccurate, becomes paranoid and delusional as she prepares to conquer Satan and 'transfix him with the cross' (200). At night her boat drifts ashore, and she feels omnipotent and eager to fight Lucifer, whom she believes has taken the form of the monster in the lake. Then, believing the sea creature has come ashore to battle her, she strips off all of her clothes and grapples with him. After an intense struggle, the naked Pauline, armed only with a rosary, strangles Lucifer, 'his long tongue dragging down my thighs' (202). In the morning she realizes that she has killed Napoleon Morrissey, the father of her child, but she does not feel any guilt for his death since she rationalizes that the devil had assumed Napoleon's form when she had battled and killed him. It is important to note the intensity of her violence, and that when she was strangling Napoleon with a rosary she was conscious of his long tongue dragging down her thighs. The implication is that her religious fervor should be construed as a sublimation of repressed sexual impulses, and that the fanatical violence against Lucifer/Napoleon should be regarded as displacement of her self-hatred. In any case, with her hallucination over, she hides the corpse of Napoleon in high weeds near Fleur's cabin, knowing full well that the Morrisseys will assume that Fleur is the one who murdered him. Aware that she is naked and must cover up before she can return to the convent, she rolls in slough mud, leaves, moss, feathers of a torn bird and 'the defecation of animals'. Despite Pauline's megalomaniac proclamations of her religious purity, clothing herself in this filth suggests that on some level at least she sees herself as no better than 'shit'. She herself notes that when she finally arrives back at the convent, she is 'nothing human, nothing victorious, nothing like myself' (204).

The phrase 'nothing like myself' is a signal of Pauline's identity problem – her self-image is unstable. She concludes her narrative by announcing her transformation. She now sees herself as 100 per cent white and sanctified. Sublimating her unacceptable sexual drive into an acceptable religious one, she proclaims, 'Christ will take me as wife' (204). She states that she conquered the lake monster that night and expresses no regrets that the Morrisseys, who found the body of Napoleon behind Fleur's cabin, blame Fleur for the death. She will be sent out to teach Indian children in Argus and intends to save their souls and thus is 'an agent of colonization', as John Purdy observes (21). To underscore that her old self, Pauline, is dead, she announces in the final lines of her narrative that she will now go by the name of Leopolda, a name that aptly suggests her 'perverted nature' with its echo, as Robert Morace points out, of Leopold von Sacher-Masoch, an 'index of her masochistic (and later sadistic) personality' (51). In her troubled mind her transformation from ambivalent mixed-blood girl to white saint is complete, and she would have us believe that this rebirth is miraculous.

In reality what we have seen is a process of psychological deterioration. Pauline's low level of differentiation led to her emotionally cutting herself off from her family of origin and unsuccessful attempts to become part of a new family. Repeatedly she failed in interpersonal relationships, and, as she alienated others, her psychological state deteriorated, and she destabilized the families with which she was associated. As her borderline personality disorder increases in severity to the point of paranoid ideation and temporary dissociative state, she commits a murder for which she assumes no responsibility. Finally, she employs emotional cutoff again, totally repudiating those in her past, and creates a new fraudulent identity and denies her family, her ethnicity and her heritage.

CHAPTER 3

'I knew there never was another martyr like me'

Pauline Puyat, Historical Trauma and Tracks

Connie A. Jacobs

While trauma is clearly not new to the human condition, a language describing the long-reaching effects of trauma on survivors and their families began only in the nineteenth century with the early psychologists. Within the past 150 years, trauma theory has gained such currency that it has become a critical component of literary, historical, sociological and psychological studies. Why? Because trauma theory provides us, the listener, the observer, the reader, with valuable ways to attempt some comprehension of that which is lodged deep in the human psyche: the unnamed, the psychic wound, the site of trauma. Trauma outlives the actual event. If untreated, the initial trauma keeps coming back, unsolicited, and manifests itself behaviorally in unhealthy patterns that get passed down inter-generationally. The mind may not remember, but the trauma lives on in the reactions to it. Unless the trauma is addressed, the cycle of reactivity and suffering cannot be ended. What matters most for the children who inherit their parents', grandparents' and even earlier ancestors' trauma is that we try to understand and to respond to the initial loss and to the possibility of healing from it. As the Acoma poet, Simon Ortiz, reminds us, 'It is time and not too soon nor too late / A child again will be born into the midst / Of history, his and your history, our history' ('History's Midst', lines 26–28).

The first part of this chapter presents an overview of the field of trauma theory, its history, its major tenets and some important theorists. The second section looks at a branch of trauma theory, historical trauma, and its importance in understanding contemporary American Indian culture. A reading of the character Pauline Puyat in Louise Erdrich's novel, *Tracks*, as a victim of historical trauma concludes the study.

Trauma Theory

Critical theories emerge out of historical, cultural and intellectual necessity, and they are not recent companions to literature and aesthetics; they stretch back to Plato's *Republic* and Aristotle's *Poetics*. New theories arrive at an opportune time to fill a void, to provide answers, to give context and, in many contemporary theories, to help us bear witness. New theories are conquerors; they take from existing theories what they need and then set out to establish new territory. Such is the case with trauma theory that has borrowed from the fields of postcolonialism, feminism, cultural studies, New Historicism, Marxism and psychoanalysis.

Trauma theory studies the effects of an event so devastating to the human psyche that it cannot be processed in any ordinary way and which continues to repeat itself symptomatically through flashbacks, nightmares and 'the marks of psychic numbing' (Brown 100). As Cathy Caruth describes, 'The trauma is a repeated suffering of the event, but it is also a continual leaving of its site' ('Trauma and Experience: Introduction' 10). The roots of trauma theory can be traced to the efforts of early psychologists – William James in America and Pierre Janet in France – who sought to understand the effects of psychic trauma. These men studied the ways in which the mind processes memories and the extent to which some memories become insurmountable impediments to an emotionally healthy life. James observed how certain memories keep returning, unsolicited, randomly and destructively. Janet 'proposed that traumatic recall remains insistent and unchanged to the precise extent that is has never, from the beginning, been fully integrated into understanding' (Caruth, 'Recapturing the Past' 153). Because the traumatic event has no precedent, and therefore no way for the psyche to integrate it, the unresolved trauma keeps returning over and over again. Janet concludes that in order for healing to begin, the trauma has to be integrated (Caruth, 'Recapturing the Past' 153). Another important observation by Janet is that some traumatic events are so intense that the brain stores them differently and does not allow for them to be 'retrieved under ordinary conditions' (Caruth, 'The

Intrusive Past' 160). Later, when portions of the event do surface in the conscious, they are often accompanied by some sort of behavioral reaction.

It was Sigmund Freud who laid the foundations for the current field of trauma studies. In his work, Freud became interested in how and why the reactions to traumatic experiences tended to repeat themselves in a person's life. For Freud, 'the term "trauma" is understood as a wound inflicted not upon the body but upon the mind' (Caruth, *Unclaimed Experience* 3). His work with First World War veterans brought him an understanding of the nature of traumatic events, 'war neuroses', that kept reoccurring in dreams and became 'an impossible history within them' (Caruth, 'Trauma and Experience: Introduction' 5). It is in Freud's seminal work of Jewish history, *Moses and Monotheism*, that he develops the word 'latency' to describe the condition that occurs if events are repressed. The paradox, Freud notes, is that since a traumatic event cannot be fully experienced when it occurs, it can only be experienced at a different time and under different conditions, thus its 'latent' or delayed response. Additionally, Caruth describes another of Freud's most important insights, 'The historical power of the trauma is not just that the experience is repeated after its forgetting, but that it is only in and through its inherent forgetting that it is first experienced at all' ('Trauma and Experience: Introduction' 9).

The aftermath of the Second World War with its genocidal horrors and Hiroshima, followed by the Viet Nam 'conflict' brought the field of trauma studies to the fore, and with it many of the leading trauma theorists: Robert Jay Lifton, Dori Laub, Cathy Caruth, Michele Balev, Dominick LaCapra, and Kalí Tal. The early 1960s saw the first full-length studies of Holocaust survivors, and in 1980 the DSM-III (*Diagnostic and Statistical Manual*) first included a definition of Post-Traumatic Stress Disorder (PTSD), what Laura Brown calls, 'the psychiatric syndrome that arises out of the experience of trauma' (100). The DSM-III defines PTSD as the experience of 'an event that is outside the range of human experience' (Brown 100), a foundational concept in the field. The 1990s brought trauma theory into the realms of literature, history and culture with the publication of Cathy Caruth's collection *Trauma: Explorations in Memory*, and *Unclaimed Experience: Trauma, Narrative, and History*; Dominick LaCapra's *Representing the Holocaust: History, Theory, and Trauma* and *Writing History, Writing Trauma*; and Kali Tal's *Worlds of Hurt: Reading the Literatures of Trauma*. These contemporary theorists and others have made significant contributions to the understanding of trauma and its impact on the human psyche.

For this chapter, the following selected critical concepts and terms from trauma theory are fundamental to an understanding of the fictional character, Pauline Puyat:

'acting out versus working through' traumatic events. That is, how does a victim respond? Does s/he become 'fixed' in the trauma or move beyond the event? (Dominick LaCapra, *Representing the Holocaust: History, Theory, Trauma*, 188)

'the burden of his/her history' that a victim carries within, even though s/he does not have possession of that history (Freud)

'the capacity to remember [that] is also the capacity to elide or distort . . . or may mean the capacity simply to forget' (Caruth, 'Recapturing the Past: Introduction' 153–4)

'an enduring state of mind. . . . The moment becomes a season, the event becomes a condition' (Erickson, 'Notes on Trauma and Community' 185)

'fantasme' – used by the French psychoanalysts, and attributed to Freud, is a way to describe the 'intangible phenomena' of dreams, delusions, complexes, fantasies, daydreams, hallucinations and sexual wishes originating out of some kind of unresolved experience or trauma (Rapaport 17–18)

'internalized oppression' – Pablo Freire's theory that people who have been victimized may begin to identify with their oppressors and feel hatred towards other people (groups) like them, as well as hatred of the self (Brave Heart, 'American Indians and Alaska Natives in Health Careers')

'loss of confidence in self, family and community' (Erickson, 'Notes on Trauma and Community')

'mastering' trauma [which] is not possible since trauma resides 'outside or alongside the "integrated" ego' (Hartman, 560)

'pathologies' – resulting from a traumatic event and taking the form of amnesia, disassociation and even rejecting aspects of one's experience and identity (Caruth, 'Recapturing the Past: Introduction')

possession by the past (Caruth, 'Recapturing the Past: Introduction')

'psychic numbing' and 'psychic void' – Henry Krystal in his work with Holocaust survivors refers to conditions that occur if a person does not acknowledge the traumatic event ('Trauma and Aging: A Thirty-Year Follow Up')

'transference' – one of LaCapra's major contributions. At its best, transference acts out the past in new, healthy relationships, such as therapy, and promotes healing. However, if the event is not acknowledged and dealt with, the individual stands in danger of remaining a victim to its potential destructiveness (*Representing the Holocaust: History, Theory, Trauma*).

Historical Trauma

Laura Di Prete opens her book *Foreign Bodies: Trauma, Corporeality, and Textuality in Contemporary American Culture* with a description of the Jewish Museum in Berlin designed by architect Daniel Libeskind, whom she heralds as 'a master of architectural commemoration' (1). The museum presents a cultural and historical history of the Jewish people since their arrival in Germany in the fourth century. A visitor walking into the museum encounters a series of empty spaces, room after room, which are accessed by a series of bridges or 'roads'. You travel from empty space to empty space over empty space. The main focus of the museum is what Libeskind terms 'the Holocaust Void' (1): a room located in a tower outside the museum where there are no exhibitions. His structure is a homage and testimony to the victims of the Jewish Holocaust, especially the Jewish citizens of Berlin, and what visitors experience is an overwhelming sense of emptiness and horror at all the lives that have been lost.

Libeskind's visual representation of absence provides an effective way to begin thinking about the effects of historical trauma caused by the mass killing of one group by another. Examples come too easily to mind, and the twentieth century has witnessed the wholesale destruction of millions of people. The names of the most infamous leaders ordering the killings are familiar: Mao Ze-Dong, Jozef Stalin, Adolf Hitler, Leopold II of Belgium, Pol Pot, Saddam Hussein, Suharto, Tito and Idi Amin.[1] When you factor in civilians killed in war as well as regional and internal conflicts, the numbers become numbing. The survivors of these mass exterminations are victims of historical trauma; they have survived but carry with them overwhelming loss and permanent psychic scarring.

Trauma theory is generally applied to one horrific event, such as Stalin's pogroms or Pol Pot's 'killing fields'; one war, World War I, World War II, or Viet Nam; or a finite period of mass trauma such as the Armenian or Jewish Holocausts. Leading scholars and clinicians cited above have contributed to building a field of knowledge of the long-ranging effects on survivors of mass trauma and their descendants. However, when the focus turns to American Indians, the scope of trauma theory requires expansion in order to understand and to begin treating a trauma that is 500 years old, and ongoing. Nancy Van Styvendale forcefully expresses this very point: 'The intergenerational trauma of Native peoples raises serious questions about the assumption of trauma as rooted in event, where "event" is understood to refer to a distinct experience that happens in one specific location and time. Cumulative and collective, this trauma is more properly understood as both "insidious" . . . and trans/historical' (205). Aaron Denham provides a useful definition of historical trauma: the 'process of transferring the characteristics of trauma to subsequent generations. These include but are not limited to collective trauma, intergenerational PTSD, historical grief, an acute reaction to colonialism, intergenerational trauma, and multigenerational trauma' (396).

Maria Yellow Horse Brave Heart, a sociologist, has been instrumental in bringing about public recognition of the collective effects of historical trauma as they relate to American Indian populations. Her definition includes 'cumulative emotional and psychological wounding over the lifespan and across generations, emanating from massive group trauma. . . . Historical Trauma [is] [t]he collective emotional and psychological injury both over the life span and across generations, resulting from a cataclysmic history of genocide' ('Welcome to Takini' n.p.). Her work in this area began in the 1970s when she became aware of the enormity of the grief and sorrow American Indians, including herself, were carrying with them and passing on to future generations. Her professional career was built upon helping 'our people heal from this trauma we carry' ('Historical Trauma'). Brave Heart's work was influenced by research from Jewish scholars on the Holocaust, especially Eva Fogelman, who focused on children of survivors and the need to educate them about their history so they could confront and control it. Some of the main symptoms of historical trauma that Brave Heart addresses in her work are survivor guilt, depression and psychic numbing, fixation on trauma, hyper-vigilance, compensatory fantasies, preoccupation with death, internalization of ancestral suffering and internalized oppression ('From Intergenerational Trauma'; also see Grant).

The causes of historical trauma in American Indian populations are numerous, but all are a result of colonization. The various phases of colonization can be organized into categories that help orient a reader to the scope of historical trauma among American Indian populations:

contact that brought diseases (measles and smallpox)

war and invasion of American Indian tribal homelands, resulting from the doctrine of 'Manifest Destiny', the gold rushes, and the building of the transatlantic railroad

reservations where the US military removed tribes from traditional homeland, roles, and livelihoods and relocated them to
government reservations

boarding Schools where officials from the US Government often
forcibly removed children from their homes, causing ruptures
in family and tribal life as well as loss of transmission of tribal
language

lack of religious freedom and prohibition of ceremonies, resulting
in loss of cultural memory of traditional ceremonies

relocation where the Bureau of Indian Affairs (BIA) officials
moved families off reservations to urban centers

adoptions of American Indian children into non-Native families.

The long-lasting effects of historical trauma on American Indian communities testify to the extent of the damage wrought by colonization
and, as Les Whitbeck declares, 'After military defeat, American Indians
experienced one of the most systematic and successful programs of ethnic cleansing the world has seen' (121). It is important to note, as many
scholars have done, that not all of the 550 federally recognized American
Indian tribes were affected similarly by historical trauma and that there
is not one American Indian community (see Duran, Duran and Brave
Heart; Palacios and Portillo; and Denham). However, the results of historical trauma have, unfortunately, produced similar problems that are
pan-tribal.

A survey of the lives of American Indians today, especially those living on reservations, demonstrates the degree to which many have been
affected by historical trauma. There are lower rates of completed education, an absence of healthy family environments, high unemployment,
poverty, alcoholism, violence, low self-esteem, high suicide rates and
dependence on the government that results in a lack of self-reliance. As
James Berger notes, 'The idea of trauma also allows for an interpretation of cultural symptoms – of the growths, wounds, scars on the social
body, and its compulsive, repeated actions' (n.p.).

Whitbeck and his group devised a study that would measure the
effects of historical trauma as defined by Brave Heart and others. In a
longitudinal and ongoing study with a group of American Indian elders
on two reservations in the upper Midwest, Whitbeck's group sought to
document the types of historical loss they experienced as well as their
emotions surrounding these losses. Of prime importance to the elders
was the loss of language resulting from the boarding school era, when
the children were punished for speaking their tribal language. Also
related to the boarding school era was a breakdown in family and

community. The other major area the elders talked about was loss of land due to broken treaties. The main feelings resulting from these losses are predictable: anger and depression (119–24).

Statistics bear out the ongoing problems in American Indian populations:

> alcohol and drug addictions that result in more than 60 per cent of deaths among American Indians (Duran, Duran and Brave Heart 61)

> suicide rates often 70 per cent higher than the national average. Among American Indian youth, some suicide rates are up to '10 times the national average' (Daly, 'Senate Looks at Suicide', n.p.)

> lower median household income – around $19,890 – according to Janelle F. Palacios and Carmen J. Portillo. The average national household income is $30,056 (15)

> likelihood of American Indian women experiencing violence and poor health. Brown's point that trauma is gendered is made painfully clear when looking at the lives of American Indian women. Palacios and Portillo document the grim reality for many American Indian women who tend to experience higher rates of violence (twice the rate of the national average); are often pregnancy risks; have poor parenting skills due to the boarding schools and lack of experience of growing up in a family unit; and are more likely to die from cancer, diabetes, stroke, liver disease, heart disease and internal injuries (16).

The news from Indian Country, however, is not all bleak. There are a growing number of tribal and pan-tribal healing programs that seek to reduce the effects of historical trauma. Leading this effort is Brave Heart and her Takini Network. Her initial work in 1992 was for her Lakota people, and it involved a four-day workshop. That experience made Brave Heart realize the inherent power in communities that attempted to confront their problems, mourn their losses and start a healing process. Brave Heart hoped that her model could be used with other tribal nations and formed The Takini Network; '"Takini" is the Lakota word meaning survivor or one who has been brought back to life' (Brave Heart, 'American Indian and Alaska Natives in Health Careers', n.p.). Since 1992, Brave Heart has conducted over 100 workshops where she works with elders in a specific tribal setting. Once she and her group leave, the community members she trained are then responsible for following up. In these workshops, Brave Heart seeks to help indigenous people to 'heal from the historical unresolved grief' and she sees her work both as intervention and healing. Herb Grant notes that, 'Generally, discussion of the multigenerational transmission process of historical trauma is focused on aspects of parenting and alcoholism' (127). Accordingly, in their workshops, Brave Heart and her colleagues have been increasing their 'focus on the rebuilding of positive parenting and attachment' (Grant 127). Working with parents, she addresses reasons for their poor parenting skills and seeks to help them realize the effects the boarding schools had on their parenting skills. Her goal is to effect a change that can help their children lead more productive lives and be better role models themselves when they become parents.[2]

A Reading of Pauline Puyat as a Victim of Historical Trauma

How can we who have not experienced historical trauma begin to bear witness and to understand the enormity of the loss for American Indians? I would argue that literature is a most effective means to draw us into a story that is not our own and help us to 'read the wound' (Hartman 537). Van Styvendale asserts that 'literary constructions of trauma' are important to American Indian texts as a means by which to understand the oppression, despair and hopelessness felt by American Indians (204). Laura Di Prete goes further and argues for the efficacy of the literary approach to trauma that she believes can serve as a type of psychoanalysis. It becomes the text, and not the therapist, that opens up the memories and allows the retelling, and, perhaps, the healing. As readers, we then become participants in the healing process through our awareness and our understanding of what has taken place.

Louise Erdrich's stories demand that we pay attention and listen to them. Even if they are fictional, Erdrich's stories represent and come from Anishinaabe history. As I have argued elsewhere, Erdrich is continuing the tradition of a tribal storyteller by passing on Anishinaabe history to all who read her books. Nowhere is this more evident than in her North Dakota novels. Erdrich's novels have a prolific cast of characters, and their lives are intertwined through blood, marriage, friendship and love (see Barton and Beidler).

One character stands out from the others, not only because she plays a role in five of the novels, but also because she is destructive, unlikable, self-righteous and resolutely anti-Indian. I refer, of course, to Pauline Puyat/Sister Leopolda. Drawing upon the tenets of trauma and historical trauma theories as a lens by which to take a close look at Pauline's character, I hope to demonstrate the degree to which this character is Erdrich's most extreme representation of a victim of unresolved historical trauma. *Tracks* is the novel where readers first learn key events in Pauline's life story.

With its alternating narrators, the format of *Tracks* pits Nanapush's version of history against Pauline's. Nanapush is modeled after the Anishinaabe culture hero Nanaabozho who is trickster and healer. Nanapush is also a trickster and healer as well as storyteller, jokester, traditionalist and grandfather figure to Lulu. He is telling Lulu Pillager Nanapush where her story fits into the larger story of both tribe and family. Nanapush is the keeper of history, of the stories. In the opening paragraphs, Nanapush recounts the losses from disease, of the land, of removal from traditional lands in Minnesota and of depletion of the animals. He wants Lulu to know her history, to know why her mother, Fleur Pillager, sent her to a boarding school away from the reservation. He needs her to understand both her history as well as tribal politics so she will not make a bad marriage to an enemy of her family.

The other narrator is a Métis, Pauline Puyat, on the fringes of the community, a misfit, and 'born a liar' (53). She is humorless and friendless. Pauline does not seem to know her family or tribal history, other than that her grandfather was Canadian, and she wants to be like him, to look like him: to be 'all white'. While neither narrator is entirely reliable, Erdrich definitely privileges Nanapush's version of history over Pauline's. Nanapush wants to remember; Pauline wants to forget.

Pauline's denial of her Anishinaabe blood and of the impact colonization has had on her family and tribe marks her as a victim of historical trauma, a tribal member who has no sense of the degree to which history has affected her. As Hartman describes, her trauma has become 'displaced from memory' (546). Brave Heart discusses this situation in an interview with Tina Deschenie who asks how Brave Heart deals with people in her workshops who deny any effect from historical trauma. Brave Heart explains, 'We let those in denial know that we carry this trauma, even if it is not conscious. It affects our health, our emotions, our behavior, our relationships, and our children' (3). As Caruth has pointed out in her work, if the trauma is not assimilated into the consciousness, there can be no healing. She writes, 'What returns to haunt the victim . . . is not only the reality of the violent event but also the reality of the way that its violence has not yet been fully known' (*Unclaimed Experience* 6).

Pauline keeps reenacting historical violence through her fixation on pain; according to LaCapra's theories, she is acting out her trauma rather than working through it. She denies the source of her trauma and yet keeps reliving it through her addiction to bodily deprivations. She does not wash, only goes to the bathroom twice a day, wears her shoes on the wrong feet, drinks only hot water, never touches or scratches herself, wears a hair shirt, puts burrs in her armpits, screwgrass in her stocking and nettles in her headband and lets her toenails grow. She has identified with the oppressor in the form of the Catholic Church, not realizing she is symbolically replicating the pain inflicted upon her tribe, especially the pain meted out to the children in the Catholic boarding schools where children were removed from their families, forbidden to speak their tribal language, were shorn of their long hair, forced to wear uniforms, deprived of food, endured harsh punishments, were beaten and even sexually abused, all in the name of God.

Pauline sees the Catholic Church as a place where she can belong. She feels, and is, alone, without family and without land. She reasons, 'Where else would I go but to the nuns?' (142). In the church she can find a place that will accept her bizarre behaviors, even sanction them. Pauline aspires to martyrdom and, as Susan Friedman discusses, she 'models herself upon the early Christian martyrs and medieval Catholic saints, whose suffering recapitulates the anguish of the crucifixion' (120). Friedman clarifies, however, that a reason why female saints would often practice extreme mortifications of the flesh was in order to prove their worthiness in a very patriarchal institution. Yet, paradoxically, often that same institution condemned the women for heresy or witchcraft for their penitential excesses (122).

'Excessive' is an instructive way to think about Pauline. In *Tracks*, she refers to several saints, yet asserts that she is different from them, even as she tries to simulate their sacrifices. There is Saint Perpetua who is exposed to a mad heifer, Cecilia who outlived her own beheading, Saint Blaire who was 'combed to death by an iron rake' and Saint Catherine who incessantly whirled. She even mentions a man, Saint John of the Cross, who was shut in a closet for a year (152).[3] The deprivations endured by these saints were for a higher service: as penance for sins and as help to prepare their body for the 'visionary experience' (Friedman, 121). Pauline explains the reason behind her excesses: 'Suffering is a gift to God!' (144). Yet it is hard to find the religiosity driving her actions. Nowhere do we see her actions as rites of purification in order to bring her closer to God and to better act as his agent in the world. There is no compassion, no love for her neighbors, for her Sisters and for tribal members, no humility and no piety. She has taken on the bodily suffering but not the love of fellow beings. She is rather a victim of trauma acting out what Di Prete terms the 'traumatized body' (2) and not Christ's bride. She aspires to be the best sufferer – 'I knew there never was a martyr like me' (192). She assumes the trappings of sacrifice but lacks the heart and Christian love necessary to accompany any real act of submission.

It is also through the Catholic Church that Pauline can aspire to martyrdom as well as to pit the supremacy she feels the Catholic Church bestows upon her as a novice against the power of the traditional medicine woman, Fleur Pillager. Again we see historical trauma being reenacted as the Catholic Church specifically and Christianity generally seeks to conquer and to eliminate Native religion. Pauline believes Fleur holds the key to Misshepeshu, the powerful underwater *manitou* who controls the waters and the destiny of all who would venture out upon them. Therefore, it is Fleur, as representative of the traditional ways, whom Pauline must defeat. When Pauline goes out onto Lake Matchimanito to conquer the Lake Man, she is delusional and filled with fantasies of her powers, what Freud terms 'fantasme', that are brought on by trauma. Believing her own outrageous sacrilege that Christ and God were too meek to confront Misshepeshu, she becomes the savior, the one to bring 'The Indians' (138) into the Christian fold. Instead, in her delusional state, she murders the father of her child, Napoleon Morrissey. Friedman's interpretation of this murder is noteworthy: 'Killing Napoleon represents the attempt to erase the sin of carnality, of life in the body she would deny. . . . As Christ's champion, Pauline commits murder, a metonym for missionary erasures of indigenous religions' (115).

There are other examples in *Tracks* that mark Pauline as a symbol of historical trauma. One is her denial of being Anishinaabe, as when she announces to the Mother Superior that despite her 'deceptive features, I was not one speck of Indian but wholly white' (137). Franz Fanon describes in *Black Skin, White Masks* how people with a hatred of themselves as oppressed can seek to identify with the oppressor. Rather than seeing herself as partially white, Pauline identifies herself as all white, echoing Fanon's theory of one effect of a caste system imposed by the colonizers. He writes, 'This colonization of the mind produces the desire – often expressed symptomatically – to be white as a response to the racist imperative to "turn white or disappear"' (100).

Her disassociation from her native heritage is another indication of a fissure of self brought on by trauma. Hartman believes such a rupture allows fantasy to enter 'to repair a breach' (543). The fantasy becomes a truth owned by the victim, however outrageous. In order to bring about this revised version of self and history, Pauline must continually forget, distort and disavow (see Caruth). As Nanapush describes, 'The practice of deception was so constant with her that it got to be a kind of truth' (53). She not only denies she has Anishinaabe blood; she also denies any damage her meddling has caused. She disavows her role in the Eli/Sophie affair and the terrible consequences of it; she accepts no responsibility for her ineptitude which contributes to the death of Fleur's second child; she will not speak her tribal language; she tells tales of both her aunt and Bernadette Morrissey mistreating her; she initially 'forgets' locking Dutch James, Tor Grunewald and Lily Veddar in the meat locker in Argus; she 'remembers' how Christ forgives her for her affair with Napoleon and the child born from it; she feels God has singled her out for special service to bring 'Indian' souls to him; she believes she not only cut the rope connecting Mary Pepewas to life but also that after the death, she flies up into a tree. These 'compensatory fantasies' (Brave Heart, 'Wellbriety Conference' 7) are one response to trauma, an attempt to try to make up for and to recreate a better past.

Brave Heart identifies 'a preoccupation with death, death identity' as another sign of historical trauma ('Wellbriety Conference' 7). Usually, however, the death fixation is a way of mourning and grieving for those who have passed on. For Pauline, this is not the case. In aiding death at her sickbed watches, she feels a release; death 'brought [her] peace' (69), and she 'made death welcome' (69). Pauline even chooses to become death's carrier. She passes death from family to family by not washing after being in a death house, thus replicating the US government's practice of spreading disease through the distribution of diseased blankets to tribes. Hartman's theory of death as a cathartic experience in trauma literature can be applied to Pauline's perverse behaviors: 'At most, the act of killing, like kids stoning a dog or hanging a cat, is provocative of what is missing: it challenges a conscience or moral design' (542). Clearly, Pauline is without a conscience.

Erdrich's descriptions plainly identify Pauline as a scavenger bird, another way of associating her with death. Nanapush describes her as 'the crow of the reservation, she lived off our scraps' (54). Pauline sees herself in this role: 'I had the merciful scavenger's heart' (69) and believes she is capable of flight. Susan Scarberry-García in her article on animal and bird representations in *Tracks* considers that, 'because of her need to transcend her earthly circumstances' (48), Pauline fancies herself as a bird, and Scarberry-García reads Pauline as both crane and crow. Pauline seems to be everywhere: in the corners, in the shadows, waiting and watching. In Argus, she 'blended into the stained brown walls' (16) and could be found lurking near the stock pens, butcher shop and meat locker. She observes, but does not participate. She is cut off from others by her scavenger-like personality. Her family has either died or moved away; she does not know. She is alone and a victim of psychic numbing (see Krystal) brought on by her isolation, her lack of connection to family and to land and her inability to have meaningful connections with others. She compensates by scavenging as a way to live off others.

Pauline's name is carefully chosen. Friedman relates Pauline to Paul who as a Jew converted to Christianity and repudiated his 'prior identity . . . as Saul' (114). Paul was an enthusiastic missionary who traveled throughout the region bringing in people to the new Christian church. Likewise, Pauline feels she has a mission to help 'the Indians' by converting them to Christianity and bringing as many souls as she can into the church, away from their traditional religious practices. When she is sent to teach at St. Catherine's school in Argus, her focus is to 'add their souls to those I have numbered' (205). An even more interesting name choice is the one she draws when she enters the convent, Leopolda. There are two historical figures referenced by this name. First is the brutal King Leopold II of Belgium, who was responsible for the deaths of up to 15 million Congolese in the nineteenth century. Historic accounts tells us that he felt he bore no responsibility for these deaths, yet he has gone down in history as one of the worst killers of humanity. The other Leopold is Leopold von Sacher-Masoch, an Austrian who also lived in the nineteenth century. He was a writer who incorporated masochism into his stories, and the term 'masochism' derives from his name. Pauline's name, therefore, alludes to historical figures who proselytize, massacre and inflict self-pain.

It is through this disturbing, lonely and dangerous woman, Pauline, that we can recognize a history of American Indians as victims of overwhelming oppression by the US government which sought their extermination in order to clear the country for European settlers. Pauline is a literary reminder of the degree to which victims of historical oppression can act out their trauma. There can be healing, but only if trauma is recognized and recovering from trauma is desired. Pauline never does acknowledge her trauma but rather transfers all of the worst effects of colonization onto a new character, Sister Leopolda. It is interesting that the character of Pauline/Sister Leopolda lives to a ripe old age and is even considered for sainthood until the truth of all of her wrongdoings comes out. Erdrich includes this unlikable character in most of her early novels and positions Pauline against some of her most endearing characters: Nanapush, Father Damien and even Pauline's daughter, Marie Lazarre Kashpaw. Pauline is historical trauma writ large, Erdrich's testimony to 500 years of historical oppression of American Indians.

CHAPTER 4

'To become a bureaucrat myself'

History and Law in Tracks

David Stirrup

This chapter will examine the historical, particularly the legal-historical, contexts of *Tracks*, Erdrich's third novel and the earliest in the chronology of her 'North Dakota series'. The attempted 'shaping' of Native American communities through such mechanisms as the Bureau of Indian Affairs (BIA), the establishment of reservations and policies of removal, assimilation and termination through the nineteenth and twentieth centuries figures the singular nature of the legal-political relationship between the United States government and what Justice John Marshall called the 'domestic dependent nations' of its original inhabitants. I will briefly describe the nature of law and literature studies, paying particular attention to the benefits to literary study of taking account of the law and its rhetorical, as well as judicial, implications for indigenous peoples. I will then outline the key legal-historical contexts in which Erdrich's novel, and Native American literatures more broadly, sit, examining the novel itself through this dual lens. My argument is simply that engaging with the legal-historical framework of allotment and treaty rights helps to open up the significance of *Tracks* for the rest of Erdrich's 'tetralogy' for the Anishinaabeg people specifically, and for Native–white relations more broadly. In doing so, one explores not merely a representation of a difficult time in Anishinaabeg history, but also a representation of the assertion and importance of, and threat to, indigenous sovereignty, and, in turn, one examines the ways in which this and other books address the ongoing ramifications of Indian policy and law central to questions of self-determination.

Kristen Carpenter's claim in this regard is simply that 'the study of literature has the potential to contextualize certain Indian law cases'; indeed, she confirms that 'a number of scholars argue that reading literary works . . . alongside relevant legal texts can deepen our understanding of the law' (606). For literary, rather than legal, scholars, of course, the reverse is also true. Reading historically, particularly in relation to a historical novel such as *Tracks*, necessitates an understanding of the legal conditions active in the historical moment being represented. Understanding this, law can deepen our understanding of the contexts and issues at stake in the fiction.

Law, History, Literature

The historical novel has the potential to draw into focus both the historical moment it depicts and the moment in which it was written. It permits, in that sense, a process of reflection on the causes and consequences of temporally distant contexts. Such inherently comparative positions open up all sorts of interesting interpretive questions, not least around questions of contingency and (in)determinacy, teasing open the political agendas and social consequences behind apparently inevitable, or ineluctable, events. Approaching literature in these terms is essentially historicist, placing the social and material conditions and discursive milieu of a text's production, and/or the moment it depicts, in central focus.

Given the nature of case law and the potential for precedents to be over 100 years old (Gulig and Harring 87), the capacity of literature to lend a sense of the lives upon which these laws impact, too often obscured by time, jargon or pure abstraction, is clear. Much Native literature touches on legal impositions upon indigenous lifeways, whether indirectly – the dams in McNickle's *Wind from an Enemy Sky* (1978), Linda Hogan's *Solar Storms* (1997) and Thomas King's *Green Grass, Running Water* (1993), for instance, which depend on a particular set of legal conditions around Native land, resources and other rights – or directly, such as allotment in S. Alice Callahan's *Wynema* (1891), the court case concerning the display and repatriation of Native American remains in Gordon Henry's *The Light People* (1995) or John Tatakeya's trial in Elizabeth Cook-Lynn's *Aurelia: A Crow Creek Trilogy* (1999). Further examples might include Gerald Vizenor's tricky focus on treaties, gambling and the liberation of his characters from codified 'crossblood' taxonomies, or the light shed on environmental law by those texts – fictional and non-fictional – that deal with the impact of uranium mining and waste dumping in Indian reservations. 'In 1985', observes Jace Weaver, 'in one of the leading cases of environmental law, the Ninth Circuit Court of Appeals observed, "Indian reservations may be considered as potential locations for hazardous waste disposal sites . . . because they are often remote from heavily populated areas" ' (2001 190). Such decisions have proven disastrous for some Native communities, particularly in the Southwest, and literary texts, along with other kinds of 'testimony', have the capacity to lay bare these consequences for broad audiences.

The combined study of literature, law and history has the potential to inflect the study of all three, addressing what Ian Ward sees as one of the key disputes in law and literature studies: the 'historicity of legal texts' (4). This chapter will deal with law *in* literature, since my focus is a novel, but the literary implications for law *as* literature, particularly around matters of style and rhetoric and the critical theory that informs literary hermeneutics, are neatly encapsulated in Ward's summary of James Boyd White's work:

> White's central concern is with the method of reading and understanding, and it is this concern with method which . . . unavoidably relates the twin projects of the law and literature movement – law *in* and law *as* literature. When we read narrative fiction, according to White, we do so with a more immediate sense of style and rhetoric, and it is rhetoric which, in many ways, is the keystone of White's thesis. (6)

There is a double turn implicit in this kind of comparative study, then. White, for instance, notes his focus on law 'not as a system for producing material results in the world, but as a system of meaning, or . . . occasions and opportunities for the creation of meaning' (52). I will not develop the theoretical debate here – which breaks down an opposition between the literary text as aesthetic play and the legal text as documentary fact – but many legal scholars have balked at the application to the law of critical theory's emphasis on the provisionality of language and rhetoric's emphasis on the function of form as conditioner of and contributor to meaning.

Reading Native literatures within this framework may aid understanding of the rhetorical implications of the law itself, not least within the context of what Chadwick Allen calls 'Treaty Discourse' (1997), which has been repeatedly tied up in property law, in legal and political definitions of sovereignty and in legal definitions of identity. For instance, as one of many consequences of severalty, 'People are classified by their tribe, the family, or the government as "full-bloods", "half-bloods", "one-fourth", "one-eighth", and so on. This is the genetic distinction' (Hobson 8). Of course, it is not a genetic distinction; it is a legal one. If treaty discourse provides a divisive taxonomy it also, somewhat ironically, provides a vehicle for resistance, not forgetting that, despite a slightly different interpretation under US constitutional law, treaties are conventionally enshrined in international law.

Alternatively, in the abstract to their 'Native American Literature, Ceremony, and Law', Cristine Soliz and Harold Joseph suggest that 'The joint study of law and literature offers a platform for Indigenous studies and other programs to explore divergent philosophies and systems of law that have marked the Americas since 1492.' This kind of comparative study posits a learning possibility for scholars and practitioners of US law that is iterated in different terms by other scholars. There is an ethical imperative, certainly, to understand 'law' in these contexts as not merely, or even not at all, related to Euroamerican law, but related to the systems of justice and advocacy developed by and within Native communities themselves and with the 'ethical systems' inherent in ceremony and often implicit in story. Bruce Duthu, for instance, argues, 'It is critically important that legal discourse, and particularly the legal discourse that concerns relations between Indigenous and non-Indigenous societies, incorporates the emerging and evolving narrative traditions of Indigenous Peoples' (143). Those narrative traditions begin for Duthu in the oral stories of his upbringing but extend to literary works too. Duthu's ultimate expectation from their inclusion and examination in legal discourse is that this 'encourages, and indeed often requires, lawmakers and law advocates to cross intercultural boundaries to examine the extent to which legal structures and rules respect cultural differences or reveal jurisprudential myopia' (143).

Highlighting complex and controversial court cases such as the *Cobell* series and *Lone Wolf versus Hitchcock* (1903) Carpenter claims that Erdrich 'raises important, relevant questions about "allotment"' and, in doing so, may inspire lawyers to contemplate the 'losses in socio-economic, familial, spiritual, and other realms of tribal life . . . completely ignored by *Lone Wolf*' and 'enhance understanding of the case and contemporary advocacy today' (607–8). If this does not go as far as Duthu, it at least contributes to the argument that Native people's stories must be listened to and can be learned from. In his study of American literature's relationship with law, Brook Thomas comments that to try 'to understand law "in the context of the narratives that give it meaning" is to try to reconstruct the cultural narratives that grant the law its authority' (5). Importantly, in the context of Native American literatures, the literature stands in relation to, despite *and* in explicit dialogue with, the legal-political hegemony.

The preservation of sovereignty in relation to land title is key in Indian country, both politically and culturally. As Kahnawake activist Taiaiake Alfred notes, 'We cannot preserve our nations unless we take action to restore pride in our traditions, achieve economic self-sufficiency, develop independence of mind, and display courage in defence of our lands and rights' (9). That latter action, the display of courage in defence of lands and rights, has been borne out time and again in North American courts, and nowhere more so than in the monumental *Lone Wolf versus Hitchcock* Supreme Court case. Originally brought by Kiowa leader Guipago (Lone Wolf) in 1868, the plaintiff argued that the unratified Treaty of Medicine Lodge (actually three treaties dealt with collectively) between the Kiowa, Comanche and the US government, had been abrogated. Providing for allotment, the treaty's twelfth article required that three-quarters of adult male members of the tribes must sign the document for it to be valid. *Lone Wolf* argued that the latter had not occurred and therefore subsequent agreements to allot and then cede 'surplus' lands were a violation of the original treaty.

Finding in favor of Secretary of the Interior Ethan A. Hitchcock, the court ruled that Congress 'has "plenary power" over Indians and can dispose of Indian lands at will', a decision that 'more narrowly construed, refused to apply the Fifth Amendment's Taking Clause to protect Indian property rights' (Gulig and Harring 87). This represents a radical departure from earlier findings, most notably the findings of the 'Marshall trilogy', which asserted that tribes represented 'domestic dependent nations', meaning that the Supreme Court had no jurisdiction over Native nations.[1] L. Scott Gould asserts that 'The first and foremost doctrine in federal Indian law is the doctrine of inherent sovereignty' which holds that tribes, under the ruling of *Cherokee versus the State of Georgia* 'may exercise powers free of the strictures of the Constitution unless limited by treaty or Congress' (Gould 809; qtd in Seibert 393). That the *Lone Wolf* decision chose to emphasize the power of Congress in land cases was significant.

The class action *Cobell* case also testifies to the need for historical contextualization in cases like *Lone Wolf*. Settled in 2010 in favor of the plaintiffs, *Cobell* sought to 'address the government's breaches of trust which resulted in the loss, dissipation, theft, misdirection, misappropriation and unaccountability of several billion dollars of monies held in trust . . . in Individual Indian Money (IIM) accounts' (*Cobell versus Salazar*). Those IIM accounts were created as part of the General Allotment Act, to manage the sale income for tribal individuals of surplus lands and other resources. '*Cobell*', says Carpenter, 'has raised widespread

awareness about the injustice of federal mismanagement of allotment';
its settlement constitutes an albeit tiny reparation for an equally tiny
proportion of property lost during, or as a direct result of, allotment
(Carpenter 2006 619). The Dawes Severalty, or General Allotment, Act
of 1887, hastened in Minnesota by the Nelson Act of 1889, divided up
tribal lands into individual parcels of 40 to 80, and then 160 acres
(depending on the type of land and its usage).[2] These parcels were then
distributed among enrolled members of reservation bands, to be held in
trust by the US government for a period of 25 years. Although billed as
intending to provide skills and a livelihood off the land, Allotment was
described by Theodore Roosevelt as 'a mighty pulverizing engine to
break up the tribal mass' (Larson 573). In *Tracks* we bear witness to the
rapid erosion of the land base through tax forfeiture and foreclosure.

Carpenter's point more broadly is that 'When *Tracks* and *Four Souls*
tell the multi-faceted and intergenerational stories of an allotted community, they suggest that narrow claims, such as the claim for a taking
of property in *Lone Wolf*, fail to capture the losses of allotment' and that
such stories operate to redress the case findings themselves, which
characterize 'allotment as a policy that simply changed the manner in
which tribes owned their real property and did not cause any losses at
all' (622, 607).

Other cases of peripheral import to the peoples and places depicted
in Erdrich's fiction include *Minnesota versus Mille Lacs Band of Chippewa Indians* (1999), which dealt with usufructuary rights on lands
ceded in the 1837 Treaty. The Treaty's fifth article contained the clause:
'The privilege of hunting, fishing, and gathering the wild rice, upon the
lands, the rivers and the lakes included in the territory ceded, is guar-
antied [sic] to the Indians, during the pleasure of the President of the
United States' (Krogseng 2000 773). Two subsequent agreements – an
Executive Order in 1850 revoking those rights and requiring the Mille
Lacs Band to withdraw from ceded lands in Wisconsin and Michigan,
and a second Treaty in 1855 in which the Band ceded further territory
and agreed to the establishment of their present-day reservation –
along with Minnesota's statehood in 1858, appear to remove the 1837
treaty rights (Krogseng 773–4). Krogseng notes, 'the state's Enabling
Act is silent as to Indian treaty rights. Thus there is no record of the
status of the Mille Lacs Band's treaty rights at the time Minnesota
became a state, nor is there any legislative history pertaining to the
Act's effect on those rights' (774). The Mille Lacs Band themselves
argued that the record did exist: it was the 1837 Treaty. As Wenona
Singel and Matthew Fletcher note, those usufructuary rights, reaffirmed by the Eighth Circuit Court of Appeals are particularly powerful: 'they can trump private property rights, state regulation, and even

state criminal laws' (1290). Although *Tracks* does not directly raise these specific issues, these cases and the ongoing tensions in the Great Lakes illustrate the key importance of treaties to the legal status of Native relationships to specific places and resources, while also demonstrating the potential awareness-raising function of literature around these topics.

Tracks, Land Claims and Treaty Rights

The legal backstory most pertinent to *Tracks* begins in the nineteenth century, with the settlement of the Anishinaabeg on reservations in the United States and reserves in Canada. US reservations were largely established through treaty prior to the 1871 Indian Appropriations Act and by statutes and executive orders thereafter, and by treaties from the 1870s onwards in Canada. The historical narrative of Erdrich's fictional reservation and its geographical indeterminacy, not to mention Erdrich's insistence in *Last Report on the Miracles at Little No Horse* (2001) that it is not based on a single real place, point towards an amalgam of several North Dakotan and Minnesotan reservations. Of these, Turtle Mountain in North Dakota and White Earth Reservation in Minnesota are arguably the most prominent sources.

Always controversial, reservations were nevertheless seen as a way of enabling the continued independence of tribal groups. Gulig and Harring note: 'Indian lands were not simply important as property, but they were places where Indians could live. Following from the tribes as sovereign nations, Indian land was a place for Indians to exist as Indians, to carry on their lives in ways consistent with their own unique cultures' (96). Reservations came to the Anishinaabeg in the 1860s and 1870s: in 1867 at White Earth in northwestern Minnesota under treaty between the US government and the Mississippi band of Chippewa Indians, and in 1882 in the Turtle Mountains, where executive orders (in 1882 and 1884) and the McCumber agreement (1892) set aside land for their sole use.[3] The original agreement ceded some ten million acres of wheat land to the government, while the 1884 agreement saw the land base reduced further to 'two six-mile square townships of untillable brush-covered hills' (Debo 1995, 354). The mixture, in Erdrich's novels, of Ojibwe, Cree and Métis (mixed French and Cree predominantly), certainly reflects the tribal roll at Turtle Mountain at the time. The specific issues at stake in *Tracks*, however, are better illustrated by turning to what is often called the White Earth timber scandal, not least because the momentous events at the end of *Tracks*, where the lumber companies move in to the Pillager 'parcel', are highly evocative of that episode.

White Earth Reservation was established to home the majority of Minnesota's Anishinaabeg, an intended concentration that drew serious opposition from many traditionalists, including the Leech Lake Band of Pillagers who, although finally relocating, did so at the outer edges of the land base. That separation is broadly reflective of what developed into a strong factionalism at White Earth in the wake of allotment. Initially split down apparently denominational lines (largely either Roman Catholic or Episcopalian), ultimately 'ethnic differences marked the genesis of community relationships at White Earth' (Meyer, 5). Those 'ethnic differences', largely designated by 'mixed-blood' and 'full-blood' would become particularly significant in the early years of the new century.[4] In 1904 the Steenerson Act and Clapp Rider, reinforced by a second Clapp Rider in 1906, removed many of the trust restrictions on sale of resources, especially timber, for mixed-bloods.[5] The Nelson Act had 'preserved' timberland by preventing the apportioning of pine-rich parcels, to be held in trust, while forcing the relinquishment of other tribal lands. Clapp and Steenerson, along with the 1906 Burke Act, which permitted land sales by 'competent' allottees, enabled the sale of that lumber. Essentially, the Steenerson Act granted further acreage to the tribe, including timber-rich parcels, to the delight of many Anishinaabeg who had protested at the earlier loss of land, while the Clapp Rider 'provided for disposition of the timber' (Meyer, 142).

The inevitable catalog of abuses – from illiterate tribespeople being conned out of their parcels by unscrupulous lumber companies, to crooked representatives writing in their own claims – is considerable. The Burke Act itself also created a layer of legitimate abuses based on a nebulous notion of 'competency', which was often identified with blood quantum. Michael McNally notes the inherently corrupted nature of this process:

> A particularly insidious aspect of White Earth's dispossession was the prominent role played in it by the nation's leading physical anthropologists. In the 1910s, Ales Hrdlicka and Albert Jenks were summoned to settle investigations of fraud in land sales by scientifically determining the blood quantum of White Earth residents. . . . Equipped with samples of hair and calliper measurement of skulls, the scientists dismissed half the fraud claims, determining that four hundred claimants had been of 'mixed blood' after all and therefore were unprotected by the trust clause of the legislation. In many cases, these findings completely disregarded the testimony that claimants themselves made concerning their family trees. (85–6)

Any factionalism that pre-existed allotment was pushed to its limits during this period. Berninghausen reflects on this policy in relation to *Tracks*:

> It was well understood that communal tribal land was essential to Native American identity in general and Chippewa identity in particular. Yet instilling the ethic of competitive individualism, essential for assimilation into the dominant culture, seemed to require individual private land ownership. . . . Altering the relationship between people and land was essential to the success of the federal policy, transforming 'home' into 'real estate', commodifying the sacred so that it becomes property. (199)

The privatization of communal lands was a major catalyst for the foment at White Earth and is essential background to the internal conflicts Erdrich represents. However, that factionalism, particularly in the Euroamerican version of the historical record, has tended to overshadow more positive elements of the tribal narrative, a representation of reservation history that Gloria Bird rejects as 'a static moment in the process of our colonization' (46). It derives from what Ledwon calls the 'legally sanctioned appropriation of property rights' (579).

Reservation-formation and Allotment, then, present the immediate historical contexts for *Tracks*, which, beginning in 1912, opens 25 years after the Dawes Act. Not quite in line with the end of the trust period of either White Earth or Turtle Mountain, since allotment on both reservations occurred slightly later, nevertheless the implications of that period resound strongly in the text. There are several key instances: the proliferation of Lazarre land claims following their purchase agreement with the Turcot Lumber Company; Nector and Margaret Kashpaw's sleight of hand with Pillager tax money, leading to the forfeiture of the Matchimanito parcel; Fleur's own act of revenge on the surveyors and lumber teams that move in; and Nanapush's acknowledgement that the only way to tackle the legal machinery of the United States is to 'become a bureaucrat' (225) himself.

The often-quoted opening of *Tracks* is a key passage:

> We started dying before the snow, and like the snow, we continued to fall. It was surprising there were so many of us left to die. For those who survived the spotted sickness from the south, our long flight west to Nadouissioux land where we signed the treaty, and then a wind from the east, bringing exile in a storm of government papers, what descended from the north in 1912 seemed impossible. (1)

The opening of the novel depicts what Sidner Larson calls the fragmentation of a tribal people. That fragmentation hangs on those specific historical contexts described above and persists to the 'present-day' (1980s) setting of *Love Medicine*, in which patterns of enmity and dysfunction between and within families are fully settled. We meet these characters for the first time in 1912, in the fuller contexts of their vulnerability, exposing their openness to manipulative forces: 'There were so few of us who even understood the writing on the paper. Some signed their land away with thumbs and crosses' (99). The first narrator, Nanapush, is marked out early as an 'old-time' character, working tirelessly to save Fleur Pillager, almost the last remaining of her disease-ridden clan, and recounting recent momentous events as a kind of mythic commentator: 'In the years I'd passed, I saw more change than in a hundred upon a hundred before' (2). The events he chooses to recount are at first startlingly generic: 'I guided the last buffalo hunt. I saw the last bear shot. I trapped the last beaver with a pelt of more than two years' growth' (2). As Bird notes, 'that Fleur Pillager, her cousin Moses, Pauline and Nanapush are all the last of their respective bloodlines is a manifestation of "The Vanishing Red Man" syndrome' (42). But Nanapush makes one key observation, absent from Bird's analysis, that places his stories within a far more politicized discourse: 'I spoke aloud the words of the government treaty, and refused to sign the settlement papers that would take away our woods and lake' (2). Later we learn that he advised Rift-In-the-Cloud not to 'put [his] thumb in the ink' at the Beauchamp Treaty signing (100). Later still, he demonstrates his distrust of the legal systems imposed on the reservation when he reluctantly opts for violent reprisal over the Lazarres, inferring to Nector that the tribal court holds kinship sympathies with their 'enemies' (118), highlighting one of many ways in which the novel demonstrates an imbalance of power between the maintenance of lands and traditions and the 'sell-out' to the Turcot Lumber Company.

The evocative metaphors of the opening locate the narrative in a long arc of dispossession implicating various European-derived diseases, migration, the effects of treaty signing and the bureaucratic strangulation of tribal peoples that ensued. The 'wind from the east' that produces 'a storm of government papers' and exile elevates the historical to the mythic but there is a highly significant syntax here. The long second sentence begins with the phrase 'For those who survived', emphasizing the endurance of those who experienced, and now bear witness to, what, in 1912, 'seemed impossible'. This is a deeply interesting opening to the novel, given the collapsing of documentary into figurative registers, and the interweaving of a historical sweep with more personal and *literary* narrative.

In the light of a narrative sequence that conforms to the 'inevitability' scenario of US conquest, Nanapush's moment of resistance is a jarring rejoinder – a reminder that there is and was nothing 'natural' or inevitable about the displacement of indigenous peoples. The romanticism of the natural metaphors of 'lastness' that Erdrich employs here – fundamental to the grand narratives of manifest destiny – is interrupted by a different kind of narrative: in part bureaucratic, in part rebellious, overall resistant to the consuming narrative of tribal dissipation.

It is not an easy story Erdrich is telling, for it focuses on internal politics, on the inherently corrupting nature of learning to 'reinvent the enemy's language'.[6] What is at stake here is the conflict established within this particular community as a clear and direct result of the kind of pitting of forces generated by the allotment act. Historical and legal studies highlight the conflict that developed either because parties felt duped by treaty representatives (*Lone Wolf*) or because the community was divided (McCumber); in the latter case, the victors generally were those who had the legislators and corporations on their side, as often happened at White Earth. In *Tracks*, the introspective nature of the narrative provides another kind of conflict between Kashpaw opportunism and Pillager/Nanapush naivety. While the Kashpaws agree with Nanapush that 'Land is the only thing that lasts life to life' (33), they ultimately do not share his misplaced faith in the system: 'I know about law. I know that "trust" means they can't tax our parcels' (174). Although the serious competition in the novel occurs between the older generation of Nanapush and Margaret, and the younger generations of the Lazarre/Morrissey families, the Matchimanito inhabitants are ultimately disenfranchised by the Kashpaws who seize the opportunity to pay off their own allotment fees by using the money Nanapush has entrusted to them, leading to tax forfeiture on the Matchimanito parcel. The external pressures are clear when Nanapush talks of the reservation being 'nibbled at the edges and surrounded by farmers waiting for it to go underneath the gavel' (99), but the novel also refuses a too-simple 'colonial' narrative of white agency subjugating powerless Natives.

Early in *Tracks*, shortly after the deaths of Fleur's family, Nanapush describes the relatively recent effects of 'competency' regulations, illustrating in the process the impact of material reservation conditions on the outcome of allotment:

> Starvation makes fools of anyone. In the past, some had sold their allotment land for one hundred poundweight of flour. Others, who were desperate to hold on, now urged that we get together and buy back our land, or at least pay a tax and refuse the lumbering money that would sweep the marks of our boundaries off the

map like a pattern of straws. Many were determined not to allow
the hired surveyors, or even our own people, to enter the deepest
bush. (8)

The kind of collective action suggested here is ultimately what is under
scrutiny in Erdrich's work; a counter might be Nector's rise to tribal
chairman under mixed motives of Kashpaw pride and power, or Fleur's
act of revenge in *Four Souls* as an act of individual vengeance at the
expense of her children, both in contrast to Nanapush's drive to figure
out the bureaucracy in order to bring Lulu home from school – to liber-
ate her from the government's grasp and reconstitute the family unit.
Fleur's general behavior in *Tracks*, on the other hand – her defiance,
sabotage, neglect and abuse of medicinal gifts – is described by Lawrence
Gross as misusing her personal power:

> she cannot be blamed for being angry, as she initially isolates her-
> self in the woods and uses her powers to make others fear her. Yet
> for all her strength, by the end of *Tracks* she is divested of what
> matters the most in Anishinaabe life: community, children, and
> land. Her ultimate failure speaks to the shortcomings of using
> great blessings to do great harm. (51)

Such a reading further stresses the tension between individualistic and
collective action.

The importance of this, alongside Nanapush's earlier comment about
the desire of some to buy back land is significant. *Tracks* resonates with
the intense political struggles of the 1960s, 1970s and 1980s, though it
does not explicitly confront them. While the novel does not reflect the
activities of groups like the American Indian Movement, which was
formed in the late 1960s (though it is there, in *Love Medicine*, in the
figure of Gerry Nanapush), there is a general reference in the novel not
only to the despoliation scandals of the early twentieth century, but also
the tense conflicts in the Great Lakes over issues such as walleye
spear-fishing.

Court decisions like the 1972 Wisconsin Supreme Court ruling that
the Bad River and Red Cliff Anishinaabeg had fishing rights on Lake
Superior, or the 1983 *Voigt* decision that reaffirmed off-reservation
hunting and fishing rights in northern Wisconsin (which had been
ruled against in 1978) characterize this conflict. The back and forth
between courts and the judiciary, with arrests frequently made for
spear-fishing in particular, carried on until 1985 and reflect the strong
feeling at the time, expressed in often violent protests and clashes
between traditional spear-fishermen and women and non-Native sports

fishermen. Although, again, Erdrich does not explicitly address these issues, they offer an important backdrop to the immediate contexts of the novel's production. And again, they demonstrate the close relation between the historical and legal contexts of reservation life in the twentieth century. Several non-Native protest groups galvanized around these issues, eventually moving towards, and even on to, White Earth, 'concerned with the protection of their "private property" and the exercise of Native rights on the reservation, whether to land or to natural resources' (LaDuke 123). The 'Protect Americans' Rights and Resources' (PARR) lobby is still protesting what they see as the injustice of the above rulings, referring to 'legally dead' treaty rights. Clearly, on the contrary, those treaties are still very much a live issue, with external definitions and defences of 'rights' and 'private property' still the driving concerns.

Erdrich has long resisted outright polemics in her fiction. Understanding these issues, however, enriches our reading of the novel, inflecting the tension of the 1970s and 1980s and sense of transition of the 1910s and 1920s, while further contextualizing Fleur's anger and explaining how easily the Kashpaw deception might have been enacted with so few contemporary disincentives in place. And notable, of course, is Erdrich's decision to focus the novel so clearly on interaction within the community, while alluding to events that might have encouraged a novel of direct confrontation. As Carpenter might argue, the literature of allotment brings insight into the experiences of individuals in relation to these large cases, often abstracted into case law; certainly *Tracks* portrays the easy duping of a group unversed in the minutiae of Euroamerican law. The novel implies, even where it does not state it, an inherent injustice and legal vulnerability around questions of land tenure.

Erdrich offers another implicit criticism, since the sequence in which Nanapush learns of the deceit emphasizes a cold, callous aspect of the mediating function of the federal agency and its role in the contest between those closest to the bureaucratic center (in other words, those more 'cooperative' members) and those at its edges:

> I banged my stick next to [the Agent's] round-toed shoe. 'How much of that good price [secured on the land], that illegal late fee [paid by the Kashpaws] perhaps, splashed into your pockets? How much is stored in the walls of my old cabin, which you gave the Lazarres? How much cash did you stuff into the mattress of Bernadette [Morrissey]?' (208)

All of this informs an implicit critique of the external conditioning behind the conflicts – an admixture of particular culturally determined outlooks and other material factors such as the pecuniary incentive to support land sales – a critique dependent on knowledge of those legal and historical contexts.

Nanapush's response is ultimately most instructive. Describing his regret at not taking Father Damien's advice more seriously, he tells Lulu, 'He was right in that I should have tried to grasp this new way of wielding influence, this method of leading others with a pen and piece of paper' (209). This statement, an assertion of change, an awakening to the mechanisms imposed on him by outside influences, is key to examining the restrictions placed on indigenous sovereignty in *Tracks*. Very much tied to the land – how can one exercise sovereignty with no land base, after all? – reading *Tracks* in this light allows us to tease open the ways in which pressure from settlers and investors has the capacity to shuffle allegiances, encourage duplicity and prevent coherent and cohesive resistance. But as Nanapush realizes, those same mechanisms offer potentially viable solutions in reality. In 1989, the White Earth Land Recovery Project (WELRP) was formed by Winona LaDuke, an affiliate of Anishinaabe Akiing, with the express aim of 'return[ing] White Earth land to the Anishinaabeg by supporting the transfer of public lands back to the White Earth tribal government, buying land from willing settlers, and other mechanisms' (LaDuke, 126).[7] More importantly – and here is that ethical imperative I mentioned earlier – the novel brings to light, albeit subtly, a hint of the alternative systems Duthu mentions, through two means: first, those repeated instances of Nanapush's resistance, whether it be his bid for self-governance, or his standoff with the Lazarres, 'we old-time Indians were like this, long-thinking but in the last, forgiving, as we must live close together, as one people, share what we have in common, take what we're owed' (180); And, secondly, and equally explicit, the collapse of Morrissey status through intermarriage and loss of respect, all implicit in their association with the Lazarres, the corruption of greed and exploitation writ large in 'all of them grown stout and greasy from the meat supplies that they had pilfered from their neighbors and the lard from the Agent's storehouse' (184). Importantly, this kind of alternative-to-contest narrative is crucial to the demands of tribal scholars interested in prioritizing self-governance: 'The state's power', writes Alfred, 'including such European concepts as taxation, citizenship, executive authority, and sovereignty, must be eradicated from politics in Native communities. In a very real sense, to remain Native – to reflect the essence of indigenous North Americans – our politics must shift to give primacy to concepts grounded in our own cultures' (11).

Conclusion

From minor connections to major intersections, this essay only touches the legal-historical narratives that arise from a novel like *Tracks*. Few scholars of Native literatures have yet embraced law and literature methodologies, although it is arguable that the critical-theoretical approaches of numerous writers and scholars in Native studies implicitly do battle with the legal philosophies of Western jurisprudence. Further studies in this area, which would seem both timely and fruitful, will best be set in the direction of Duthu's aspirations, taking up dialogue with law and literature's own set of conventions. There is one remaining caveat in this context that concerns me as a literature scholar, and that is the very serious danger of treating text *as* context. Indeed, Carpenter comes close at times in her essay to ruminations that would belie the *fictional* nature of Erdrich's novel. Although ultimately she acknowledges its fictionality and seems to advocate that the fiction is a means of remembering that the *real* stories need to be heard, it stresses the need for scholars engaged in law and literature studies to be alert to the essential differences between the texts they seek to compare and, more importantly, to the danger of subsuming lived experience to textual witness. Scholars in Critical Legal Theory are, as the name suggests, alert to the provisional and conditional nature of textuality: that no single text is representative, that no single representation is comprehensive and that no single position can be entirely ideologically neutral must always be held in mind when grand, generalizing claims for the value of literature to law are made. Literary texts are valuable and potentially useful to examinations of the law, but they must be treated with the same caution as any other piece of 'evidence'; perhaps more so, since they are not generated for the purposes of legal redress or explication and are produced often in spite of, not because of, the law.

PART II

The Last Report on the Miracles at Little No Horse

Introduction

The Last Report on the Miracles at Little No Horse continues Erdrich's North Dakota cycle of novels, providing background about the early lives of characters such as Nector Kashpaw and Pauline Puyat. Indeed, the occasion for the narrative is the series of letters sent by Father Damien to Rome over a period of many years and the arrival on the reservation of a papal envoy, Father Jude Miller – the Adare baby who was separated from his family in *The Beet Queen* – to investigate the possible canonization of Pauline/Sister Leopolda. The novel also provides some key details of Fleur's marriage to John Mauser, the rapacious logging company owner in *Tracks*, whose marriage to Fleur is told in *Four Souls*; the latter days of Nanapush and his death; and the death, finally, of Father Damien through whom much of the narrative is focalized.

The revelation that Father Damien, the reservation priest in the cycle of novels, is a cross-dressing woman has been the focus of much of the critical discussion of *The Last Report*. As Mark Shackleton shows, Agnes DeWitt/Father Damien occupies a position that is not only that of an outsider, as she is 'transfigured' from woman to priest, as a priest s/he is also an 'insider'. This liminal position allows the enjoyment of the patriarchal privileges made available to priests but also offers Father Damien a point of view from which to critique the unspoken conditions that facilitate the exercise of European patriarchal power. In the chapter 'Postcolonial and Critical Race Theory', Shackleton questions why

Native American literature has been neglected in the context of postcolonialism and critical race theory, given that the deconstruction of discursive strategies of power and control is central to both. David Stirrup, in his chapter on *Tracks*, engages Erdrich's critique of US law which authorizes the appropriation of Native lands and the containment of the exercise of Native sovereignty. Stirrup's chapter is in conversation with Shackleton's in that both address Erdrich's exploration of the impact on Native communities of Western liberalism, legal reasoning and Enlightenment rationalism, limiting Native American sovereignty and Native rights. In Erdrich's work, the subversion of Eurocentric binary categories of race, ethnicity, gender and sexuality is central, as Hollrah and Hafen go on to show in their chapters.

Much of the novel is concerned with exposure. In his final reports to the Pope, Father Damien wants to confess the subterfuge that he has sustained during his life as a priest, he wants to reveal the evil that Sister Leopolda represents – a murderer and a putative saint – and in the process of writing he exposes the discursive operations of colonial power in the specific context of the Native reservation where he has ministered. Shackleton shows that it is in Father Damien's access to two languages – the language of the Church which compels subservience, even when Father Damien wants to write critically, and the *Ojibwemowin* learned from his Native parishioners – that allows him to think and speak outside the confines of dominant discourse. Father Damien learns more than Native language from Nanapush; he also learns to use that language in order to question and subvert assumptions of authority, in a mode that Shackleton likens to the Ojibwe trickster. This trickster discourse, like the 'two-spirit' motif – male and female spirits inhabiting the same body – is seen by Shackleton as an example of the 'hermeneutical impasse' (Rainwater) characteristic of Erdrich's writing: Damien uses Christian and Ojibwe terms of reference in the same utterance, creating for the reader an epistemological divide that cannot be bridged with any simple interpretation of cultural adoption or belonging.

In both form and theme, *Last Report on the Miracles at Little No Horse* challenges Eurocentric binaristic modes of thinking. Rachel Lister has analysed the dialogism of this novel, describing how 'Agnes' narrative constitutes a series of dialogic encounters' (Lister 224); however, the trajectory of the novel moves towards a wider questioning of the 'truth' of any discursive construction. The variety of kinds of texts included in the narrative, and the framework of Father Jude's attempt to gather authoritative 'evidence' of Sister Leopolda's sainthood, subverts the assumption of fixed meanings and definitive accounts of events. Agnes learns the performative dimension of gender identity, which she comes to describe as 'heavily manufactured of [sic] gesture and pose' (76), as she first dons the dead Father Damien's clothes and then begins to imitate masculine gestures and poses. But the novel also emphasizes the dimension of gender as bodily experience: the menstruation that Agnes prays will end or the whiskers that fail to grow as Father Damien lies in his weeks-long coma.

Father Damien/Agnes occupies a liminal position not only in relation to gender categories, but, as a priest who describes himself as having been 'converted' by Nanapush, he lives between Ojibwe and European cultures. Native people (Kashpaw and Nanapush, Fleur, Mary Kashpaw) know of her cross-dressing and accept it. Through his experience of the vision quest and sweat lodge Father Damien learns the relations among Native shamanic religion, ceremony and land. As his awareness of the destructive impact of colonialism increases, Father Damien seeks forgiveness and absolution – which, together with faith, love, sin and saintliness – are among the concepts that P. Jane Hafen sees tested in the context of Ojibwe experience and specifically through the profound Ojibwe influence of Nanapush upon the priest's spirituality. Self-forgiveness for complicity in colonial destruction, represented by the Catholic Church, is what Agnes/Damien seeks. However, Hafen's discussion in 'Indigenous Traditions in *The Last Report on the Miracles at Little No Horse*' nuances these concepts by focusing on the ways in which Erdrich complicates Catholic rituals and practices with Ojibwe characters and their traditions and beliefs as a strategy of literary decolonization. Father Damien is the human point where Church doctrine meets the daily spiritual lives of his Native parishioners, and by living that intersectionality Damien comes to 'practice a mixture of faiths' (276); s/he is a living example of reconciliation on many levels. In his growing awareness of Damien's holiness Father Jude begins to wonder whether he is investigating the wrong candidate for beatification and suspects that Father Damien may be the true saint.

Hafen argues that sacred interconnections between identity, place and objects form a network of indigenous relations that Father Damien can witness but cannot experience. Similarly, Patrice Hollrah shows how some critics have been misled by using the Native term 'Two-Spirit' to describe the non-Native character Agnes/Father Damien. While the transformation from woman to man may seem to invoke this Native status, in fact the regrets that Father Damien voices concerning the children he (in his life as Agnes) never had, as well as his desire to 'confess' in his last report the 'lie' that he sees his life as having been, and his desire in death to dispose of his body so that no one will ever know his biological sex, all powerfully suggest that Father Damien is not 'Two-Spirit'. Rather, the figure of Agnes/Father Damien serves to put into question the nature of sexual attraction and the nature of the relationship between love and sexuality. Hollrah cites a number of examples in Erdrich's fiction of characters who want to live in loving, sexless hetero-sexual relationships while pursuing homoerotic relationships, and other characters who, at different points in their lives, move between hetero- and homosexual relations. Reflected in the title of her chapter, 'Love and the Slippery Slope of Sexual Orientation', is Hollrah's point that, in Erdrich's writing, there are no fixed relations among love, gender and sexuality. Those relations are fluid and changing, along with the iden-tity categories that support them, such that 'Agnes/Father Damien defines herself as a person who at the core of identity eliminates gender altogether.'

CHAPTER 5

Power and Authority in the Realms of Racial and Gender Politics

Post-colonial and Critical Race Theory in The Last Report on the Miracles at Little No Horse

Mark Shackleton

In Louise Erdrich's *The Last Report on the Miracles at Little No Horse* (2001), Sister Cecilia, a former nun (née Agnes DeWitt) takes on the clerical robes and identity of Father Damien and becomes the priest to the Ojibwe on the Little No Horse reservation. In the subplot the life history of Pauline Puyat is traced from her origins in a bitterly divided mixed-blood family to her rise as Sister Leopolda, a powerful figure at the convent near Little No Horse. Both rises to power and authority are based on deception – Father Damien is a woman, and Pauline must pass as white in order to enter the order. Both have a 'double vision' that allows them to perceive the workings of power and authority and the intricacies of gender and racial politics from a privileged position as well as through the eyes of a liminal outsider looking in. As a number of critics (Barak, Keenan) have suggested, Louise Erdrich frequently plays with borders and distinctions, deconstructing, undermining and questioning essentialist markers of power, authority, gender and race.

This chapter will argue that a number of the rhetorical strategies of post-colonial theory can be applied to *Last Report*, and by implication to a wider range of Native American writing, at the intersection between post-colonialism and critical race theory. Critical race theory (CRT) has its origins in the 1960s and is concerned with racism, racial subordination and discrimination, and, in particular, the socially constructed nature of race. It offered a radical critique of the American legal system, for by studying and seeking to transform the relationships between race, racism and power, it in effect questioned the very foundations of liberalism, legal reasoning and Enlightenment rationalism. Race is, of course, also a central concern of post-colonial studies, as shown in the work of Franz Fanon, Edward Said, Homi Bhabha, Cornel West, Toni Morrison, Barbara Christian, Gayatri Spivak, Chandra T. Mohanty, Stuart Hall, Paul Gilroy and others. Post-colonialism meets critical race theory in their joint attention to discursive strategies of power and control and in their aim to decolonize essentialist categories of race, gender and ethnicity.

Most recent writing on race in post-colonial theory has focused first on the Black experience, be it in the United States (West, Morrison), the Caribbean (Fanon), the United Kingdom (Hall) or in the so-called Black Atlantic, which links Africa, America, the Caribbean and Britain (Gilroy). Second has been the Asian experience (Said, Spivak, Bhabha, Mohanty). By contrast, relatively little has been written about First Nations/Aboriginal experience or the so-called 'Fourth World'. In a recent anthology, *Race Critical Theories*, only one contributor mentions Aboriginals. CRT has also been primarily concerned with Black (African American) experience, though it has been used as a critical tool to promote Native American sovereignty and to defend indigenous peoples' rights and land claims. Issues of race, nevertheless, are at the heart of the primary texts of the Native American Renaissance and the post-Renaissance generation. Racial conflict and difference are central to N. Scott Momaday's *House Made of Dawn* and Leslie Marmon Silko's *Ceremony*; all Gerald Vizenor's work concerns stereotyping and the deconstruction of racial mindsets; Pauline Puyat's mixed-blood traumas link Erdrich's *Tracks* and *Last Report*, and Sherman Alexie charts the psychic breakdown of a 'white' Indian in *Indian Killer*. Given that race is central to post-colonial theory, and racial (primarily mixed-blood) identity is such a dominant theme in Native American writing, it is worth briefly discussing why post-colonial and race theory has not been more widely applied to Native American writing.

Post-colonialism has not always been a welcome term in the context of Native American studies. This is partly because major post-colonial critics seem to have turned a blind eye to this area of study, and partly because there has been resistance among a number of Native American writers to the use of the term. None of the three major post-colonial theoreticians, Edward Said, Homi Bhabha and Gayatri Spivak, have directed serious attention to the existence of Native American voices. As Louis Owens ('As If' 13) has pointed out, in *Culture and Imperialism* Said himself writes in imperialistic tones of 'that sad panorama produced by genocide and cultural amnesia which is beginning to be known as Native American literature' (304). There is additionally little or no discussion of Aboriginality in the work of Spivak or Bhabha, though, having said that, post-colonial approaches have been productively applied to Native American writing by such critics as Arnold Krupat and Elvira Pulitano.[1]

The main critique of post-colonialism among a number of Native American writers raises the question of whether in the context of American imperialism the term 'post-colonial', implying a 'post' condition of decolonization and independence, can be applied to Native Americans. Among First Nations writers, warnings about viewing Native literature through post-colonial lenses have been made by, among others, Lee Maracle, Jeannette Armstrong and Thomas King.[2] In his frequently cited essay, 'Godzilla vs. Post-Colonial' (1990), Thomas King objects to the assumptions that the term implies. These assumptions, as he sees it, include the notion of 'progress and improvement' from a 'pre' to a 'post' condition; the fact that the terms of discourse are those of the colonizer and hence reek of 'unabashed ethnocentrism'; and that essentially Native literature is seen as a 'reaction' to the arrival of European settlers. The latter in particular ignores the vital elements of Aboriginal oral culture that flourished in pre-contact times, and are still active today. As a corrective, King offers four 'vantage points' from which to view the range of Native North American writing: tribal, polemical, interfusional and associational. Tribal literature is presented in the Native language and is directed towards the members of that community; polemical literature concerns the clash of Native and non-Native cultures; interfusional literature blends oral expression and literature; and associational literature concentrates on the daily activities of Native life, organizing plot elements along a flat narrative line and eschewing the climaxes and denouements commonly found in non-Native writing. These suggested categories, King argues, serve to base the critical focus on the culture from which the works arise, rather than to see Native writing as a reaction to the dominant culture.

Definitions of post-colonialism are inevitably wide-ranging and here a distinction between temporal and topological approaches is useful. Discussing the term 'post-modern', Robert Wilson distinguishes between two 'archives' of primary and secondary texts, while at the same time acknowledging that the two archives do overlap. The first 'archive' constructs the post-modern as a period; the second is a flexible analytical term designed to isolate conventions, devices and techniques across a wide range of cultural products. Applying Wilson's terms to post-colonialism, the first archive focuses on the writing produced by societies that have been affected by European colonization, while the second conceives of the post-colonial more in terms of discursive practices, such as resistance to colonial forms and legacies. Thomas King's critique of post-colonialism emphasizes the temporal dimension of the term, and downplays the critical analysis of culture that the term also implies, but in fact his own definition of 'polemical literature' is very close to the topological approach of the post-colonial 'second archive'. When he writes that polemical literature 'chronicles the imposition of non-Native expectations and insistences (political, social, scientific) on Native communities and the methods of resistance employed by Native people in order to maintain their communities and cultures' (13), he is in fact using the terms of post-colonial theory.

In what follows I shall explore Erdrich's *Last Report* in terms that combine key elements of post-colonial and race critical theory. I shall cover notions of voice and who is heard or not heard; notions of race and the perpetuation of stereotypical notions of race from generation to generation; Erdrich's adoption and deconstruction of notions of race; Erdrich's exploration of living on the margins and the power that living liminally permits; and, finally, her use of discursive strategies, which I refer to as trickster discourse, which appropriate the language of the dominant culture in order to expose its inherent structures of power and control. In these following sections the focus is not on post-colonialism as a period of time (Wilson's first 'archive'); instead, as in Wilson's second 'archive', my focus is on Erdrich's manipulation of the conventions and devices of language through which she provides a post-colonial critique of power and control in the realms of racial and gender politics.

Whose Discourse Prevails?

A central concern of both post-colonial theory and critical race theory is the question of whose voice is heard. Both theories are concerned on the one hand with revealing the interests which lie behind the production of knowledge and power, and, on the other hand, with retrieving what Foucault has called 'disqualified knowledge', primarily the voices of silenced minorities. Father Damien, a woman in man's robes, a non-Native who has partial access to, and understanding of, Ojibwe ways, is one of these minority voices, and the novel opens with him seething in silence.[3] He is about to write his 'Last Report' to the Pope because, nearing death, he wishes to reveal his identity as a woman, to confess his charade, and to expose Sister Leopolda, a supposed saint, as a murderer.

Damien's life has been spent writing 'fierce political attacks, reproachful ecclesiastical letters, memoirs of reservation life for history journals, and poetry' (2) all of which have remained unpublished and quite possibly unread. Writing his 'Last Report' in 1996, he has addressed every Pope since coming to the reservation in 1912 without a single reply.

Damien's discourse operates on two levels. Inwardly he angrily chastises the Pope: 'Apparently, one couldn't hope for a reply, oh no, that would be all too human, wouldn't it!' (3), while his actual letter, although showing signs of irritation, is ultimately conciliatory and humble. Towards the end the Pope is addressed as 'Fountain of Faith', and the writer concludes the letter with the suggestion that the pontiff's silence is perhaps a test of faith: 'Perhaps the silence from beyond these poor boundaries has been a test, a shrewd marker of my endurance, my belief' (4). In this way Damien employs self-censorship, self-silencing, bending to the full weight of Rome by adopting the approved symbolic language of the Catholic Church ('Fountain of Faith') and by taking on the conventional role of the humble supplicant whose faith is unshaken even when no light is shown: 'let this last report confirm my lack of [religious] doubt' (4). Damien's true feelings and his challenge to the power and wisdom of the Church are at odds with his final written statement, thus instancing Foucault's claim that discourse controls, selects and organizes information. Damien the rebel here becomes complicit with the power of the Catholic Church by reinscribing its values and language. In this way the official discourse of power is seen, in Foucault's words, to ward off the dangers of doubt and avoid the 'ponderous, formidable materiality' of fact: in this case the material evidence of Damien's gender and Leopolda's murder. In the example given here, Damien is seen to challenge this power, but ultimately succumbs to it.

Post-colonial and critical race theory are both concerned with the way discourses of power serve to uphold prevailing beliefs and social values. Critical race theory in particular has been primarily concerned with legal discourse and the way it sustains embedded conceptions and encourages individual 'counter-storytelling' as a corrective. *Last Report* foregrounds clashes of discourse primarily shown through the investigation of Leopolda's supposed sanctity. Father Jude has come to Little Horse to investigate the 'official' story of Leopolda, and his language and approach is couched in legal terms. He has come to look for 'firsthand and thoroughly witnessed fact' (50), and asks whether 'proofs had yet been furnished of Leopolda's intercessions' (51). By contrast Damien offers a continuous 'counter-story' that unnerves Jude's official procedures. Jude's gravity meets with Damien's 'prideful glee' at which Jude is 'nonplussed' (50). Challenging Jude's set procedures at every turn, Damien himself adopts the language of law, asking 'who will form the council' (the jury on Leopolda's case), and inquires shrewdly of 'the status of any petitions or people's acclamations' (50). The counter-examination continues with Damien requiring Jude to define the terms of sanctity, a trickster-like inversion of the rules as he suddenly breaks into the Ojibwe language, followed by an immediate return to the 'tones of firm analysis' with the assertion that he, Damien, would like to establish himself 'as the crucial witness' (51). Under this barrage Jude's securities begin to dissolve. Jude is forced to acknowledge the truth of Damien's/Agnes's perception that 'Pauline was a creature of impossible contradictions' (123) leading Jude to wish that there was 'just one thing that Leopolda did that was not of an ambiguous nature' (147).

What these textual examples show is the flexibility, revealed through discourse, of Erdrich's understanding of power relations. When Damien uses the language of the Catholic Church he is bound by its constraints; its diction takes over his mind, forcing him into patterns of subservience. On the other hand, Damien's use of Ojibwe, and his trickster strategies of appropriating the language of legal authority in order to subvert its assumptions of power and authority, shows the way in which 'counter-story' provides access to an alternative and resistant speech.

What's Race Got to Do with It? The Impossible Contradictions of Pauline Puyat

When Father Jude complains of the impossible conundrums surrounding Pauline Puyat/Sister Leopolda's 'ambiguous nature', Damien replies, 'But that is just exactly what the Puyats are . . . not one thing or the other. Contradictory . . . you must look at the name and the clan to assess the person, even a mixed blood like Leopolda. For she was shaped by the double nature of her mother, and who knows what else' (147–8). Damien here locates race as a key concern in determining character and destiny, specifically the notion of the divisions and hatreds caused by interracial antagonisms which are passed down from generation to generation. Pauline has been 'shaped by the double [mixed-blood] nature of her mother' and the words 'who knows what else' allude darkly to the hatred and violence which figure so strongly in Pauline's mixed-blood family origins.

Readers of *Tracks* have been given a full picture of Pauline's psychological development, locating her need to identify with whiteness as a force which is so dominant in her life that it encompasses strangling her mixed-blood ex-lover and abandoning her mixed-blood child. The central scene here is Pauline's vision of Christ, a figure with dark hair but Aryan blue eyes, who comes to absolve her from the taint of race: 'He said that I was not whom I had supposed. I was an orphan and my parents had died in grace, and also, despite my deceptive features, I was not one speck Indian but wholly white' (*Tracks* 137). The Christ-figure also absolves her from the responsibility of raising her child in view of her greater task of ridding heathenism from the land, the pagan 'enemy' being the Ojibwe, seen as 'a devil in the land, a shadow in the water'. Here the 'shadow in the water' is the Ojibwe water monster Misshepeshu, which Pauline believes she has strangled with her rosary beads after an epic nighttime battle, though when light breaks she realizes that it is Napoleon Morrissey she has killed, the father of her child. Pauline conceives the fight on the epic level as the triumph of Christian good over pagan evil: 'I believe that the monster was tamed that night' (*Tracks* 204). On the personal level she has killed the Indian in herself, leaving the mixed-blood Pauline behind and becoming the all-white Sister Leopolda.

Pauline's history chimes with key notions in race theory. In *Colonial Desire*, Robert J. C. Young shows how patterns of thought about culture and race laid down in the nineteenth century continue to persist in contemporary cultural theory. Young shows how culture and race developed together and that the categories of the past still influence the present. He closes his first chapter by quoting Foucault's 1982 essay, 'The Subject and Power': 'we have been trapped in our own history,' and concludes, 'The nightmare of the ideologies and categories of racism continue to repeat upon the living' (210). Ann Laura Stoler, in *Carnal Knowledge and Imperial Power*, a study of colonial Indonesian society in the late-nineteenth and early twentieth centuries, like Young, shows the centrality of notions of sexuality at the heart of Victorian racial theory. But whereas Young characterizes colonial desire as an obsession with hybridity and transgressive fantasies of inter-racial sex, Stoler emphasizes the extent to which rules and taboos of inter-racial intimacy at the individual and family level underpinned imperial politics at large. In their separate approaches both owe a debt to Foucault's *The History of Sexuality* and its exploration of the links between sexuality and power.

What is interesting in *Last Report* is that Erdrich's representation of *métissage* (the mixing of races) through the history of the Puyat family to some extent repeats the tropes of nineteenth-century race theory. In relation to Pauline this can be interpreted in terms of her internalization of the values of the mainstream culture, but in Erdrich's representation of Pauline's family background, and even in her representation of Pauline, some familiar tropes are reworked. I shall return to this point, but first the section of *Last Report* that most directly represents the issue of the irreconcilable tensions and effects of mixed-blood identity needs to be discussed.

Midway through *Last Report*, and concluding Part Two ('The Deadly Conversions'), Father Damien provides a ten-page 'History of the Puyats', providing the reader for the first time with a fuller picture of the racial tensions behind Pauline's bloodline. Characteristically, the information Damien gives is 'disqualified knowledge', namely 'a tattered and stained, unevenly typed article addressed to the North Dakota State Historical Society' to which 'one or two rejection letters' (148) are attached. Strife and discord based on the alliance of Native and non-Native bloodlines are foregrounded. In Damien's 'partial history' (150), the first figure presented is Pauline's mother (also called Pauline), 'a young girl in whom the bitterness of seven generations of peasant French and an equal seven of enemy-harassed Ojibwe ancestors were concentrated' (150), and we learn that her Ojibwe mother and French-Canadian father hated each other. When a hunting party of Bwaanag (Lakota) Sioux meet the girl's band of Ojibwe and French-Indian Michif, the two parties agree to settle their scores in a race rather than a battle. Both parents see in this race an opportunity to kill their spouses, as the price of defeat in the race is death, an end that the first Pauline's mother achieves unexpectedly when a Bwaan woman stabs her husband after he has won his race. The father's dying words to his daughter are to kill the mother, establishing a pattern of mother–daughter hatred and violence that will be passed down from generation to generation. The first Pauline does indeed bring about the death of her mother by pouring foul boiling soup down her throat, brutally inverting the starvation that the daughter had received at the mother's hands. The final violent mother–daughter relation is represented by the murderous duels between Sister Leopolda and her unacknowledged daughter, Marie. Both Paulines are marked by 'twisted energy' (155) and the inability to love or be loved. Both are their mixed-blood mothers' daughters, what Damien refers to as 'the warped result of all that twisted [the] mother' (158).

Erdrich's reprise of the Elektra theme, however, differs from the classical original in its attention to the part played by racial tensions, in particular the effects of the volatile mixing of two embattled minorities frequently struggling for survival, namely poor French peasant stock and generations of 'enemy-harassed Ojibwe'. The volatile racial mix is maintained, moreover, when the latter-day Pauline is born of the union of her matricidal mixed-blood mother and a Polish aristocrat visiting the wilds of Canada. Damien speculates gothically on the 'unknown capacities' and 'secret Old World cruelties' of the titled Pole, and the fearsome genetic inheritance that is tangled in the last Pauline's 'simmering blood' (157). Indeed, Erdrich in both *Tracks* and *Last Report* presents Pauline as a *windigo*, feeding on, and gaining sustenance and vitality from, the dying.[4] Pauline's care for the dying constitutes the 'Deadly Conversions' in which she brings Indian souls to Christ. On the other hand, her tireless ministrations are yet again an aspect of her 'impossible contradictions', for '[t]he ugliness of death brought out of her an angel' (122).

Damien's 'History of the Puyats' is not only phrased in terms of mixed-blood strife, however, for his 'History' is framed by the 'central astonishment' (148) of the final large-scale buffalo hunt of the Ojibwe in which the buffalo trample their own dead and run down and destroy their calves. The 'History of the Puyats' is thus not an individual story but is symbolic of the self-destruction of the Ojibwe as a nation: 'the history of the Puyats' says Damien, 'is the history of the end of things' (158). It is associated with despair, suicide and the tragic destruction of future generations: 'what occurred when some of our grief-mad people trampled their children' (158). Leopolda again is presented in terms of impossible contradiction: 'Leopolda was the hope and she was the poison' (158). She is the hope in that mixed-bloods potentially present the way forward by symptomizing what Louis Owens has called 'the dynamism, adaptability, and syncretism inherent in Native American cultures' (*Other Destinies* 167). She is, however, the poison in that she perpetuates the notion of the 'tragic mulatto'. Trapped in her own history of racial denial, spreading the poison in her daily life, she represents the end of things. At the celebration of the Feast of the Virgin she is an image of death, a walking *memento mori* that sends a shock of agitation to the heart of Damien: 'The Puyat – dressed in her own homemade habit – staggered past, her arms piled with buffalo skulls. Jutting from the veil, raw and planar, her face, like another of those skulls, stared out with deep, unseeing hollow eyes' (108).

I argued above that in *Last Report* Erdrich's representation of *métissage* through the history of the Puyat family in some ways repeats the tropes of nineteenth-century race theory. One such trope is the association of mixed-bloods with hypersexuality, most obviously embodied in literature in the figure of Rochester's mad Creole wife in *Jane Eyre*. Ann Laura Stoler writes: 'colonial discourses of desire contrasted lower-class men of passion and bourgeois men of character. . . . These discourses attributed sexual excess to those of creole, lower-class, and mixed-blood background – "fictive" and not properly embourgeoised Europeans' (157). In *Last Report*, after the first Pauline has administered foul boiling stew to her mother, the mother's grace wanes, the nerves on one side of her face collapse, and she becomes suddenly 'frightening to men' (156). By contrast, her daughter, although no beauty, 'suddenly becomes irresistible to men' (156), although they are confused by their attraction to this strange 'pop-eyed' child. Erdrich locates the girl's insatiable sexual appetite, her 'famishment', as an expression of inner emptiness, a hungry void created by her mother's cruelty. Her inability to love or be loved gives her a ferocity and a disturbing attractiveness. Erdrich thus takes a familiar colonial trope, but provides it with an added layer of psychological motivation, in some ways redeeming her image of the sexually ravenous mixed-blood from racial stereotyping. The second Pauline Puyat, born late in the mother's life, is also raised in 'purified bitterness' (157). Her equally intense sexual hunger, like her mother's the product of lovelessness, cannot find satisfactory expression. Men sense her manic strangeness, and her first lover, Napoleon, removes himself in mid-embrace 'like a dog sensing the presence of a tasteless poison in its food' (*Tracks* 73). Denied direct expression, her sexuality becomes voyeuristic and intrusive, and, by spiking the food of her would-be lover, Eli, with love medicine, and by entering the body and mind of his young lover, Sophie, they become her puppets, the objects of her perverted play. Once again Erdrich has taken the same colonial trope of the sexualized mixed-blood, but treats it with sophisticated psychology (along with Ojibwe lore concerning love medicine) to lift her characterization above stereotyping.

Pauline Puyat is a multiply marginalized individual whose impossible contradictions, located primarily in her mixed-blood background warring with her need to be all white, causes fragmentation and insanity. In the next section, I suggest links between ethnicity and sexuality and the extent to which living on the margins is discriminating but also provides access to a certain degree of power.

Living Liminally and the Power That It Can Give

Critical race theory recognizes that race and racism work with and through the intersections among gender, ethnicity, class and sexuality as systems of power. Pauline Puyat feels herself to be trebly marginalized in terms of race, gender and class, and her need to access power at all costs is caused by her sense of exclusion. Thus her desperate need 'to be like my grandfather, pure Canadian' (*Tracks* 14) is motivated by her desire to avoid the marginalization and shame of being reared in the Puyat family, which she describes as 'mixed-bloods, skinners in the clan for which the name was lost' (*Tracks* 14). Compounded with this is her sense of being invisible to men on account of her unattractiveness: 'I was fifteen, alone, and so poor looking I was invisible to most customers and to the men in the shop' (*Tracks* 15). But being on the margin of things can confer power. As she herself says, invisibility can be an 'advantage'. Being on the edge of things allows one to cross boundaries, access forbidden knowledge and operate unseen: 'Because I could fade into a corner or squeeze beneath a shelf I knew everything' (*Tracks* 16). Pauline dramatically demonstrates this hidden power when, unseen, she locks in the meat freezer the three men who had raped Fleur, causing the immediate death of two of them and the lingering death of the third.

Agnes/Father Damien does not suffer exclusion on the grounds of race, but after donning the robes of a priest, she is immediately aware of the privileges and power allowed men but denied to women. This is even extended into being given more personal space, allowing greater freedom of physical and mental movement: 'It was as though in priest's garments she walked within a clear bell of charged air' (62). In his essay, 'Of Other Spaces', Michel Foucault distinguishes three kinds of social spaces in society: real spaces, utopias and heterotopias. Damien's sensation of liberation, as though walking 'within a clear bell of charged air' is an instance of heterotopia. A heterotopia (literally 'other place') is a space of otherness that has multiple layers of meaning and functions where different social forces and ways of life can come into contact with each other without hegemonic control. As Foucault expresses it, heterotopia is a counter-site, 'a kind of effectively enacted utopia in which the real sites, all the other real sites that can be found within the culture, are simultaneously represented, contested, and inverted' (24). Foucault uses the image of a mirror in this context to evoke a sense of personal space that is both 'here' and 'there', real and unreal, and involves the way one relates to one's own image. Meeting people for the first time dressed as a priest, Damien is observing himself as through a mirror, a kind of double vision in which he notes the way he himself reacts to the way other people react to him.

Foucault's image of the mirror can by extension be allied to the way in which identity is based on social constructions, on the way society sees us and the way we wish to view ourselves. When looking in a mirror, Foucault writes, 'I begin again to direct my eyes toward myself and to reconstitute myself there where I am' (24). When Damien remarks, 'Agnes was surprised to find that this [deferential] treatment entirely gratified her, and yet seemed familiar as though it was her due' (62), it is a complex reflection of a woman in man's clothing noting the pleasures of living in a man's world and accepting the preferential treatment as befitting her chosen role as priest. Put simply, donning robes or roles not only affects the way others see us but also affects the ways we see ourselves.

Erdrich is clear-sighted about the way gender is engineered and socially constructed from our earliest years, as shown in Agnes's understanding of the roles women are conditioned to play in love and life: 'She had . . . learned her share of discipline and in addition – for the heart of her gender is stretched, pounded, molded, and tempered for its hot task from the age of two – she was a woman' (18). Initially, adopting the identity of Father Damien throws Agnes/Damien into confusion, a sense that she has no identity at all, though it is aligned with the insight that male and female identities are both 'manufactured' rather than essences. Later, Agnes reaps the benefit of her ready access to traditional male codes and behavior usually denied women. Relying on her female 'wits' and male 'strength', Agnes throws her power into the 'voice and demeanor of Father Damien' (167) and with the additional aid of a whip dispels a group of reservation troublemakers from her church like Jesus expelling the money-changers from the temple. Mental agility and physical strength are here allied in such a way as to dispel familiar gender stereotypes of male activity and female passivity.

Erdrich's questioning and deconstruction of essentialist notions of gender are paralleled by her play with essentialist notions of nation or cultural identity. Catherine Rainwater has written convincingly about the way Erdrich deliberately raises conflicting interpretative possibilities which lead to 'an hermeneutical impasse' ('Reading between Worlds' 410) for the reader in which no single cultural code (either Ojibwe or Western) is privileged and false syntheses of antithetical possibilities are resisted. Applying these notions to Father Damien in Last Report would at first sight appear to be difficult. The novel would seem to endorse a reading in which Damien adopts the codes and spiritual practices of the Ojibwe nation, and discards non-Native religion. Damien wears moccasins, calls the Ojibwe 'her people', and, in a direct statement to the black dog, an emissary of Satan, states directly, 'There is no one I want to visit except in the Ojibwe heaven, and so at this late age I'm going to convert, stupid dog, and become at long last the pagan that I always was at heart' (310). One of Damien's final visions is to see the universe in terms of Ojibwe creation cosmology: 'She no longer saw the constellations as she had before knowing them in Ojibwe, but saw the heavens as her friends defined them. Saw the otter. Saw the hole in the sky through which the creator had shot down at a blistering speed' (348). The evidence would seem incontrovertible that Damien has totally adopted an Ojibwe way of seeing the world, but looking at his choice of diction would belie that judgement. Words like 'heaven', 'convert' and 'pagan' come from a Western/Catholic frame of reference, so that to a large extent Damien's Ojibwe world is perceived in terms of Christian discourse. Following Rainwater's argument, we have here a 'hermeneutical impasse' in which the overt meaning of the text is at odds with the language in which that meaning is expressed. The clearest example of this is when Damien rows out to Spirit Island, which she conceives as her last resting place, where perhaps she might escape the black dog. Here 'her soul might slip past the cur's slimy teeth and sneak by the hell gates and pearly gates into that sweeter pasture, the heaven of the Ojibwe' (346). Once again, the colloquial 'pearly gates' and the biblical 'hell gates' and 'sweeter pasture' are all Christian in reference. The Ojibwe heaven is seen as the 'green pastures' of Psalm 23. The reader need not question whether Damien gains spiritual strength from her adoption of Ojibwe ways. The support he finds among the Ojibwe reflects the acceptance of two-spirits, that is, a masculine and feminine spirit co-existing in the same body, and the important cultural roles two-spirits could play in Native North American tribal society. Having said that, Erdrich's subtle textual play undermines simplistic assumptions concerning the adoption or rejection of nationhood or culture. Damien's rejection of his Western Christian self in language which reaffirms the presence of Christian worldviews is a classic instance of a key theme of self-critical post-colonialism, namely that to deny the dominant reaffirms its strength; the anti-colonial stance couched in Western discourse is in fact a form of re-colonization.

Trickster Discourse beyond the Hermeneutical Impasse

If Damien's language at times denies what he affirms, there are other sections of *Last Report* which provide both a subtle and direct critique of colonialism without becoming enmeshed in the very language and codes which it would attack. Such a section is Nanapush's story entitled 'Nanabozho Converts the Wolves', which he tells Damien during their first meeting. The Ojibwe trickster Nanaabozho (another name for Nanapush) is supplied by a French fur trader with blankets, coats, a gun and poisoned fat. Meeting with a wolf, Nanaabozho tells him to sum-mon as many foxes and wolves as he can and proceeds to tell the assem-bled group that if they eat the fat they will gain eternal life, and if they do not they will die. In a parody of the communion service, he places the fat in their willing mouths and the last words they hear are those of Nanaabozho as he pronounces 'Long may you live!' Returning to the Frenchman to collect his pay for the furs he has acquired in this devious fashion he comments, 'Truly . . . I have converted them – to money' (85). In this story, in which Nanaabozho is the priest and the foxes and wolves are the gullible Indian congregation, what is clearly evident is the appropriation of the language of Christianity to sharp critical effect. The Christian paradox of dying into eternal life is here equated with 'deadly conversion' (the second part of the novel in which this story is told is entitled 'The Deadly Conversions') in which money and power are directly implied as the motivating forces behind colonizing Christianity on the North American continent.

In Erdrich's work the trickster Nanapush is associated with survival – primarily through storytelling, wit and verbal trickery. He is what Paula Gunn Allen (51) has called 'a word warrior'. Nanapush tells his story of Nanaabozho and the wolves when he and Fleur are close to death and when many in the reservation have already succumbed to tuberculosis. The timely arrival of Damien at their cabin and the challenging story he sends Damien's way restores his will to live. Barbara Babcock associates the trickster with the power and vitality that living on the margins provides. The trickster's power, she says, 'endows his group with vitality and other boons', and as a 'criminal' culture-hero he 'embodies all possibilities – the most positive and the most negative' (154). In the tribal context the trickster's violation of all rules and boundaries means that he stands as a negative example, a warning of how not to act. Because of his rule-breaking he is forced to wander aimlessly on the fringes of society. However, in the colonial context in which an embattled minority struggles for survival, this marginal figure can be a figure of resistance and takes a central role as cultural survivor. According to William J. Hynes, one of the characteristics of the trickster is his ability to invert situations, confusing and escaping the structures of society and overturning any person, place or belief no matter how prestigious; he is 'the official ritual profaner of beliefs' (17). Nanapush's story of the wolves illustrates this power inversion: the language of Christianity is robbed of its doctrinal power and its hidden agendas are revealed. In Erdrich's work as a whole, however, Nanapush does not become the officially sanctioned voice of dissent. Like the traditional trickster, Erdrich's Nanapush is fallible. In a later novel, *Four Souls* (2004), Nanapush's buffoon-like aspects are even enlarged: he gets drunk, exhibits his hindquarters, cross-dresses and at points acts absurdly when his sexual confidence ebbs. Nanapush is a figure of paradox; continuously evading restrictive definitions, he remains part rogue, part wise leader, part teacher, part clown.

As an image of what Babcock calls 'creative negation' (182), the trickster embraces all contradictions and all possibilities. Deconstructing essentialisms also involves acknowledging paradox and contradiction, and continuously deferring false synthesis or resolution. These notions link post-colonial and critical race approaches to race, gender and ethnicity. In *Last Report* race is a central issue in the character of the mixed-blood Pauline Puyat who, by denying her Indianness and insisting on 'whiteness', splits her racial self into irreconcilable and essentialist categories that lead to madness. By contrast, Father Damien's border existence between maleness and femaleness allows her a unique perspective on the constructed nature of male power as well as a degree of access to that power.

In my approach to *Last Report* I have emphasized discourse as a major site of power struggles, including the counter-hegemonic force of Damien's and Nanapush's trickster discourse. It is thus ironic that Louise Erdrich both has and does not have the last word. In the closing 'End Notes' of the novel, a fax from the Vatican accuses Erdrich of appropriating Damien's confessions into her novel. Erdrich artfully attributes her work to voices which spoke to her in dreams, and defers simplistic notions of authorial power with the final questions, 'Who is the writer? Who is the voice?' (358).

CHAPTER 6

'We Speak of Everything': Indigenous Traditions in *The Last Report on the Miracles at Little No Horse*

P. Jane Hafen

The literary reinterpretation of religious institutions is part of Erdrich's process of decolonization. Erdrich explores Ojibwe/Christian relations by examining who qualifies for sainthood. Ostensibly the investigation to assess the saintly qualities of Sister Leopolda compels much of the plot development. However, the conversion and transformation of Agnes DeWitt into Father Damien and the process of sanctification through life's journey reveal qualities of holiness that transcend structures of religious institutions. Erdrich complicates Catholic rituals and practices with Ojibwe traditions, beliefs and characters, such as Nanapush, the incarnation of an Ojibwe trickster, and Mary Kashpaw, the embodiment of charity.

Father Damien becomes the intersection of the organized religion and the spiritual lives of his Ojibwe parishioners. In a subtle backdrop, Erdrich utilizes tropes of music to hone ideas of physicality and spirituality, and, rather than embodying a quintessential battle between the flesh and spirit, demonstrates holistic resolutions. Complexly interweaving characters, events and transitions with DeWitt/Damien at the center, Erdrich tests Christian beliefs of faith, love, sin and forgiveness and eternal life by reframing those ideas in Ojibwe experiences.

Indigenous Critical Theory

The Last Report on the Miracles at Little No Horse presents particular theoretical challenges. The text appears to be grounded in Euroamerican religiosity with the main character Agnes DeWitt/Sister Cecilia/Father Damien fulfilling roles in the Roman Catholic Church. Of course, the obvious ritual violation occurs when Agnes assumes the gender specific, male exclusive role of priest in the persona of Father Damien. Indeed in the 'End Notes', the Erdrich narrative voice acknowledges Kenneth L. Woodward's *Making Saints: How the Catholic Church Determines Who Becomes a Saint, Who Doesn't, and Why* (*Last Report* 357) as a source for the novel. The richness of Catholicism in the text has been the subject of critical discussion by Allison Chapman, Thomas Matchie and others. Chapman in particular argues convincingly for a reconstruction of saintly hagiography in Erdrich's characters.

To focus solely on the Catholic elements of the story and characters is, obviously, to ignore that this novel is indigenous. However, to claim that Father Damien becomes Native is to ignore tribal sovereignty and the details of Ojibwe spirituality that Erdrich does not include explicitly in the text. While Father Damien certainly comes to believe and to validate aspects of Ojibwe spirituality, he is not 'converted' in the traditional Christian sense (55) of giving up one faith for another; he becomes part of an integrated worldview that accommodates multiple spiritual experiences. He continues with his Catholic ordinances, and, 'In turn, Father Damien had been converted by the good Nanapush. He now practiced a mixture of faiths, kept the pipe, translated hymns or brought in the drum, and had placed in the nave of his church a statue of the Virgin–solid, dark, kind eyed, hideous and gentle' (276). Additionally, he writes to the Pope, 'I have discovered an unlikely truth that may interest your Holiness. The ordinary as well as esoteric forms of worship engaged in by the Ojibwe are sound, even compatible with the teachings of Christ' (49). This accommodation undercuts the hierarchy and authority of the Catholic Church, but does not displace it. As Dee Horne observes: '[Father Damien] does not perpetuate the unequal power imbalance or disavow Catholic traditions that have informed him; rather, he reexamines Catholicism within the context of Anishinabe [sic] traditions' (278). Father Damien continues to function as a priest and continues, through his letters to the Pope, to express confidence in the institution.

Therefore, focusing solely on Western methodologies such as structural applications, cultural materialism or post-colonialism in a colonial Ojibwe world, further removes the text from its indigenous heritage and further colonizes Ojibwe literatures. Erdrich's narrative takes on the task of decolonization. As mentioned above, the colonizing power of Christianity is diffused by the transformation of Father Damien. Maori scholar Linda Tuhiwai Smith outlines in *Decolonizing Methodologies: Research and Indigenous Peoples* additional narrative strategies that undermine the colonial powers. Those strategies include: claiming, testifying, storytelling, celebrating survival, indigenizing, intervening, revitalizing, reframing and so on.[1]

Part of that indigenizing project includes an integration of elements, a wholeness that runs counter to the Christian theology of Saint Paul that divides and compartmentalizes, as will be discussed later. Although tribal specificity is crucial, certain commonalities appear in these commentaries by native scholars. They consider cosmologies of tribal beliefs, interrelationship of objects, genres and peoples. They acknowledge the vitality of land, language and survival. Seminole scholar Susan Miller notes the living correlation between all things:

> In Indigenous thought, people are seen as families or communities rather than individuals. The pervasive importance of the family surpasses even its considerable importance in American and other non-Indigenous worldviews. Indigenous family encompasses the entire cosmos. . . . Every element of the cosmos has a place in the family. Everything is alive and has needs and rights. People must therefore concern themselves with the health and well-being of everything in the cosmos just as they concern themselves with their families and communities. (27–8)

By identifying the interconnectedness of all living things, Miller distinguishes indigenous cosmology from Judeo-Christianity where elements exist in a hierarchical order with dominion over all things and in the Great Chain of Being. Additionally, in the Ojibwe worldview, Erdrich explains that nouns are 'alive or dead, animate or inanimate. The word for stone, *asin*, is animate thus expanding the relationships of biological beings with elements of the earth itself' ('One Language', italics added).

LeAnne Howe, Choctaw writer and scholar, describes the combining process in creative works as 'tribalography'. Through her definition she also designates the inherent differences among tribes and with non-natives as well:

> Now I have come to the place where I must tell you what my term tribalography means and how it achieves a new understanding in theorizing on Native studies. This is a tall order for a storyteller, but here goes. Native stories, no matter what form they take (novel, poem, drama, memoir, film, history), seem to pull all the elements together of the storyteller's tribe, meaning the people, the land, and multiple characters and all their manifestations and revelations, and connect these in past, present, and future milieus (present and future milieus mean non-Indians). I have tried to

show that tribalography comes from the Native propensity for bringing things together, for making consensus, and for symbiotically connecting one thing to another. It is a cultural bias, if you will. (42)

So not only are the elements of the earth interrelated, but they emerge through literary forms. Those forms can be the traditional oral stories that explain the origins of the universe and establish boundaries of social and moral behaviors or they can be more modern expressions of literary genres. Literary forms also reflect changing cultures and interactions, and affirm tribal sovereignties.

Another Choctaw scholar, Clara Sue Kidwell, outlines the foundational premises of American Indian Studies: land, historical discourse, sovereignty and revitalization of languages:

> The first premise is that the relationship between people and the land is the shaping force in American Indian cultures (we accept the reality of cultural differences among tribes). For reservation-based communities in contemporary society, these relationships persist. The second premise is that in historical contact between Indian and European cultures, the story must be told from both sides. The second premise leads to inclusion of oral traditions and oral history as valid sources of historical information about the human actions and motivations that historians seek to record. The third premise, which is particularly problematic for the U.S. government to comprehend, is that sovereignty is an inherent right of Indian nations. In contemporary America tribal sovereignty is grounded in treaties with the U.S. government that assured tribal rights to control of land. The fourth premise is that language is the essential key to understanding culture and that American Indian languages, which are disappearing at an alarming rate, should be preserved and revitalized as much as possible. Language embodies Native epistemology. The final premise is that contemporary Indian music, dance, art, and literature express long-standing values of tribal cultures while adapting them to modern media. (4)

Erdrich herself discusses the importance of indigenous language as both revitalization and conveying sovereignty and utilizes it in a decolonizing strategy: 'There is a spirit or originating genius belonging to each word. . . . [Ojibwemowin] is a language that also recognizes the humanity of a creaturely God, and the absurd and wondrous sexuality of even the most deeply religious beings' ('Two Languages'). Informed in the traditions of Western civilization, including Christian Catholicism, yet rooted in Ojibwe storytelling, language and worldview, clearly Erdrich exploits the narrative to reaffirm decolonizing processes.

The application of indigenous critical principles is twofold. Not only do they decolonize standard theories of literary criticism, but they center indigenous power and indigenous voice. This does not mean that indigeneity exists in a vacuum or is essentialist as native peoples enter and live in the modern world. On the contrary, reclaiming tribal traditions within modern realities is part of a pattern of survival and persistence. Nowhere is this more important than in spiritual matters. Historically, where Judeo-Christianity has been equated with civilization, indigenous practices have been misunderstood and reviled, categorized as savage. As a practical matter of basic survival, many tribes accommodated Christianity, but made their own definitions of spiritual practices. Acoma Pueblo poet and scholar Simon Ortiz explains:

> Obviously there is an overtone that this is a Catholic Christian ritual celebration because of the significance of the saints' names and days on the Catholic calendar. But just as obviously, when the celebration is held in the Acquemah community, it is an Acquemah ceremony. It is Acquemah and Indian (or Native American or American Indian if one prefers those terms) in the truest and most authentic sense. This is so because this celebration speaks of the creative ability of Indian people to gather in many forms of the socio-political colonizing force which beset them and to make these forms meaningful in their own terms. In fact, it is a celebration of the human spirit and the Indian struggle for liberation. (7–8)

In other words, the ritual in tribal communities is no longer purely European or Euroamerican Catholic, but has become part of the native nation in a significant way; it has been reclaimed. This is not hybridity, but a survival strategy. As Linda Tuhiwai Smith argues against an artificial authenticity that predates European contact, she notes that cultures are 'complicated, internally diverse or contradictory' and must adapt while maintaining their essential characteristics: 'In [authenticity], claiming essential characteristics is as much strategic as anything else, because it has been about claiming human rights and indigenous rights. But the essence of a person is also discussed in relation to indigenous concepts of spirituality' (74). Spirituality in *The Last Report on the Miracles at Little No Horse* is rooted in indigenous concepts of integrated wholeness and the idea that spirituality decolonizes institutional religion despite its overtly Catholic themes.

Indeed, Erdrich deals with this strategy of decolonization in the first section of her poetry collection, *Baptism of Desire* (1988). The title of the collection indicates a transcendence of the actual ritual of baptism or conversion with an acceptable desire for reconciliation with God. In a series of poems that address major Catholic figures – Christ, Mary Magdalene and Saints Clare, Agnes and Teresa de Avila – Erdrich reinterprets and undermines their sanctity. A sequence of poems in 'The Sacraments' not only parallels the sacred ordinances of Catholic practices, but deconstructs them through personal and unconventional subject matter while integrating personal questions of faith and belief.

One of the primary tropes Erdrich uses to demonstrate that integration is the elimination of the polarization of spirit and body. Traditional Christianity advocates the triumph of the spirit over the flesh of the body, mostly through the writings of Saint Paul and Saint Augustine. Saint Paul writes to the Romans:

> Those who live according to the sinful nature have their minds set on what that nature desires; but those who live in accordance with the Spirit have their minds set on what the Spirit desires. The mind of sinful man is death, but the mind controlled by the Spirit is life and peace; the sinful mind is hostile to God. It does not submit to God's law, nor can it do so. Those controlled by the sinful nature cannot please God. (*NIV* 8.5–8)

These ideas are further cemented as the early Christian Church became institutionalized: 'In their amalgam of Greek and biblical ideas, the fathers believe that the human perfection lay in recovering as nearly as possible the spirit's control over the flesh, which they imagined Adam and Eve enjoyed before the fall' (Woodward 338).

The Last Report on the Miracles at Little No Horse begins with conventional expectations of gender, structure, authority, body and spirit. Father Damien, a familiar figure from Erdrich's earlier novel, *Tracks* (1988), is the primary character. In typical Erdrich style, the narrative begins with place rather than character. The distinction of place over people is a subtle indigenous emphasis, but it also demonstrates the ontological and integrated role of landscape in all of Erdrich's writings. In 1996, Father Damien has lived beyond his expectations. As an aged priest writing to the Pope and describing his holy duties, Father Damien reinforces the ritual and structures of Catholicism. However, the situation soon turns awry as the wine he drinks seems more like water, an inversion of the miracle at the wedding at Cana where Jesus turned the water into wine. As he undresses, he removes the moosehide moccasins from his feet, and removes an Ace bandage from his chest to reveal 'his woman's breasts' (8). Father Damien has undone the authority of the Church, crossed gender lines, crossed cultural boundaries and witnessed the physical transformation of wine into water. While a deconstructionist analysis would be tempting, an indigenous interrelating makes all of these elements clear in their interdependence. As Maria Orban and Alan Velie observe, 'Making Father Damien a woman exposes the arbitrary nature of the ways oppositions like man/woman, moral/immoral, sacred/sacrilegious are culturally constructed' (28). While the oppositions are exposed and indeed culturally constructed, these oppositions are also transcended in the reconciliation of those differences.

The first full section of the novel, titled 'The Transfiguration of Agnes', is full of allusion. The Transfiguration as a singular Christian event refers to the change in appearance of Jesus on the mountain (Matthew 17.2; Mark 9.2–3). The title foretells the changes that will occur in the main character, Agnes. Agnes as a proper name is the cognate of the Latin *agnus* or lamb, with *Agnus Dei* meaning the Lamb of God, or Jesus. Saint Agnes was a third-century Christian saint who preserved her virginity (Englebert 38). The name refers, however, to the main character, Agnes DeWitt.

The subtitle of the first section, 'Naked Woman Playing Chopin' is also a foreshadowing of the gender transference that will occur. Pianist Frederick Chopin (1810–49) was famously involved with a cross-dressing, name-changing woman, Aurore Dupin (1804–76), who wrote under the pseudonym George Sand. Like the Prologue, the narrative begins with place and a foreshadowing description of a baptismal 'flow of water' (12). Erdrich gives great detail to Berndt's farm, animals and equipment, and, again, foreshadowing Berndt's death, notes, 'The spirit of the farm was there in the lost breath of the horses' (12). The line is subtle but it demonstrates the blurred line between spirit and physicality.

The narrative backtracks to Sister Cecilia. Agnes is a novice and is named Cecilia for the patron saint of music who is also known for a sexless marriage (Englebert 444–5). She lives in a convent that is built of yellow bricks stamped 'Fleisch' by the manufacturer. The obvious irony, of course, is that 'Fleisch' is the German word for 'flesh' and the physical bricks construct the walls around the spiritual duties of the sisters. Sister Cecilia's piano playing will be discussed later, but the struggle between flesh and spirit, body and soul is constructed not only in the individual characters, but in the physicality of the place. Erdrich draws attention to the seeming contradictions, however; in tribal application, the yellow bricks taken from indigenous soil, the spiritual work, the farm and the life therein are all part of a cohesive universe.

Sister Cecilia's devotion to Chopin usurps her vows to God and she leaves the convent only to fall into the arms of Berndt, the farmer. Their sexual relation is intense, belying the celibacy of both of her namesakes. Rather than leading a chaste spiritual life, Agnes/Sister Cecilia finds herself fully enjoying the pleasures of the flesh without apparent guilt, although she does stop taking communion at the church.

After the disastrous bank robbery that plants in Agnes the idea of masquerading as a priest and Berndt's subsequent violent death, a great flood assails the land. Agnes is carried away with images of matrimony, her night dress billowing in the water 'like a wedding train', and baptism: 'I drowned in spirit, but revived. I lost an old life and gained a new' (43). The new life also alludes to the earthdiver origin stories of the Ojibwe and the sacrificial transition Agnes is making to an integrated world (Hughes 613). In this transcendent experience, Agnes is revived by an unnamed Christ figure. Not only does he nourish her, but in their intimate encounter, their physicality overcomes rather than succumbs to the spirit. Agnes's life is forever transformed: 'Having met Him just that once, having known Him in a man's body, how could I not love Him until death?' (43). The food and intimacy are not merely metaphorical, but are precise realities, just as Agnes understands, 'I took [His words] literally to mean that I should attend Him' (43).

The first time Agnes celebrates the Mass, performing as Father Damien, she also experiences that literalness of transubstantiation: 'the dry, thin consecrated Host turned into a thin mouthful of raw, tender, bloody, sweet-tasting meat' (69). Although Agnes sees this event within the context of her new function as a priest, from an indigenous point of view it both verifies her gender transgression in functioning with the authority of a priest and acknowledges Christ's sacrifice in real, not metaphorical, physical and spiritual terms.

In a separation of bodily functions, though, Agnes loses her menses, but not without a reminder of the adhesive spirit and body connection. She prays to God to 'stop the useless affliction of menstrual blood' (78). Her prayers are answered, but, as she cleans herself with snow 'She shivered with shock and a lost sensation gathered, swept through her, and was gone with a shimmer of musical notes. She closed her eyes, tried to make the physical climax into a prayer, but her mouth dropped and she cried out in a quiet voice, feeling the ghost touches of her lost lover' (78). The lost lover is ambiguous – is it Berndt? Christ? Chopin? Despite the bodily cessation of menses, her orgasm is a sexual reminder of the bond between body and soul. As Erdrich explains:

faith is erotic in the sense that our yearning is toward union, toward the absolute. Toward a transcendence – not of the body – but of all of the concerns that grab us from every side from day to day. Transcendence of the ordinary or an acceptance – a love of the ordinary part of faith. So I interpret erotic to be a much more inclusive and embracing word than say purely sexual. ('Interview')

In describing 'all concerns' and 'inclusive[ness]' Erdrich is reaffirming Miller's sense of all parts of the universe and Howe's compilation of genres and narrative in tribalography. She is indigenizing and decolonizing the division between sexuality and organized religion.

Love and Passion

Central to Christian theology is the concept of love. The conversation between Father Damien and the respected elder, Kashpaw, about love drives home the differing worldviews between the ideas of Western civilization and Ojibwe ideas. Kashpaw, who already knows about Father Damien's gender disguise, asks, 'what makes you walk behind this Jesus?' Damien's thoughts 'wheel together like a flock of startled birds' (99). In a profound condensing of major themes, ideas and images of the novel, Damien 'contemplate[s] the pattern of the flock of which the great logos of his passion was written' (99). The 'flock' could be the congregation of which Father Damien was the shepherd. 'Flock' could also be the startled birds, implying an order to chaos, as suggested by the next image, 'the great logos'. The Greek root of *Logos* implies logic, order and organization, but it is also translated in the New Testament as 'the word', particularly as it begins the Gospel according to Saint John.

> In the beginning was the Word, and the Word was with God, and the Word was God. He was with God in the beginning.
>
> Through him all things were made; without him nothing was made that has been made. In him was life, and that life was the light of men.
>
> The Word became flesh and made his dwelling among us. We have seen his glory, the glory of the One and Only, who came from the Father, full of grace and truth. (*NIV* 1.1–4, 14)

Perhaps as much as any biblical scripture, these verses figure the embodiment of the creative power and spirit of Christ. Like LeAnne Howe's ordering of story, Father Damien/Agnes's musing is the Euroamerican way of seeing the world fitting into an ancient Native way of seeing this wholeness. Or, in the context of *Last Report*, Erdrich's narrative is decolonizing by collectively depicting idea and body.

Father Damien's 'passion' alludes to the many sections that are titled 'Passion' and the last section of the book, 'Father Damien's Passion'. Passion in this context refers to the suffering and sacrifice made by Jesus, yet, in *Last Report*, many Ojibwe characters suffer and sacrifice as well. So in this flicker of reasoning and allusion, Father Damien answers Kashpaw's question – 'It is love' – with confidence in the rightness of his work, and with sincerity and commitment. The responses of Kashpaw and the community are 'uncertian' [sic]. Damien's 'love' is layered and complex in the traditions of Christianity. However:

> In the Ojibwe language, the word does not exist in the same sense – there is love out of pity, love out of kindness, love that is specific to situations or to the world of stones, which are alive and called our grandfathers. There is also the stingy and greedy love that the white people call romantic love. This love of Christ, this love that chose Agnes and forced her to give up her nature as a woman, forced Father Damien to appear to sacrifice the pleasures of manhood, was impossible to define in Ojibwe. (99)

The stark contrast between the understandings of the definition of 'love' demonstrates how Erdrich can decolonize a religious-based idea and reframe it in Ojibwe language and context.

Another basic tenet of Christianity is charity or *agape*, the love of one's fellow man. While Father Damien, in his ecclesiastical duties, is a prime candidate and actor for the embodiment of charity, and while he is foiled by the self-serving acts of Sister Leopolda, the surprising character who represents charity is Mary Kashpaw. As Lakota scholar Debra Barker observes: 'Erdrich develops her character to reinscribe standards of saintliness, goodness, and self-sacrifice, qualities often associated with Christ' (266). Mary's service and giving, unlike Father Damien's, is not complicated by a hidden agenda of identity protection or by institutional motivation. In this context, Mary accompanies Father Damien in ministering to the sick. Many will be buried in the holes that Mary obsessively dug after the tragic death of her parents. Although Father Damien has been working tirelessly, saving the lives of some, losing others, he and Mary are on the road 'due west', the Ojibwe direction of death. Struggling to keep up with Mary, he sees her in the light:

> Agnes saw beneath the girl's disguise. She saw that the face of her constant companion, Mary Kashpaw, was the face of the man with the horn spoon. Then she knew. Christ had gone before the priest, stamping down snow. Christ had bent low and on that broad, angry back carried Father Damien through sloughs.

Covered him when he collapsed at the bedsides of the ill. . . .
Christ was before him right now, breaking the trail. (123)

When Mary transfigures into Christ, Agnes recognizes the purity of her love and sacrifice. Indeed, when Agnes falls into deep depression after the departure of her lover, Father Gregory Wekkle, Mary protects Agnes's identity. In a final act of compassion, Mary finds Father Damien's body and disposes of it so that Agnes's secret will never be known. Her acts protect not only Father Damien, but the order of the Ojibwe community from the outside colonizers. Most of the Ojibwe already know about Agnes's true identity, and, through Father Damien, the rules of Catholicism regarding forgiveness are mildly enforced. The repercussions of Father Damien's ecclesiastical acts would have been devastating, and Mary protects against their exposure.

Nanapush the Trickster and Community

In contrast to the overtly Christian values displayed by characters in the text, the trickster Nanapush exists in the domain of Ojibwe culture. Derived from the mythic Ojibwe Nanaabozho, Erdrich's character has a rich history throughout her North Dakota novels. In true trickster fashion, his deeds and appetites are excessive, in part to instruct how the consequences of behavior without boundaries lead to misfortune. His banter is frankly sexual. He is a born storyteller who works to preserve the land, language and heritage of the traditional Ojibwe. His character helps to establish the tribal community. Simply put, in order for a collective community or oneness to exist, hierarchy must be balanced by liminality and that creates a sacred space for the trickster. As Victor Turner explains in *The Ritual Process*:

> For communitas has an existential quality; it involves the whole man in relationship to other whole men. . . . Communitas breaks through the interstices of culture, in liminality; at the edges of structure, in marginality; and from beneath structure, in inferiority. It is almost everywhere held to be sacred or 'holy', possibly because it transgresses or dissolves the norms that govern structured or institutionalized relationships and is accompanied by periods of unexpected potency. (372)

Even though Father Damien tries to create a sense of community, especially when he drives the competing factions out of the Church like Christ drove the moneychangers out of the temple, Nanapush's roguish behaviors truly unite the spiritual community, even in his death.

In the epigraph to the novel, Nanapush speaks the indigenous framework:

> There are four layers above the earth and four layers below. Sometimes in our dreams and creations we pass through the layers, which are also space and time. In saying the word nindinawemaganidok, or my relatives, we speak of everything that has existed in time, the known and the unknown, the unseen, the obvious, all the lived before or is living now in the worlds above and below. (n.p.)

Nanapush defines, in an echo of Susan Miller, LeAnne Howe and Clara Kidwell, the unifying factors of indigenous cosmology. He also represents traditional Ojibwe power:

> The spiritual connection among all these living things created a universal bond, a kinship which ethnologist Mary Black-Rogers termed *bimaadiziwad*, from the Ojibwe verb 'it lives'. But bimaadiziwad signifies more than simply 'living'. It also signifies that the person has 'power'. In other words, those things that have power are considered to be living. (Angel 25)

The primary narrative of *Last Report* is about Father Damien, but Nanapush is also a central character who openly challenges the colonial aspects of religion, politics and land theft. As the trickster who binds the tribal themes across the novels of Erdrich's North Dakota saga, Nanapush is fundamental in initiating Father Damien to the tribe. Gerald Vizenor calls Nanaabozho a 'comic holotrope' that represents indigenism through narrative and a communal sign (187).

Agnes/Father Damien learns the complications of tribal politics, especially in regard to losing land. Sister Hildegarde describes the dire circumstances: 'They'll lose all the land, of course, being unused to the owning of land. Incredibly, it makes no sense to them. They avow, in their own peculiar way, that the earth is only on loan' (72). In a decolonizing observation the third-person narration notes: 'Into this complex situation walked Father Damien, with only the vaguest notion of how the ownership of land related to the soul' (76). Through the narration, Erdrich explains ideas of sovereignty and land that Father Damien cannot see. Additionally, while affirming indigenous principles, the relationship to the land as a living entity transcends the notion of property or real estate. The land defines who people are and gives them life, especially through language.

In the 'End Notes' at the conclusion of the novel this association is reiterated through Nanapush's voice:

> If we call ourselves and all we see around us by the original names, will we not continue to be Anishinaabeg? Instead of reconstituted white men, instead of Indian ghosts? Do the rocks here know us, do the trees, do the waters of the lakes? Not unless they are addressed by the names they themselves told us to call them in our dreams. Every feature of the land around us spoke its name to an ancestor. Perhaps, in the end, that is all we are. (362)

Not only does Nanapush aver indigenous interconnectedness and the role of language, he speaks in a decolonizing voice that Father Damien cannot. He sees a sacred bond between identity, place and objects that Father Damien, despite his eventual fluency in Ojibwemowin and his translation of Nanapush's words, can witness but not experience.

Transcendence through Music

Although music might seem peripheral to this discussion of decolonizing and indigenous discourse in *The Last Report on the Miracles at Little No Horse*, because there is an absence of Ojibwe specific music, its use underscores some of the same principles already discussed. Through a number of her novels, Erdrich displays a musical literacy in the choruses of *The Master Butchers Singing Club* (2003) and the piano repertoire in *Last Report*. The main point is fairly simple. Music consists of physical elements: sound waves that combine in time. However, the combination of tones, harmonies, rhythms, tonalities and structures combine together to make the whole greater than the sum of the parts. Like the battle between body and spirit in traditional Christianity, musical expression has to transcend the limitations of the physical elements. Chopin's music works exceptionally well in this regard. Like Turner's creation of community through structure and anti-structure, Chopin's musical style has the steadiness of one hand in the other hand and the fluidity of uneven and asymmetrical patterns.

Sister Cecilia's playing of Chopin leads to her passion and introduces her to trouble: 'Her phrasing described her faith and doubt, her passion as the bride of Christ, her loneliness, shame, ultimate redemption' (14). Erdrich catalogues the characteristics of other major composers: Brahms, Schubert, Debussy, Bach and Beethoven. For Sister Cecilia, '[h]owever, when it came to the Chopin, she did not use the flowery ornamentation or the endless trills and insipid floribunda of so many of her day. Her playing was of the utmost sincerity. And Chopin, played simply, devastates the heart' (14). So intense is her Chopin performance that she experiences orgasm, much to the consternation and disturbance of the other sisters of the convent: 'Such was her innocence that she didn't know she was experiencing a sexual climax, but believed rather that what she felt was the natural outcome of this particular nocturne played to the utmost of her skills' (15). The unquantifiable aspects of Chopin produce a physical completeness and response.

After leaving the convent and living with Berndt, she acquires a piano so grand that a side of the house must be removed to move it in. In her grief after Berndt's death, she would practice to the neglect of other duties. Now, sexually experienced, she would remove her clothes, 'express[ing] her pure intent' (34). Ironically, the big, expensive Caramacchinone grand piano becomes the instrument of her salvation. Not only does she float away on it in the grand flood, popping up like Queequeg's coffin, but it housed money sequestered from the bank robbery. Yet in her transformation to Father Damien, 'she had lost the vast gift of her music' (45). She does not lose everything, though, just her apparent piano skills and the accompanying eroticism (Hughes 606). When Agnes celebrates the Mass as Father Damien, she recalls the ceremony because of the musical structure of the Ordinary: 'The Mass came to Agnes like memorized music' (68). Years later, in her recovery from the loss of Father Gregory, she recovers through piano playing: 'God had taken the music away for a time to bring her closer, then returned it when removing the last sexual love she would ever have. . . . Music poured out in a rational waterfall' (219).

Music also calls to the snakes. Traditionally a Judeo-Christian image of temptation and evil, the snake also represents transformation and new life. Additionally, Saint Patrick drove the snakes from Ireland (Chapman 155). In practicing her sermon before the snakes in the chapel, Damien reiterates her Christian understanding: 'What is the whole of our existence . . . but the sound of an appalling love?' (226). By preaching about love to the archetypal representation of good and evil, Damien transverses boundaries and presents a discourse that, like the music, transcends those divisions.

Although the Ojibwe, like other Indian Nations, adapt and interpret Christian hymns, Erdrich does not address this issue other than with a small mention of the original Father Damien. He tells Agnes early in the narrative: 'Miss Dewitt, it is said that God often enters the dark mind of the savage via musical pathways. For that reason, I've studied translations of the hymns laid down in Ojibwe by our studious Father Hugo' (36). Indeed, many traditional hymns are transformed linguistically to reflect Ojibwe understandings.[2] Erdrich's silence about these Ojibwe hymns opens a space for the more abstract classical music that envelopes the main character, Father Damien/Agnes, and demonstrates the themes of transcending physicality.

Sainthood

One of the framing plots of the novel is the investigation by Father Jude Miller into claims that Sister Leopolda should be beatified in preparation for sanctification. In the course of his investigation, Father Jude discovers the complicated history and relationships among many of the Ojibwe parishioners. He falls victim to the seduction of Lulu Nanapush, inheritor of the trickster tradition. He finally understands the futility of the separation of physical desire and the spirit: 'The great burden of his feeling pressed up all around him in a buzz of noise. Saying it lifted away the burden of strangeness. Relieved, he smiled at her, and then she was staring straight into his eyes, with an easy, knowing sympathy that made his blood hum in his ears' (336). In his final evaluations, Father Jude realizes that the true saint is Father Damien: 'The life of Father Damien also included miracles and direct shows of God's love, gifts of the spirit, humorous incidents as well as tragic encounters and examples of heroic virtue' (341). What Father Jude does not see is the relationship of Father Damien to the earth, to the sense of tribal community, to recognizing the inter-relationship of all things.

Father Damien's final act to hide his true identity as Agnes DeWitt is a suicidal plan to drown himself. This act is the strongest argument against his full conversion to Ojibwe cosmology because 'drowning was the worst death for Chippewa to experience' (*Love Medicine* 291) and would engage the Ojibwe 'sinister role of water' (Noori 91). However, self-drowning would also disempower the Catholic taboo of suicide and echo Agnes's original baptismal transformation. As things turn out, though, Father Damien does not drown but laughs himself to death, anticipating his reunion with Nanapush. Agnes's last conscious image though is a 'bigger, work-toughened hand' grasping hers and pulling her across (350). The image of pulling across reconnects to *Love Medicine* where Marie Kashpaw forgives her philandering husband, Nector. As he looks across her freshly waxed floor, she observes:

He stood there looking at me over that long, shiny space. It rolled and gleamed like a fine lake between us. And it deepened. I saw that he was about to take the first step, and I let him, but halfway into the room his eyes went dark. He was afraid of how deep this was going to become. So I did for Nector Kashpaw what I learned from the nun. I put my hand through what scared him. I held it out there for him. And when he took it with all the strength of his arms, I pulled him in. (162)

In both *Love Medicine* and *Last Report*, images of the fear and danger of water, of reconciliation by being pulled across a chasm of forgiveness, transcend specific religious imagery.[3]

Indeed, forgiveness and reconciliation are the fulfillment of Agnes's understanding of her purpose for her life on the Little No Horse Reservation:

Here it was – the reason she'd been called here in the first place. The reason she'd endured and the reason she'd been searching for. This was why she continued to live. . . . [She] drew strength from the massive amounts of forgiveness her priest had dispensed in his life. She saw that forgiveness as a long, slow soaking rain he had caused to fall on the dry hearts of sinners. Father Damien had forgiven everyone, right and left, of all mistakes and shameful sins. (309)

Although forgiveness is dispensed through Catholic authority and ritual in the confessional, Father Damien also realizes that he has been forgiven by non-Christian Nanapush for 'stealing so many souls' (310). Erdrich recognizes the universal power of forgiveness, the ritual process, while decolonizing institutional religion with Father Damien's awareness of Nanapush's Ojibwe values. Fittingly, at her death, Agnes/Father Damien thinks of Nanapush. Mary Kashpaw carefully and lovingly buries him in the lake. The last sentences of this part of the novel unify the masculine and feminine lives of Father Damien/Agnes DeWitt: 'As the dark water claimed him, his features blurred. His body wavered for a time between the surface and the feminine depth below' (351).

The religious elements of *The Last Report on the Miracles at Little No Horse* are layered and complex. Seemingly Catholic, the characters and plot undermine the institution by decolonizing its power and supplanting its premises with indigenous wholeness. Land, language, history and narrative are inter-related to affirm survival among the Ojibwe peoples on this fictional reservation, but in circumstances reflecting contemporary Indian life.

CHAPTER 7

Love and the Slippery Slope of Sexual Orientation

L/G/B/T/Q etc. Sensibility in The Last Report on the Miracles at Little No Horse

Patrice Hollrah

Introduction and Critical Theory

The first half of the title for this chapter, 'Love and the Slippery Slope of Sexual Orientation', refers to the indeterminate nature of language; specifically, the inability of labels and/or sexualities to define whom one will love or with whom one will have an erotic act. The same indeterminacy applies to the second half of the title, 'L/G/B/T/Q etc. Sensibility', because these sexualities do not include all possible categories, such as trisexual, pansexual and Two-Spirit, just to name a few. Furthermore, the title does not indicate a consideration of gender identities, a separate and distinct category from sexual orientations that should be included in the discussion of love relationships, as Erdrich presents them in *The Last Report on the Miracles at Little No Horse*. This chapter deals with the argument for an Indigenous theoretical approach in discussing Agnes DeWitt/Sister Cecilia/Father Damien in *Last Report*. Ojibwe novelist Louise Erdrich defies neat definitions and simplistic categories of gender identities and sexual orientations.

Thus, terminology in a discussion of Agnes/Father Damien is problematic, whether from a Native Two-Spirit theoretical approach or a

Western cultural perspective. In the collection of essays titled *Two-Spirit People: Native American Gender Identity, Sexuality, and Spirituality*, editors Sue-Ellen Jacobs, Navajo scholar Wesley Thomas and Sabine Lang discuss the history of the term 'Two-Spirit' and how it was 'coined in 1990 by Native American individuals during the third Native American/ First Nations gay and lesbian conference' (2). Muskogee Creek/Cherokee scholar Craig S. Womack writes:

> Many Native gays and lesbians have begun to use the term 'Two-Spirit' to describe themselves. Although the term is pan-tribal, because each nation has its own word for homosexuals in its tribal language, 'Two-Spirit' is a metaphor, a trope, that reflects the fact that many traditional cultures see gays as between genders, doubly empowered because they can see from both male and female perspectives. . . . [E]specially significant is the idea behind the word that gayness is a blessing, as well as that the choice of the term is an act of self-definition. (301–2)

The term has since been appropriated by non-Natives; however, scholar Sue-Ellen Jacobs today argues that ' "Two-Spirit" belongs only to Native Americans who accept it as a cultural response to the diversity of terms used in non-Native societies for a variety of sexualities and gender performances' (Jacobs e-mail). According to these definitions, using 'Two-Spirit' to describe Agnes/Father Damien is incorrect and inappropriate. Sheila Hassell Hughes considers that the transgendered priest belongs to 'the tradition of the Catholic "transvestite saint" ' and the 'Native American "two-spirit" . . . that Indigenous, sacred tradition of gender diversity' (599). Although critics tend to combine Western and Native theories to arrive at some kind of hybridity or 'gender syncretism' (600), the destination does not necessarily include ideas important to Native sovereignty: the misappropriation of Native knowledge and identity being only two.

Queer theory, according to Womack, 'is most interested in the gray areas, those identities and practices that are the hardest to characterize as gay or straight' ('A Single Decade' 39). But, as scholar Clark Hafen notes, in Native American communities 'third and fourth gender classifications are not queer. Indigenous communities have known this for centuries. [Diverse genders are] integral parts of society' (1). Although Queer theory seems as if it would be a convenient way to examine how Agnes/Father Damien disrupts and resists normative values (Womack, 'A Single Decade' 39), the post-modern/post-structural paradigm does not necessarily include consideration of what makes life worth living: power, identity and desire/sexuality (Bornstein), particularly in the novel's reservation setting of Little No Horse where Ojibwe ontological identity is embedded in the land and there is a traditional history of Ojibwe women holding power. Despite Agnes/Father Damien's assimilation into Ojibwe culture, Queer theory does not necessarily work as the most appropriate theoretical approach for *Last Report*.

Scholar Lisa Tatonetti's review essay, 'The Both/And of American Indian Literary Studies', gives a useful overview of 'the imagined divide between proponents and detractors of contemporary literary nationalism' (277). Tatonetti places Elizabeth Cook-Lynn (Dakota), Robert Warrior (Osage), Jace Weaver (Cherokee) and Craig Womack (Muskogee Creek/Cherokee) among those who argue for tribally centered readings of Indigenous literatures; Arnold Krupat, Elvira Pulitano and David Treuer (Ojibwe) are among those who privilege combinations of theoretical approaches that include either non-tribal and tribally centered readings or a sole focus on Western textual aesthetics. Because one of Erdrich's questions in *Last Report* is 'who is a saint – Ojibwe nun Sister Leopolda or Agnes/Father Damien' – and again because the novel's setting is Little No Horse, I would argue for a tribally centered reading, which would include the cost of colonization and conversion to Christianity for the Ojibwes. Dee Horne writes about the complexity of the colonial context in the fictional reservation of Little No Horse:

> In her portrait of a colonizer, Agnes DeWitt-Sister Cecilia-Father Damien, a woman who becomes a nun at a convent in Minnesota only to leave later and disguise herself as Father Damien, a priest, Erdrich critiques unequal power relations whereby the colonizer assumes superiority and power over the colonized. Agnes-Damien, through the interplay between artifice and art, colonizer and colonized, masculine and feminine, male and female, Catholicism and Anishinabe [sic] spiritual traditions, negotiates the social constructions of gender and race and defines her identity. In this respect, her story is a celebration of self-determination and demonstrates that identity is not stable but involves ever-shifting, complex negotiations that allow for co-existence with differences. (277)

Erdrich manages to break through the binary oppositions and shows how Agnes/Father Damien achieves her goals of living as a Catholic priest, ministering to the Ojibwes on the Little No Horse reservation, learning their language and spiritual traditions and, most importantly, becoming their friend and believing the Ojibwes to be '*His people*' (5).

Annette Van Dyke proposes that Agnes/Father Damien could have used the power of the priesthood to continue colonizing the Ojibwes:

'There is always the chance that she might be corrupted with the power given a priest' (65). In an act of sovereignty, Erdrich creates a priest who does practically the opposite and assimilates into the Ojibwes' world-view of spiritual traditions and healing practices. Indeed, Debra Barker (Rosebud Sioux) admonishes readers to admire the Ojibwe character Mary Kashpaw for her 'unwavering devotion to Father Damien, par-ticularly when she invokes her spiritual power to guard and protect his soul and sanity. . . . Mary's spirit finds and draws him back from the trails leading to madness and death, back to the physical realm of their lives of service and responsibilities' (268).

In his essay, 'Towards a National Indian Literature: Cultural Authen-ticity in Nationalism', Acoma Pueblo scholar and poet Simon Ortiz writes about resistance: 'Indian people have creatively responded to forced colonization. And this response has been one of resistance. . . . [I]t is this literature, based upon continuing resistance, which has given a particularly nationalistic character to the Native American voice' (10). He goes on to write about the responsibility of Indian writers 'to advocate for their people's self-government, sovereignty, and control of land and natural resources; and to look also at racism, political and economic oppression, sexism, supremacism, and the needless and wasteful exploitation of land and people' (12). Erdrich certainly includes these issues in her work, and, in particular, she pays attention to sexism in *Last Report* and challenges the authority of the Catholic Church to ordain only men into the priesthood, arguing that a woman can administer sacraments as effectively. Erdrich's challenge to the Catholic Church is a form of resistance and echoes the ideas of gender complementarity, where there is gender balance, power and equality. In arguing for the permeability of boundaries between the individual and the group, Leni Marshall agrees that *Last Report* is a work of resist-ance: 'The porous nature of delineating demarcations informs Erdrich's entire text and, I argue, is her message of resistance' (45). Hence, Agnes/Father Damien is an example of resistance to rigid boundaries and the continual negotiation and fluidity of gender identities and sexual orientations.

Jace Weaver, Craig S. Womack and Robert Warrior agree with Ortiz in their collection of essays, *American Indian Literary National-ism,* which includes the Ortiz essay noted above. They write, '[W]e believe that being a nationalist is a legitimate perspective from which to approach Native American literature and criticism. We believe that such a methodology is not only defensible but that it is also cru-cial to supporting Native national sovereignty and self-determination, which we see as an important goal of Native American Studies gener-ally' (xxi). Again, Erdrich's work falls within this methodology because her fiction presents ideas of self-determination, showing how Ojibwes respond to the colonizing influence of the Catholic Church, a period of history that too often has been narrated by non-Natives.

In *Decolonizing Methodologies: Research and Indigenous Peoples*, Linda Tuhiwai Smith (Ngati Awa/Ngati Porou) writes about the assumptions that non-Natives bring to research about Indigenous peoples:

> Research 'through imperial eyes' describes an approach which assumes that Western ideas about the most fundamental things are the only ideas possible to hold, certainly the only rational ideas, and the only ideas which can make sense of the world, of reality, of social life and of human beings. It is an approach to Indigenous peoples which still conveys a sense of innate superiority and an overabundance of desire to bring progress into the lives of Indigenous peoples – spiritually, intellectually, socially and economically. It is research which from Indigenous perspectives 'steals' knowledge from others and then uses it to benefit the people who 'stole' it. Some Indigenous and minority group researchers would call this approach simply racist. It is research which is imbued with an 'attitude' and a 'spirit' which assumes a certain ownership of the entire world, and which has established systems and forms of governance which embed that attitude in institutional practices. These practices determine what counts as legitimate research and who count as legitimate researchers. (56)

Tuhiwai Smith rightly acknowledges the concern that Native scholars have when people from outside the Indigenous peoples' cultures carry on research and then dictate what the 'real' history and culture are of those people. Tuhiwai Smith's critique completely supports the need for an Indigenous critical approach to Indigenous literatures.

Similarly, Seminole scholar Susan A. Miller writes about an Indigenous paradigm in historiography, 'focusing on four central concepts: Indigenousness, sovereignty, colonization, and decolonization' (10). She notes, 'Indigenous projects are designed as service to an Indigenous people or community. Service takes many forms, and even a narrative might refute stereotypes or anti-Indigenous narratives that shape outsiders' treatment of the community and its members' (16). Erdrich writes a decolonizing narrative in *Last Report*; the Ojibwes convert Agnes/Father Damien to Ojibwe spirituality as Agnes/Father Damien converts the Ojibwes to Catholicism. Simultaneously, Erdrich writes back to the history of the colonizer, showing how the whites' debasement of the Ojibwes lacks sufficient evidence. Scholar Allison A. Chapman writes about Erdrich's revision of the saints' lives:

> Erdrich's revisions urge us to rethink the relationship between such foundational stories of Catholicism and contemporary piety, including the Church's stress on heroic sexual abstinence as the defining virtue of the female saint. . . . Erdrich's revised saints' lives, however, highlight the sanctity of human physical love. Cecilia's orgasms at the piano or Agnes's pleasure in brothel-style sexual acts are not debasements of the 'true' saints' virginity. Instead, these sexual experiences form part of Cecilia/Agnes's encounter with the divine. In contrast, the most sexually continent of the Ojibwe characters, Sister Leopolda, is also the most darkly tormented and tormenting. (159)

Other Ojibwe characters, for example Nanapush, accept sexual relations as a positive and necessary part of life and do not understand the abstinence that a Catholic priest or nun must practice. Agnes/Father Damien does not practice abstinence and through her love for the Ojibwes more completely meets the criteria for sainthood than Sister Leopolda.

Choctaw scholar LeAnne Howe's literary critical theory of tribalography addresses issues that other critical approaches might exclude:

> Native stories, no matter what form they take (novel, poem, drama, memoir, film history), seem to pull all the elements together of the storyteller's tribe, meaning the people, the land, and multiple characters and all their manifestations and revelations, and connect these in past, present, and future milieus (present and future milieus mean non-Indians). . . . [T]ribalography comes from the Native propensity for bringing things together, for making consensus, and for symbiotically connecting one thing to another. (42)

In *Last Report*, Howe's definition of tribalography considers the Ojibwe history and culture, past, present and future, *and* the relationships among the Ojibwes and non-Natives, or Agnes/Father Damien. By making connections among all the things that construct Agnes/Father Damien, Erdrich's project in *Last Report* becomes clearer and is illustrated by Nanapush's definition of *nindinawemaganidok* as the epigraph to the novel:

> There are four layers above the earth and four layers below. Sometimes in our dreams and creations we pass through the layers,

which are also space and time. In saying the word *nindinawemaganidok*, or my relatives, we speak of everything that has existed
in time, the known and the unknown, the unseen, the obvious, all
that lived before or is living now in the worlds above and below.
(n.p. Original italics)

By including everything that the Ojibwe world experiences through
mythic time, Erdrich creates the possibility that anything can be imagined, particularly in terms of gender identities and sexual orientations.

Erdrich and Critical Theory

In *Red on Red: Native American Literary Separatism*, Womack argues
for Native viewpoints when discussing Native literatures because he
'rejects the supremacist notion that assimilation can only go in one
direction, that white culture always overpowers Indian culture, that
white is inherently more powerful than red, that Indian resistance has
never occurred in such a fashion that things European have been radically subverted by Indians' (12). Erdrich's body of work produces a critical theory that rises out of an Ojibwe intellectual center, resisting
mainstream notions of identities.

Sexual orientations and gender identities can be situated within the
larger concept of gender complementarity in traditional Native communities, which holds that the important aspects of men's and women's
roles complement each other and are equally valued for the contributions they bring to the community, one role not having any more importance than another. This general description of gender complementarity
allows for many variations, as gender roles are social constructs, and
more importantly tribal constructs. Lang points out, 'Gender variance
is defined . . . as "cultural constructions of multiple genders (i.e., more
than two) and the opportunity for individuals to change gender roles
and identities over the course of their lifetimes"' (qtd Jacobs 103). Contemporary Native peoples have survived the impact of colonization and
the changes it has brought, and despite those changes, gender complementarity continues to the present day, examples of which can be found
in the construction of literary characters in Erdrich's novels. This chapter, however, is also concerned with the non-Native characters in
Erdrich's work and how the critics define them.

If Native cultures do not operate from a Western perspective of an
oppositional bi-gender system – woman and man – then there are more
genders that fall into the paradigm of gender complementarity. Therefore, the same principles would apply to various gender identities, that
they complement other genders and make important contributions to

the community. As an example, Standing Rock Lakota anthropologist Bea Medicine views these sex role reversals historically as 'normative statuses which permitted individuals to strive for self-actualization, excellence, and social recognition in areas outside their customary sex role assignments. In this light, changing sex role identity becomes an achieved act which individuals pursue as a means for the healthy expression of alternative behaviors' (269). Agnes/Father Damien must pass as a Catholic priest for his healthy expression of power and spirituality. Pamela J. Rader, in her discussion of Agnes/Father Damien, argues that Erdrich explores the territory of more than two genders: 'Erdrich brilliantly examines the possibilities and challenges of living a multilayered existence that defies dichotomous categories such as Catholic-Native; Euro-Native (American); *male-female*; and simple definitions of truth-fiction' (emphasis added 222). Clearly, Erdrich presents variant gender identities and sexual orientations as normal, healthy and necessary.

Perhaps critics have assumed that Native authors are imposing their tribal views of gender variance and sexualities on the non-Native characters in their work, and this reasoning might explain why some critics take liberties with how they read those characters. Critics have viewed Erdrich's works with both Western and Native critical approaches and with varying degrees of success.

Erdrich places no labels or rigid paradigms on her characters' gender identities and sexual orientations but demonstrates how they care deeply for other people. This chapter explores the complicated relationships among Ojibwe and non-Native peoples who are in love and/or involved in sexual relationships that transcend the 'usual' definitions of gay, lesbian, bisexual, transgender and queer orientations in *Last Report* with references to how Erdrich handles characters of gender/sexual orientation variability in other novels of her North Dakota cycle: *The Beet Queen, Tales of Burning Love* and *The Master Butchers Singing Club*.

North Dakota Cycle of Novels

Writing about Erdrich's novels, Julie Barak incorrectly argues that 'Erdrich develops a fluidity of gender identities in her characters by recreating a gender role available to her through her Native American background – that of the berdache' (51), a term that Womack describes as 'degrading, offensive, and racist' (302). Louise Flavin takes a psychological approach to *The Beet Queen*, which might be appropriate for the white characters but does not apply to Celestine who has an Ojibwe worldview. Tara Prince-Hughes also writes about *The Beet*

Queen and wisely critiques both Barak's and Flavin's essays. She claims, 'Barak assumes Western ideas of femininity and masculinity when she classifies characters as mixed-gender, and as a result she tends to apply the "berdache" and "manly-hearted woman" roles too loosely' (7). Prince-Hughes maintains that Flavin's essay 'relies too exclusively on Western, and in particular Freudian, theories of psychological development' (8).

In Susan Meisenhelder's essay about *The Beet Queen*, she critiques 'the gender ideals of white culture [which] result in profound dehumanization' for women and Native Americans, specifically the characters of Sita Kozka and Ojibwe Russell Kashpaw. Although Meisenhelder rightly argues about the oppression of the dominant society's gender expectations, her essay lacks a tribally specific critical approach that might better explain Russell Kashpaw's life circumstances. She also omits any discussion of Karl Adare, a gay man, who has sexual affairs with Wallace Pfef and the Ojibwe character Celestine James. Wallace, who describes himself as 'queer' (*Beet* 161), never stops loving Karl; and Celestine has Karl's baby, Dot, and marries him, in that order. Celestine is described as 'handsome like a man' (*Beet* 67). Karl might be considered bisexual if Celestine were not described in such masculine terms and is the only woman with whom he has a sexual affair. According to Alfred C. Kinsey:

> Males do not represent two discrete populations, heterosexual and homosexual. . . . [N]ature rarely deals with discrete categories. Only the human mind invents categories and tries to force facts into separated pigeon-holes. The living world is a continuum in each and every one of its aspects. The sooner we learn this concerning human sexual behavior the sooner we shall reach a sound understanding of the realities of sex. (348)

Hence, Karl falls somewhere on a continuum and cannot be fixed in any one sexual category. Celestine, on the other hand, is an example of gender variance with a heterosexual orientation. Susan Perez Castillo writes: ' "feminine" [is] a social construct which different societies may interpret in different ways at different periods in history . . . ' (229), and continues: '[r]ather than depicting factors such as gender and ethnicity as airtight compartments or reified concepts, . . . Erdrich portray[s] them as vital, mutable discursive constructs which are eminently historical in character. In many of [her] texts, . . . Erdrich offer[s] interesting alternatives to the old binary division of Aristotelian patriarchal discourse, of power/powerlessness, self/Other, and masculine/feminine' (236). Although Castillo observes the possibilities in Erdrich's writing for gender alternatives, perhaps more accurate in describing Celestine is Prince-Hughes's assessment:

> Of Erdrich's alternative gender characters in *The Beet Queen*, only Celestine is actually of Ojibwa descent. The existence of Two-Spirit roles among the Ojibwa was remarked upon by early European explorers, and their descriptions parallel those of other Native cultural traditions. Since in *The Beet Queen*, most of the Two-Spirit characters are non-Indian, the novel suggests not only the cross-cultural occurrence of such traits, but their value to American culture as a whole. (9)

Prince-Hughes should have stopped after stating Celestine's tribal affiliation and a history of Two-Spirit roles among the Ojibwes. She makes the mistake of appropriating a pan-Native term for non-Native characters. Poet and scholar Deborah Miranda (Esselen/Chumash) objects to the use of Two-Spirit to describe non-Natives because

> Two-Spirit indicates not just a gender/sexuality difference, but the very complex issues and history of genocidal oppression that were exacerbated by being 'non-traditionally oriented' – according to the colonizers. . . . Two-Spirit as a term speaks directly to the connections between gender (what we call gender, anyway) and spirituality/religion, not just preferred sexual contact. It would be difficult if not impossible for most non-Native g/l/b/t folks to relate to all of that, in an Indigenous, historical resonance of the term. (Miranda e-mail)

Miranda is not alone in her assessment of the use of Two-Spirit by non-Natives or by critics who apply the term to non-Native characters. Scholar, poet, and activist Qwo-Li Driskill (Cherokee/Lenape/Lumbee/Osage) says, 'I identify as Two-Spirit, and even the word Trans doesn't really cover that too well. I see non-Native Queer folks appropriating the term Two-Spirit all the time. My gender is really connected to Native struggles and de-colonization movements.' Therefore, scholars should think carefully before using the term to describe non-Native characters who exhibit G/L/B/T/Q etc. characteristics in a text by a Native author.

In *Tales of Burning Love*, Candice Pantamounty, D.D.S., the third wife of the Ojibwe character Jack Mauser, has a lesbian relationship with Marlis Cook, the fourth wife of Jack Mauser. The two come together after their marriages to Jack, when Marlis is pregnant and Candice offers to adopt Marlis's baby. Erdrich presents these female characters who are in heterosexual relationships at an earlier point in their lives and later find themselves in homosexual relationships with no qualms about the change in sexual orientations. In fact, the relationship seems based more on need and convenience than anything else. Candice 'controlled other peoples' reactions, concentrated on her choice the way she perfected a patient's bite on a filled tooth' (122); and 'Marlis usually concentrated on drinking everyone around her stone-blind' (166). Candice is the responsible caretaker, and Marlis, who suffers post-partum blues, needs her (170). Candice and Marlis are examples of how people's sexual orientations can change over the course of their lives. Each of these women has something the other wants or needs, and the sexual aspect of the relationship is only one part and not necessarily the most important one.

In *The Master Butchers Singing Club*, the Ojibwe character Cyprian Lazarre is gay but loves Delphine Watzka, another strong woman. Delphine cares about Cyprian but is not strong enough to accept that he will never be able to give himself sexually only to her. Delphine tells him, 'we should stop sleeping together if you're not going to love me like a woman' (211). Cyprian is an example of the complications of focusing on only one aspect of the character – that of sexual actor. Gilbert Herdt asserts, 'The idea of an ontological or cultural reality must entail all the necessary constituents that create the desire for a genuine and satisfying life' (279). For Cyprian, a satisfying life requires marriage to Delphine (255) and his sexual encounters with other men. Sadly, he cannot have both.

Some have described Agnes/Father Damien in *The Last Report* as Two-Spirit because she adopts a male persona in order to administer the sacraments of the Catholic Church. However, Father Damien makes the decision to pass as a priest *before* he arrives at Little No Horse, as a person socialized in Catholicism and Western constructs of gender based on a binary system of man and woman. To call him Two-Spirit appropriates a pan-Native term that does not apply to him. From the beginning, Agnes considers her existence as Father Damien as 'the great lie that was her life' (61). A true Native Two-Spirit would not think of her life as a lie. During her final thoughts before she dies, she admits that she 'betrayed her nature as a woman' (347), and she feels remorse for the 'unborn children' that she never had with Berndt (348). If Agnes were truly a Two-Spirit according to Ojibwe beliefs, she would not feel that she had betrayed her biological nature as a woman. She would understand that her alternative gender is acceptable in the community.

Perhaps more interesting than Father Damien's gender construction is Father Wekkle's attraction to him, one that causes him to be 'disturbed at his own physical reaction to the proximity of Father Damien' (196).

When the two finally lie down with each other, Father Wekkle understands that in the eyes of the Church, he is willing to commit a sin equal to the sin of murder (200). Although he is relieved to discover that Father Damien is really a woman, Erdrich makes clear that people do not have control over their sexual attractions to people or over whom they love, regardless of gender or sexual orientation.

In Erdrich's novels, the emotional investment in a relationship often takes priority over the sexual element and says more about how people relate to one another in sometimes-fluid gender identities and sexualities. Erdrich understands that gender identities and sexualities are not always rigid categories that easily explain why people are attracted to one another. She creates both Native and non-Native characters who need to be defined according to how they behave, dress, work and love; in other words, they need to be considered in the totality of their lives at a particular moment in time and not carelessly grouped into some fixed category that does not accurately represent who they are.

The Last Report on the Miracles at Little No Horse

In *Last Report*, the narrative spans the life of Agnes DeWitt during the years 1910 to 1997, as she reconstructs herself into Father Damien Modeste, a Catholic priest who ministers to the Ojibwes on the remote reservation of Little No Horse. Although Father Damien is a white woman, considering how Erdrich deals with issues of gender construction sheds light on how she sees the roles of strong, powerful women. Because there is no other way for Agnes to administer the sacraments of the Catholic Church, she has no choice but to disguise herself as a man for the major part of her life, some 84 years, and live the 'most sincere lie a person could ever tell' (61).

Agnes begins her transformation when she changes places with the deceased Father Damien Modeste (the First) and dresses in his clothing: 'his cassock, and the small bundle tangled about him, a traveler's pouch tied underneath all else, Agnes put on in the exact order he had worn them. A small sharp knife in that traveler's pocket was her barber's scissors – she trimmed off her hair and then she buried it with him as though, even this pitiable, he was the keeper of her old life' (44). Her conversion begins from the outside with the accoutrements of the priest and the cutting of her hair. Like the title of this section, 'The Exchange', Agnes makes an equal trade: her former identity for the priest's. Appropriately, she buries her past along with Father Damien (the First), and is resurrected as the new Father Damien II. Agnes maintains her female sexual orientation, but changes her outward physical appearance with male clothing and hairstyle.

As people respond to Agnes-as-a-priest, she soon realizes the difference between how women and men are treated. Kashpaw drives her to the reservation, and she notices how he treats her better than she has ever known: '[T]he driver treated her with much more respect as a priest than she'd ever known as a nun. He was deferential, though not uncomfortable. . . . So this is what a priest gets, heads bowing and curious respectful attention! Back on the train, people also had given Father Damien more privacy' (62). Even as a nun, Agnes never experiences the same kind of deferential treatment that the power and authority of the office of a priest brings her. She rationalizes that she thoroughly enjoys the newfound importance because, as a human being, she deserves this kind of consideration. She feels comfortable being on the receiving end of such courtesy, as if it were perfectly natural for all human beings to treat one another this way. Erdrich implies that in an ideal world both women and men would have the power and authority enjoyed by those in positions like priests, and they would also be treated as equals, at least as they would be in a relationship structured by gender complementarity where various genders are valued. Thus, after the initial change of costume, Agnes learns that, as a priest, she can behave as though people will take her seriously, which results in the beginning of her mental adjustment, an internal one, to accompany her new external identity.

This change of thinking happens quickly and naturally, and by the time Agnes leaves Kashpaw to finish walking to her new vocation and home, she has undergone a complete metamorphosis in how she views her new identity in relationship to her future and surrounding environment: 'she was essential to a great, calm design of horizonless meaning' (65). Anything is possible for there are no restrictions on how Agnes can construct herself. Any insecurity that she might have felt about her decision to become Father Damien is put to rest once and for all: 'In that period of regard, the unsettled intentions, the fears she felt, the exposure she already dreaded, faded to a fierce nothing, a white ring of mineral ash left after the water has boiled away. . . . Father Damien Modeste had arrived here. The true Modeste who was supposed to arrive – none other. No one else' (65). Agnes has no doubts about her new skin that houses the true spirit of Father Damien, a priest who wants to attend to the spiritual needs of the Ojibwes. So convinced is she about the rightness of her re-embodiment, the stamp of approval from a higher power seems to be implied. In her self-description as the 'true Modeste who was supposed to arrive', Agnes proclaims a truth that is predestined.

While Agnes has committed totally to her new identity, she still needs to convince the community to avoid any scandalous discoveries of her impersonation. She makes a list of stereotypical gendered behaviors of how she must conduct herself in a masculine style in order to make believers of those around her; in verbal exchanges with others, body language, attitude and daily rituals, Agnes views the priest's life as one that creates a hierarchy with himself in the superior position of knowledge and power. For example, rule number five suggests that any handiwork that women do must be complimented profusely as if to compensate for the women's subordinate position in life, or lack of knowledge and power (74). Obviously, the work of the women is not valued nearly as much as the work of the men. The Western view of relations between men and women, grounded in the Christian context of the Catholic Church, dictates how Agnes sets up her rules to assist in her transformation, a system contrary to that of gender complementarity. She comes to understand that all identities involve the construction of gender politics.

Judith Butler writes about the questionable construction of gender identity: 'gender is in no way a stable identity of locus of agency from which various acts proceed; rather, it is an identity tenuously constituted in time – an identity instituted through a stylized repetition' (415), similar to Agnes's rules for her transformation. J. James Iovannone uses Butler's theory of performative gender acts to read Agnes/Father Damien as transgendered, defining the term to 'represent gendered identities that exist beyond binary categories of male and female, masculine and feminine, heterosexual and homosexual' (41). Deirdre Keenan also relies heavily on the restrictive mainstream notions of transgender identity to discuss Agnes/Father Damien but as a contrast to unrestricted Native alternative gender categories, for example Two-Spirit (2–3). Although the argument for transgender and Two-Spirit identities seems to describe Agnes/Father Damien as a heterosexual woman who lives as a male priest, I would suggest that Agnes/Father Damien defines herself as a person who at the core of identity eliminates gender altogether.

Agnes has to ask herself if she can so easily create a new masculine identity for herself, then how real was her previous identity of Sister Cecilia: 'Between these two, where was the real self? It came to her that both Sister Cecilia and then Agnes were as heavily manufactured of gesture and pose as was Father Damien. And within this, what sifting of identity was she? What mote? What nothing?' (76). Rachel Lister focuses on the dialogic encounters in *Last Report* and comments on the identities of Agnes/Father Damien: 'Agnes engages with the gendered "component" of language when she assumes the identity of Father Damien. . . . The text itself does not sustain such rigid definitions. After her transformation, Agnes seeks evidence of her ontological self and finds that her female selves are as conditioned as her masculine personae' (226).

Agnes understands that the true core of a person does not necessarily have anything to do with inherent gender traits but rather is more of an androgynous, or genderless, entity that she can construct however she chooses. This epiphany leads to her realization that she can contain a multitude of personalities, and, moreover, she can choose how she will construct them: 'She decides to miss Agnes as she would a beloved sister, to make of Father Damien her creation. He would be loving, protective, remote, and immensely disciplined. He would be Agnes's twin, her masterwork, her brother' (77). Agnes wants to create a priest who includes more feminine qualities of nurturing, thereby creating a man of God who represents a more balanced construction of various gender traits, a personality that more closely resembles the structure of gender complementarity.

Agnes's combination of gender traits becomes clear in looking at her sense of fearlessness and her menstrual cycle. First, she believes that because she has survived 'the robbery, the chase, the bullets, and the flood, then transformed herself to Father Damien, she could not be harmed. That inner assurance would make her seem fearless, which would in turn increase the respect she won among the Anishinaabeg' (78). Agnes's experiences contain valued masculine traits of adventurousness and bravery, which lead to her acquiring a sense of boldness from having survived such catastrophic events. She knows that her inner confidence emits an aura of courage that she might not have gained had she not lived through her previous escapades. Second, in dealing with the 'misery of concealing the exasperating monthly flow that belonged to her past but persisted into the present', Agnes is constantly reminded of her female sexuality (78). In order to simplify her life and ease the difficulty of hiding her menses, allowing her to continue her work, she prays for an end to her monthly 'affliction'. Whether God answers her prayers or through mind over body, her periods end. When Agnes receives her wish, however, she feels ambivalent about losing a most female reminder of herself: 'she felt a pang, a loss, an eerie rocking between genders' (78). A sense of both gender constructions, Agnes and Father Damien, is always present. Agnes successfully negotiates both personalities, no small feat, knowing that she will always be a woman but needs to be a man in order to do the public work of a priest. Maria Orban and Alan Velie suggest that Agnes/Father Damien is successful because 'Agnes is a masculine woman [and] Father Damien is a feminine man' (29).

Perhaps the most significant example of Agnes's handling of both genders takes place when she prays: 'Agnes and Father Damien became one indivisible person in prayer' (109). The complete union of her two personalities demonstrates the androgyny at her core, or, more precisely, her spirit, which is neither female nor male, but pure essence of her being. In communion with God, Agnes rises above her outward appearances and her hidden identity to move closer to a more perfect state of grace: 'Sorrows, confusions, pains of flesh and spirit, all melted into the sweet trance of the moment' (110).

Although Agnes exercises extreme measures to hide her female characteristics – binding her breasts and no longer having a monthly flow – there are people who either suspect or know that she really is not a man. Agnes assumes that Fleur knows: 'Nothing slipped by her, so he accepted that she'd known his secret from the beginning, and it hadn't mattered' (264). The Ojibwes call a woman-man an *ikwe-inini*, but they do not use the term with any ridicule or disrespect, and perhaps this explains why Fleur never mentions Agnes's secret (153). When Agnes takes medication to numb the pain of her ended relationship with Father Gregory Wekkle and sleeps for days, Mary Kashpaw also discovers the truth about her by noticing that she has no whiskers growing on her face. Rather than ignore the truth, Mary goes to great lengths to keep it hidden, watching over Agnes and pretending to shave her, so nobody will suspect (212). Once Mary knows, she goes beyond not caring about Agnes's deception and becomes even more devoted to her. In fact, of all those who know her true identity, only Sister Leopolda threatens to expose Agnes for who she really is: 'I know what you are. And if you banish me or write to the bishop, *Sister* Damien, I will write to him too' (273). Nothing comes of Sister Leopolda's accusation, and she is the only character who ever threatens Agnes's reputation.

In Agnes's initial contact with the Ojibwes, Kashpaw, her driver, 'sensed something unusual about the priest from the first':

Something wrong. The priest was clearly not right, too womanly. Perhaps, he thought here was a man like the famous Wishkob, the Sweet, who had seduced many other men and finally joined the family of a great war chief as a wife, where he had lived until old, well loved, as one of the women. Kashpaw himself had addressed Wishkob as grandmother. Kashpaw thought, *This priest is unusual, but then, who among the zhaaganaashiwug is not strange?* (64).

If Kashpaw perceives Agnes as strange because she does not have the typical characteristics of a male priest, he does not necessarily think less of her for that but instead explains it away as just another quirk of white people. According to his understanding of effeminate men, there is a socially accepted place for them within the tribal community. His attitude represents that of most of the Ojibwes who know Agnes's true identity and accept her for who she is.

While Father Gregory Wekkle knows Agnes's secret and even makes love in their youth to the 'skin that covered the body that housed two beings', on his return visit years later, he eventually treats her with subtle condescension, resorting to deeply ingrained socialized hierarchical behaviors among priests and women (208, 303). Agnes realizes that he is unaware of his patronizing attitude even though he is still attracted to her: 'Practice had perfected her masculine ease, and age had thickened her neck and waist so that the ambiguity which had once eroticized her now was a single and purposeful power that, heaven help him, he found more thrilling' (301). Despite his sincere feelings for Agnes, she resents his assumption that he is entitled to a private part of her that 'only she was meant to possess' (303). In other words, Agnes will not allow any other person to have power over her as if she is less than he.

Unlike Father Wekkle, Nanapush, an established trickster-like character, knows that Agnes is a woman, but he does not care if she wants to live her life as a man. He only uses his knowledge of her true identity when he wants to distract her enough so that he can win at a game of chess. He startles Agnes by boldly asking why she has spent her life acting as a man, and once the truth is out in the open, Agnes actually feels relieved as the heavy burden of deceit that she has carried for years lifts (230–2). Nanapush explains that he has known all along, but he still wonders why she has chosen this path: 'Are you a female Wishkob? My old friend [Kashpaw] thought so at first, assumed you went and became a four-legged to please another man, but that's not true. Inside that robe, you are definitely a woman' (231). What most impresses Agnes is that her unveiling does not really matter to Nanapush; he merely has used it to remove her bishop: 'that is what your spirits instructed you to do, so you must do it. Your spirits must be powerful to require such a sacrifice' (232); and Agnes responds, 'my spirits are very strong, very demanding, very annoying' (232). The Ojibwes embrace Agnes for who she is, reflecting an attitude of acceptance embedded in gender complementarity, valuing people for themselves and the work they do, unlike the Western Christian attitude evinced in Father Wekkle's treatment of Agnes, one of hierarchy and possession. Nanapush understands that Agnes had no choice but to obey her spirits and live as a priest, exercising her own form of independence.

Conclusion

Michael Angel writes about the role of the *Midewiwin* in Ojibwe society: 'Among the most important of Nanaabozho's gifts to the Anishinaabeg was the institution of the Midewiwin, since practitioners were promised a long life if they followed its teachings and precepts as taught by the Mide elders' (4). Nanapush adheres to the traditional spiritual practices and lives a long life. He even invites Agnes/Father Damien into the sweat lodge ceremony. Mary Kashpaw nurses Agnes/Father Damien and heals his spirit with her traditional spiritual practices. The unspoken presence of the *Midewiwin* seems to exist in the background of Little No Horse, and, as such, Agnes/Father Damien is affected by its presence. He never wants his secret identity exposed to the Catholic Church and dies in his priest's robe far from anyone's eyes; thus, he never totally rejects his Christian beliefs. Erdrich's theory of gender and sexual variance in *Last Report* without fail follows a non-judgemental course, and the traditional *Midewiwin* seems to be part of the world-view that allows such tolerance and acceptance. The political implications are that women can live autonomous lives and succeed in whatever kind of work they choose. Erdrich creates no limitations that women cannot overcome, but instead provides them with a 'great, calm design of horizonless meaning' (65), allowing them to engage in an endless number of possibilities, including changing gender identities and sexual orientations throughout their lives.

PART III

The Plague of Doves

Introduction

This part begins with Gina Valentino's consideration of the nature of critical theory in a Native American literary context. Thus, her chapter is in conversation with Mark Shackleton's discussion in Chapter 5 of the relations, both extant and potential, among post-colonialism, critical race theory, and Native literatures, particularly the question of whether Native American communities are in any sense 'post' settler colonialism. Valentino's observation that Native nationalism is motivated by the legal concept of sovereignty also places her work in dialogue with David Stirrup's discussion in Chapter 4 on the importance of law as a primary discursive context in Erdrich's work. Like P. Jane Hafen and Patrice Hollrah in their analyses of *Last Report*, Valentino discusses the issue of how Erdrich's fiction should be approached methodologically in a Native American context. Their approaches to this question are, however, quite different. Where Hafen and Hollrah explore the importance of Indigenous-centered, as opposed to non-Native, critical approaches, Valentino's discussion of gender and the critique of identity in *The Plague of Doves* asks how gender is a factor in tribal-nationalist theories of Native American literature and offers Erdrich's novel as an instance of nationalist critique. Hafen points to the importance of recognizing Ojibwe tribal spiritual practices and beliefs when assessing the role of religion in *Last Report*; Hollrah looks to the centrality of Ojibwe understandings of gender and sexual identities in order to distinguish between Native and non-Native expressions of sexuality and gender. Valentino moves the conversation to the gender politics that inflects recent accounts of Native American literary nationalism and asks how such gender conflicts might shape our reading of *The Plague of Doves*. This theoretical perspective allows her to reassess the literary heritage represented by messianic mixed-blood male protagonists in canonical works of Native American literature like N. Scott Momaday's *House Made of Dawn* (1968) and Leslie Marmon Silko's *Ceremony* (1977).

The character of Billy Peace is the focus of Valentino's account of Erdrich's feminist critique of the marginalization of women, as well as the issues of tribal sovereignty and blood quantum, in Native literary and theoretical work. Like Momaday's Tosamah, the 'Priest of the Sun', the cult that is founded by the ironically named Peace – the Kindred – offers a new vision to unify the community but also adopts a number of Native separatist ideas. Valentino argues persuasively that it is through this character that Erdrich offers a subversive interpretation of the canonical mixed-blood messiah. The subversion is effected through Erdrich's transformation of this figure into what in European terms might be called an anti-messiah but in Ojibwe cultural terms is a *windigo*: a malevolent, violent, cannibalistic spirit that particularly afflicts the starving. Shackleton, in his chapter, reminds us that the character of Pauline/Sister Leopolda has been identified as a *windigo* because of her skeletal appearance, her work in the service of death, her lack of positive emotion that is akin to the *windigo*'s association with winter, extreme physical and emotional coldness and, metaphorically, an 'icy heart' like Billy Peace's lack of affective emotions. The *windigo* spirit is said to be capable of 'possessing' humans, though humans may transform into *windigos* if they practice cannibalism. The physical representation of Billy's possession is his transformation into the opposite of Pauline's skeletal body; he eats while others go hungry, seemingly possessed of supernatural appetites, and swells to an imposing size.

Valentino shows how Erdrich uses the workings of race-based nationalism within the telling of gender-neutral histories in order to subvert the assumption of gender neutrality by introducing matrilineal histories that are in tension with patriarchal histories. What matrilineal histories do is complicate the ways in which blood relations and claims are related to land claims and sovereignty. It is the male figure of Judge Coutts who articulates an understanding of sovereignty that takes account of matrilineal narratives of history based on blood, family and community rather than messianic religion, which resist rather than instantiate destructive Native/white, male/female binaries to promote Erdrich's vision of a hybrid, inter-racial feminism.

The complex role of humor in Indian–White relations, John Gamber shows in his chapter, works to draw boundaries between Native and non-Native communities: to non-Natives the stoic stereotype of the

Indian is presented while within Native-only groups humor is rich and deep. Native humor both heals and attacks, Gamber argues, operating as 'both shield and weapon', and, fundamentally, as a strategy of resistance, adaptation and survival. As Gamber notes, the first joke of the novel takes as its butt the Norwegians who think of themselves as separate from the rest of the community but find that the doves consuming the crops make no such distinction. Throughout the chapters of this book, Erdrich's resistance of categorization, boundary-setting and binaristic thinking has been emphasized. In this part, Valentino focuses on gender, Gamber on humor and Rainwater on non-human personhood, but all three stress the narrative strategies by which *The Plague of Doves* engages in this subversion and deconstruction of fixed categories of experience.

The neglect of Native humor, Gamber argues, is an important mechanism that sustains the stereotypes of Native people as stoic and as historically 'vanished'. The myth of the 'Vanishing American' places Native communities in relation to 'untamed wilderness', the disappearance of which with the closing of the frontier suggests that no 'real' Natives currently exist. The use of sophisticated techniques of artistic humor therefore re-inscribes Native presence and represents 'a powerful and active method of pointing out and upsetting the whitestream coping mechanism of denial of settler colonial oppression'. As Gamber astutely observes, the eponymous plague of doves as large white mass consuming the landscape and starving the people bears an ironic resemblance to white settler encroachment on the land.

Relations between land and the personhood of human and non-human animals is the concern of Catherine Rainwater's chapter. P. Jane Hafen discusses the inter-connectedness of all things in tribal cosmologies where no distinction is made between the animate and the inanimate, unlike in hierarchical Western systems of belief. Rainwater explores the European colonial impulse to control, divide and master nature, other communities and themselves. In Erdrich's novel, Judge Coutts asks, 'By drawing a line and defending it, we seem to think we have mastered something. What?' (114). One of the key boundaries in the narrative is the property line that divides the town of Pluto from the reservation to which that town land once belonged. To characters like Mooshum, who view the landscape in very different terms from the European settlers, the town represents stolen land. From the eco-critical perspective that informs Rainwater's analysis, the novel exposes the limitations of European epistemologies when confronted with holistic Indigenous modes of understanding and of being that are encapsulated in the concept of 'relationship'. As Rainwater shows, the narrative draws upon a complex symbolic vocabulary comprised of biblical allusions and Christian symbolism, Ojibwe culture and history and animal imagery to challenge the legitimacy and usefulness of dividing, in order to separate, creation into contingent and arbitrary categories. Rainwater compellingly shows that in Erdrich's novel, 'to be plagued by doves, fed by a dog, or "haunted by birds" (215) is to be shadowed by insistent otherness that resists liberal-humanist, categorical definition'.

CHAPTER 8

'It All Does Come to Nothing in the End'

Nationalism and Gender in
Louise Erdrich's The Plague of Doves

Gina Valentino

Introduction

My aim in this chapter is to consider the place of gender theory in Native American Studies in general, and, more specifically, to examine its ramifications for reading Louise Erdrich's *The Plague of Doves* (2008). In considering the first, broader issue, I have been guided by the example set by King-Kok Cheung when she was asked to assess the place of feminism in Asian American studies for an anthology titled *Conflicts in Feminism* (1990). She writes, 'I believe that in order to understand conflicts among diverse groups of women, we must look at the relations between women and men, especially where the problems of race and gender are closely intertwined' (234). Cheung goes on in her article to describe the acrimony between the editors of the anthology of *Aiiieeeee!* (1974), who were all male, and Maxine Hong Kingston. In the African American context there is a comparable controversy between Ishmael Reed and Alice Walker. In ethnic studies traditions in the United States, gender theory has never been race neutral.[1] Or another way to phrase it might be that theories about race have never been gender neutral. Because of the differential treatment of men and women of color under racism there have often been tensions and conflicts between the ways that male critics and writers and their female counterparts have thought about the politics of writing. This is clearly seen in theories and formations of ethnic literary nationalism.

In telling the story of contemporary Asian American and African American literature it is almost impossible not to begin with gender wars. The same can be said for the Chicano and Chicana literature and criticism around machismo discourse. Gender war debates, however, have not been recognized as so central to Native American Studies as they have to other fields. When the story about the emergence of Native American literature is told, it tends to begin with the Native American Renaissance, and there is no gender conflict per se at the heart of the story. An explanation for this might be that the first American Indian novel to truly gain recognition and promotion was written by N. Scott Momaday. The fact that the first Native American novel to be awarded the Pulitzer Prize, Momaday's *House Made of Dawn* (1968), was written by a man seems to have circumvented uneasy questions about the 'feminization' of a particular field that emerged in other ethnic traditions with the popularity of writers like Maxine Hong Kingston or Alice Walker. This might make Native American literature appear to be an exception in the formation of a canon of contemporary ethnic literature.

While there have certainly been heated controversies that have defined Native American literature, the earliest and most public debates have been between female writers rather than between female and male writers. Paula Gunn Allen took Leslie Marmon Silko to task for her inclusion of Laguna Pueblo stories in *Ceremony* (1977) that she thought should remain within the clan. Silko, in turn, in what was eventually termed the 'Silko–Erdrich Controversy', wrote a rather scathing review of *The Beet Queen* (1986), which, among other things, accused Louise Erdrich of being more concerned with post-modern narrative technique than furthering a Native communal voice.[2] Excessive reliance on literary post-modernism, Silko claimed, was evidence of Erdrich's ambivalence towards her Native American identity. On the surface, these debates focus more on insider versus outsider status and questions of Native authenticity and location rather than outright politics of gender. Though there have been differences of opinion, male Native authors and critics like Gerald Vizenor by and large have not publicly attacked Silko or other female writers with the same vehemence as Frank Chin has attacked Maxine Hong Kingston, nor, as previously mentioned, Ishmael Reed attacked Alice Walker.

Nationalism in Native American discourse means something very different from nationalism in Asian American, African American and Chicana/o discourses. Nationalism in those other contexts is primarily a cultural matter; that is, Asian American activists like Frank Chin are not interested in creating a separate Asian American state. Native nationalism by contrast has always been tied to sovereignty and is not simply a unifying metaphor; it points to a legal discourse that animates the field. The sovereignty of tribes as nations, in principle at least, has been long recognized by the US state, though this recognition is often quite limited in its scope. Moreover, tribal self-rule pre-dates any federal US attempts at governance. As it stands, there are over 500 federally recognized tribes that are designated by the US government as 'domestic dependent nations'. In Native American Studies then, nationalism does not simply name a principle for designating an intellectual and artistic community, it also carries with it a legal distinction.

Sovereignty functions in much the same way. When Native American Studies scholars espouse sovereignty they are speaking of independent tribal self-rule within established diplomatic and legal discourse. The issue of sovereignty is literally and legally part of the ongoing struggle against the forces of settler colonialism. Most Native American Studies scholars, Jace Weaver, Robert Warrior and Craig Womack included, reject the notion that there is anything resembling a 'post' in the US colonial project as it relates to Indigenous populations.[3] In short, Native American Studies critics tend to reject post-colonial theory on two fronts: first, whatever Native America might be, it is certainly not *post*-colonial and, secondly, post-colonial criticism re-inscribes settler colonial dominance through theory that reifies European critical strategies.

What has come to be called Native, or American Indian, literary nationalism sought to rectify these and other inadequacies. In a sense, the seeds of this critical movement were planted by Simon Ortiz's essay, 'Towards a National Indian Literature: Cultural Authenticity in Nationalism', which was published by *MELUS* in 1981. It gained momentum in the 1990s with the publication of works like Elizabeth Cook Lynn's *Why I Can't Read Wallace Stegner and Other Essays: A Tribal Voice* (1996) and Craig S. Womack's *Red on Red: Native American Literary Separatism* (1999), which continued the theoretical conversation begun by Ortiz. These scholars advanced a critical paradigm that promoted the struggle, survival and legal recognition of Indigenous nations living in North America. Issues around Native nationalism and sovereignty are nothing new, of course; what *was* new was the near-exclusive emphasis that was placed on these issues as the animating concerns of Native artistic and intellectual production.

While some skeptics of this nationalist paradigm may have derided it for being 'separatist', it is important to note that, at least in its original formulations, it did not exhibit the kind of problematic gender politics that have been apparent in the cultural nationalist paradigms that shaped the emergence of other ethnic critical traditions. However, in the most recent iteration of this critical approach, namely, *American Indian Literary Nationalism* (2006), we can detect the emergence of the very kind of rhetorical strategies that have made it difficult for many feminist critics to embrace nationalism as their guiding methodological principle.

American Indian Literary Nationalism is an anthology of critical writings by senior Native American Studies scholars Jace Weaver, Craig Womack and Robert Warrior. According to the authors, *American Indian Literary Nationalism* was written to respond to the 'backlash' that 'has developed against nationalist approaches to Native literature by those, both Native and non-Native, who find them either impossible to maintain, theoretically untenable, or simply too confrontational' (xx). *American Indian Literary Nationalism* works to fix misconceptions about Native literary nationalism. In his chapter 'Splitting the Earth: First Utterances and Pluralist Separatism', Weaver provides some fundamental parameters of what the authors mean by American Indian literary nationalism. First, American Indian literary production 'is separate and distinct from other national literatures' (15). Secondly, American Indian literary nationalism 'deals with a criticism of that literature that supports not only its distinct identity but also sees itself as attempting to serve the interests of indigenes and their communities, in particular the support of native nations and their own separate sovereignties' (15). Thirdly, 'Just as Native American Literature by definition can only be produced by Native writers, so Native American literary criticism (in contrast to criticism of Native American Literature) must be in the hands of Native critics to define and articulate, from resources *we* choose' (original emphasis 17). This final point is perhaps the most controversial because, no matter how inclusive one's definition might be, race authenticates intellectual production as Native.

American Indian Literary Nationalism should be lauded for championing and fostering Native cultural sovereignty. It is hard not to commend Weaver, Womack and Warrior for their work. Few critics would quarrel with the notion that more Native American voices need to be heard in the academy, nor would many disagree that there needs to be greater focus on Native American politics. *American Indian Literary Nationalism* begins to enter troubled waters, however, when the authors single out Elvira Pulitano as a critic whose work exemplifies all that they stand against.

Warrior, Weaver and Womack in their own words were 'galvanized' by Pulitano's monograph, *Toward a Native American Critical Theory* (2003). Their primary point of contention with Pulitano has to do with Native American authenticity. The authors find that Pulitano's work 'embraces the footloose, rootless, mixed-blood hybridity . . . in which both everyone and no one is Indian. It becomes impossible to espouse a Native perspective' (xx). Furthermore, they charge Pulitano with privileging European continental theory over what they deem to be Indigenous critical methods: 'In her attempt to articulate a "Native American critical theory," she rejects nationalist approaches to Native literature in favor of doctrinaire postmodernism' (xx). There are shades of the Silko–Erdrich controversy in their argument, but what concerns me are the rhetorical maneuvers they use to characterize Pulitano's work and how it echoes the masculinism that has been so pronounced in other cultural nationalist traditions.

Regardless of the merit of Pulitano's arguments, one must question the tenor of Womack, Warrior and Weaver's critique. They write, 'This flawed text is relatively unimportant in and of itself. Yet it, like the work of her mentor [Louis Owens] before her, has begun to be taken up methodologically by those opposed to literary nationalism and by others who pay lip service to Native sovereignty, but seem to have little or no attachment to the centrality of Native nationhood to contemporary Native people' (xx). There is a muted but palpable aggression in their simultaneous dismissal of Pulitano's work and in the way she is reduced to a generic stand-in for a kind of post-modern theory they find objectionable. In this passage, Pulitano, it seems, is not allowed even basic academic agency. Elsewhere, Weaver indicates that Pulitano 'spanks' other nationalists 'for their refusal to engage high theory' (20). Weaver, Warrior and Womack display a masculinist rhetorical tendency that appears to be almost hardwired into nationalism. I can no more agree with Pulitano's assessment that Warrior and Womack's 'cultural separatism eventually leads to the hopeless project of recovering a Native essence, a project that, ironically embraces another sort of colonial invention' than I can with the manner of Womack, Warrior and Weaver's critique (62).

There is strong historical precedent for women and their allies to be cautious of nationalist theory. Even if the debates about nationalism and essentialism were not primarily couched as conflicts between men and women, the current interest in new nationalist paradigms is taking the shape of gender conflicts that have occurred in other fields. Consider Weaver's comments in the following passage, which seem to engage in an all-too-familiar linking of women of color with racial betrayal:

Too often non-Native critics want their Natives to be Squanto, kidnapped and traduced and coming home speaking the language of the colonizer; la Malinche, translator and concubine, progenitress of a fictive, thoroughly *mestizaje raza* of Mexico; or Pocahontas, sacrificing her body and her health on the altar of mediation, becoming in the process the guarantor of indignity for the Lees, the Randolphs, the Symingtons, and those who call themselves, utterly devoid of irony, the First Families of Virginia. They prefer Sarah Winnemucca to Red Cloud, Gertrude Bonnin to Richard Fields. (2)

Weaver's initial address of how Indigenous men and women function in non-Native imaginaries is valid. Native women are more palatable to dominant culture precisely because they are figured as model minorities, foresighted women who recognized the superiority of colonizing forces and thus acted as willing conduits of colonization. Weaver neglects this component in his analysis and lets the subtext linger. Weaver footnotes this passage, not to address the problems of gendered politics related to resistance and assimilation, but to name another female, Mary Musgrove, 'the Creek Pocahontas', as an example of an acceptable mainstream American Indian. In his comparisons, Weaver unfortunately re-inscribes a gendered division that pits Native female writers against Native male military leaders, setting the women up as race traitors and the men as defenders of the tribe. In doing so, Weaver shows that it is not solely the province of non-Native communities to think that Indigenous women are more inclined to facilitate colonialism.

Thus, conflict over new incarnations of Native nationalism is taking a familiar shape. As literary critic Shari M. Huhndorf has argued in *Mapping the Americas: The Transnational Politics of Native Culture* (2009), there has been a way in which male critics have marginalized Native women's concerns in the name of nationalism: 'Literary nationalism itself has been a predominantly male endeavor. Nationalist critics have devoted little attention to writing by Native women, especially those works that attend to issues of gender, and they have thereby reinforced the marginalization and political containment of Indigenous women under colonialism' (4). Huhndorf calls for a 'feminist rethinking of Native politics and culture, a task to which nationalism is inadequate' (4). It would seem that American Indian literary nationalism, and its accompanying issues of sovereignty, has not escaped the gender wars that have characterized other ethnic nationalist discourses. In the reading of *The Plague of Doves* I offer in this chapter, I show how Erdrich's novel offers a feminist critique of a Native nationalist cultural politics that echoes Huhndorf's critique of a tendency among male critics such as Warrior, Weaver and Womack to marginalize women.

Feminist Critique in *The Plague of Doves*

As I have been suggesting thus far, it would seem that American Indian
literary nationalism, despite some of the best efforts of its advocates,
does not escape the politics of blood or gender. In the reading I now
offer of *The Plague of Doves*, I show how Louise Erdrich – no stranger
to controversy or to critiques from within Native communities and
from outsiders – anticipates some of the issues and tensions I explored
in the first part of my chapter. Erdrich's narrative, I argue, should be
read as offering a critical appraisal of a contemporary Native literary
nationalism and the attendant issues of blood quantum and sovereignty.
Her feminist critique centers on the figure of Billy Peace, a resident of
Pluto, North Dakota, the fictional town in which most of the action of
the novel takes place. Like most of the characters in the novel, Billy can
trace his lineage back to both the Indigenous population and the first
white settlers. His last name indicates that Billy is related to two of the
town's founders, Henry and Lafayette Peace.

In *The Plague of Doves* Erdrich draws her attention away from the
urban locations she used in *The Antelope Wife* and returns to rural
Indian country. The town of Pluto, North Dakota lies inside the original
boundaries of a reservation, presumably Chippewa/Ojibwe, which had
once been larger. Pluto's location operates on symbolic and material levels for residents of the town and reservation alike. It foregrounds Pluto
as a contested space between white settlers and Indigenous communities. Therefore the setting necessarily engages with issues of sovereignty
and nationhood. When Neve Harp, a white local historian asks her
brother's father-in-law how Pluto came to be within the reservation, he
responds, 'What you are asking . . . is how was it stolen? How has this
great thievery become acceptable? How do we live right here beside
you, knowing what we lost and how you took it?' (84). What appears to
be a simple question about the past for Neve is a present and constant
reminder of colonial trauma for others. Mooshum frames his response
in nationalist discourse. By doing so, he restructures the trajectory of
Neve's information gathering in such a way as to highlight that the story
of Pluto's founding is the story of the reduction of sovereignty and land
rights for Native populations.

That the scene I have alluded to involves the patriarch of one of the
primary families in Erdrich's narrative explaining his view of the town's
founding to two women hints at the gendered nature of historical memory as she depicts it. Mooshum's view of history is tied to the fact that he
has a deep connection with Native nationalism. His parents supported
Louis Riel, doomed leader of the Métis resistance against Canadian
colonial expansion. Though he does not appear in the novel as a

character, the historical figure of Riel plays an important role in it since he represents a historical forerunner for the other figures of patriarchal nationalism, like Mooshum and Billy Peace. Because of their support for Riel, Mooshum's family forfeited their land and were forced to flee Canada. Resettling in what became North Dakota, his parents never fully recovered from their loss. As Evelina, Mooshum's granddaughter, retells it, 'they tried to homestead again, but the heart was out of them. They lost a baby, settled into a despondent subsistence, and were crushed when they heard Riel was tried and hanged' (21). Still an infant when these things occurred, Mooshum is haunted by this history of loss, which begins with Riel's failed nationalist uprising.

Riel has assumed iconic status for Mooshum and his family. His picture hangs on their kitchen wall with other revered figures such as John F. Kennedy and Pope John XXIII. Beyond this, Riel and his nationalist cause enables Mooshum and his brother, Shamengwa, to project an alternative version of the present that includes no loss. In an otherwise comic exchange with a priest whom the two brothers love to torment, Mooshum says, 'If we had our rights, as Riel laid 'em out, Father Cassidy, you'd be working *for* us, not *at* us.' Shamengwa adds, 'I've thought about this, brother. If Riel had won, our parents would have stayed in Canada, whole people. Not broken. We would have been properly raised up' (33). After engaging Father Cassidy in a bawdy theological conversation about 'male parts', the 'male part's wishes' and the respect for the Lord, Shamengwa states, 'Respect . . . is a much larger subject than your male parts, my brother. You referred to political respect for our people. And in that you were correct, all too correct, for it is beyond a doubt. If Riel had carried through, we would have had respect' (34). The brothers finish the conversation by toasting the nation, their people, land and women – in that order. Though a harmless and good-natured engagement, Mooshum and Shamengwa nevertheless evoke Riel as a certain kind of patriarchal nationalist hero. This personal and political history of nationalism is the subtext of Mooshum's response to Neve's question.

It is no coincidence that Evelina, the primary narrator of Erdrich's novel, was named in honor of Louis Riel's first love. She witnesses the exchange between her grandfather and her aunt about Pluto's boundaries. Aware of the tension, she absorbs the reactions of her grandfather, great-uncle and her mother, 'both of the old men's faces became like Mama's – quiet, with an elaborate reserve, and something else that has stuck in my heart ever since. I saw that loss of their land was lodged inside of them forever. This loss would enter me, too. Over time, I came to know that the sorrow was a thing that each of them covered up according to their character' (84). Evelina enters into a collective sense of Native loss through the hearing of the tale, but the complex role that gender plays in this telling and in her hearing make it clear how complicated a process is this transmission of trauma.

The loss, the literal and physical reduction of sovereignty, is transmitted to Evelina via her identification with her grandfather. Her entry into collective Native loss is initialized through a male nationalist paradigm, which provides the rationale for Evelina to reject her aunt Neve. Evelina is attracted to the moment where Native nationalism contains the power to trump cross-racial gender coalitions even within members of the same family. However, her mother interrupts this transmission when she pronounces, 'It's not her fault' (84). Evelina thinks it is Neve's fault and bases her aunt's culpability on the fact that she was once married to a Wildstrand, a descendant of the lynching party whose actions marked and formed the town. Her judgement prompts her mother to reveal the identity of the father of Evelina's own grandmother, who was half white and half Chippewa. Evelina learns that her great-grandfather was Eugene Wildstrand, who was not merely a descendant of the lynching party, but actually one of its members.

Evelina's mother intervenes in her daughter's wholesale adoption of a nationalist model of identification by revealing matrilineal family history. Race-based nationalism justifies Evelina's condemnation of her aunt precisely because it is conceptualized as gender neutral. However, her mother's revelation contradicts that assumption. Before this information, Evelina viewed her history through her grandfather and not her grandmother. Likewise, the nationalism with which she identified conformed to a male model of history and not a female one. It takes another female family member, her mother, to bring the politics of gender and blood and its direct connection to nationalism into focus. Her mother's disclosure forces Evelina to reconsider her harsh judgement of her aunt and to reconsider her nationalist ideological alliances. As Judge Coutts, another significant character in the novel and one of its narrators, explains: 'nothing that happens, *nothing*, is not connected here by blood' (115). Land claims and family blood claims are inextricably bound together.

The Plague of Doves also shows that Native nationalism and patriarchy are bound together and just as tightly. Erdrich evokes Riel in order to highlight a historically remote, nearly mythical strain of Native nationalism that is epitomized by heroic patriarchs. While the character of Mooshum is clearly among the most sympathetic in the novel, he too is in thrall to the nationalism that Riel inaugurated, making clear that the object of Erdrich's feminist critique is not men per se but a patriarchal ideology of Native nationalism that well-meaning men and women can both find themselves drawn to. With Billy Peace, however, Erdrich emphasizes the full danger of unchecked patriarchal Native nationalism.

Patriarchy and the Nationalist Messiah

Billy Peace is a descendant of Cuthbert Peace, who is one of the Chippewa men lynched by the white settlers of Pluto. Readers first learn about Billy during his interactions with John Wildstrand. Maggie Peace, Billy's older sister, becomes pregnant during her affair with Wildstrand, who was married to Neve Harp at the time. Billy confronts John at his home with a gun. John manipulates Billy and devises a kidnapping scheme ostensibly to buy Billy's cooperation. Billy agrees to the convoluted plot in order to defend his sister's honor and arrange for her financial security. Events escalate with the result that Billy joins the military to avoid being arrested. Though this incident occurred while he was still a teenager, and at the time more susceptible to John's manipulations, Billy's involvement with the kidnapping underscores his desire to assume familial male authority and function as a savior, albeit self-appointed, in that role.

Billy is shipped to Korea and stationed near the Demilitarized Zone (DMZ). While there, he has a spiritual awakening. Billy writes letters to his sister that describe his visions and tell how 'he was being contacted by powerful spirits who saved him time after time, and who promised to direct his life' (131). When Billy returns to Pluto, North Dakota it is as a traveling preacher. Billy does not narrate his own story; that is left to his wife, Marn Wolde.

Marn Wolde is the daughter of a white farming family that settled in Pluto. Marn meets Billy when she is 16 and he invites her to a church meeting. Physically attracted to him and swayed by his charismatic preaching, Marn marries Billy and leaves her troubled family. Through Marn's narration, we follow Billy's three-part evolution: from traveling preacher to reverend with a struggling but growing congregation and, finally, to cult leader. Marn supports Billy's accomplishments, and is happy with the arrival of their two children, but she increasingly regrets the estrangement from her family that her marriage to Billy caused and begins to miss the farm where she grew up.

Marn convinces Billy to return to Pluto by telling him: 'Your parents died when you were young. Your sister raised you until you went into the army, then she went to the dogs, I guess. So you don't really understand the idea of home, or folks, or a place you grew up in that you want to return to. But now it's time' (148). While it is her invocation of family and place that initially seems to convince Billy to return to the reservation, Marn comes to suspect that it is the 888 acres of land that they will possess that draws Billy back to Pluto. Regardless, Marn is thrilled with his decision until she realizes what Billy has planned – which is to bring the congregation to live on her parent's farm. Once on the Wolde family farm, Billy's spiritual message changes and his messianic aspirations take off.

Billy Peace's return to Pluto in Erdrich's novel fits with William Bevis's assertion that the homing plot comprises a central motif of Native narratives: a troubled mixed-blood, preferably male, preferably a veteran, returns home to fight inner demons and unite a divided community. On the surface, Billy Peace resembles the mixed-blood messiah of an embattled people celebrated in such works as *Ceremony*, and he does draw a new version of Native community together. However, Erdrich uses the conventions of the homing plot as a cautionary tale about the abuses of nationalism.

Billy's justification for taking over the Wolde farm is founded on nationalist claims to land rights. Marn recounts: 'The end of our land bumps smack up to the reservation boundary. This was reservation, Billy says, and should be again. This was my family's land, Indian land. Will be again' (152). Billy's attachment to the land mirrors Mooshum's and Shamengwa's. And in certain ways he is initially a sympathetic character in that we see a young man trying to reclaim a sense of native agency and sovereignty. Like Riel, Billy works to right wrongs wrought by racist colonial practices. Also like Riel, Billy wishes to create a spiritual awakening in people to reject a life based solely on accumulating material possessions. Furthermore, in the absence of Marn's brothers, who have abandoned the family, Billy helps Marn's father run the farm. Additionally, Billy gives extra care to the members of his congregation, most of whom fall between the cracks of society. These acts position him within the framework of native 'communitism', Weaver's neologism that combines the words activism and community-building and expresses aspects of Native nationalist ideology.

However, Erdrich signals there is something amiss in the nationalism Billy represents in Marn's reaction to his statement about his intention to return to his family's land. As Marn puts it, 'He says it flat out with a lack of emotion that disturbs me. Something's there. Something's different underneath' (152). In the end, it is not the lack of affect that demonstrates how problematic Billy is as an embodiment of nationalism and sovereignty. Indeed he turns out to be a *windigo*, an Ojibwe figure of excessive consumption, predatory sexual appetites and greed.

Billy's transformation into a *windigo* happens in stages. In keeping with many versions of the *windigo* story, there is a need, usually the threat of starvation, that must be filled through sustained direct action. At first Billy's actions are beneficial; he 'seems to whirl from one thing to the next, his energy blooming, enormous, unflagging', which is a good thing because there is much work to do and the farm is in danger of failing. But soon Billy's appetites outpace what the farm is able to sustain: 'The food he eats! Whole plates of spaghetti, pans of fresh rolls. . . . Billy grows as the heat withers everything else. He drinks the well dry! That summer, we borrow from the bank and sink another well' (152–3). Billy's overconsumption forces others to sacrifice and go into debt. Soon he surpasses everyone in stature: 'Billy has expanded to such a marvelous size, outweighing us all, and splendid in his new white suits' (153). In a lean time, he is the only being to thrive. Others are content to let Billy prosper because he has maintained that his leadership and spiritualism are in the community's best interest.

What is most notable about Billy's appetites is their scale, but it is important to recognize that they are all coded as masculine. In keeping with *windigo* characteristics, Billy's sexual hunger is insatiable. Billy's wife, Marn, writes, 'Another month passes and Billy's chins double so he wears a thick flesh collar. We make love every night, but I am embarrassed. He is so loud, so ecstatic. I am tossed side to side on top of him, as if I am riding a bull whale. I make him wear a sleeveless undershirt so I can hold on to the shoulder straps like handles. The bed creaks like the timber of a boat going down in a gale, and when he comes I feel heavy and swamped' (153–4). Whatever Marn gets out of these sexual encounters is clearly secondary to Billy's enjoyment. Her embarrassment indicates her discontent with her reduction to a sexual outlet for Billy. For Marn, sex cannot be merely a recreational act as it is for Billy. She confesses, 'I am afraid of getting pregnant again. I am afraid of what's happening' (153–4). Marn is frightened by Billy's excess and his growing power over the community. Billy's sexual activity eventually extends to other female members of his congregation, thus anchoring his spiritual and Native national project firmly in a traditionally patriarchal hierarchy.

Billy's complete transformation into a *windigo* occurs simultaneously with a display of his supernatural power over the people he commands and over the land they inhabit. His metamorphosis takes place as he uses his power to end a drought; he brings the rain as he is struck by lightning: 'He is a mound, black and tattered, on all fours. A snuffling creature of darkness burnt blind. We watch as he rises, gathers himself up slowly, pushes down on his thighs with huge hands. Billy is alive, bigger than before, swollen with unearthly power' (156). The *windigo* is a malevolent figure in Ojibwe stories and by casting Billy as one, Erdrich draws on this tradition to put forward a critique of the political vision he embodies.

Erdrich's point, however, is not just that Billy is a *windigo*, but that the version of nationalism he embodies requires a kind of charismatic leadership that is dangerous. That idolatry is an aspect of Native nationalism is something that the reader initially saw in a more comic light in

Mooshum's reverential relationship to Riel, whose image hangs next to JFK's and the Pope's. There's a danger in any project of community-building that depends on this kind of charismatic, iconic and ultimately patriarchal form of leadership. Billy's example shows that the desire to engage in a project of repossessing the land that was once possessed and lost can literally lead to a kind of possession. Billy is possessed, literally, by his male appetites. And his followers, The Kindred, become possessed by his vision.

Like Louis Riel before him, Billy Peace begins to cast himself as a messianic figure tied to a cause that is as nationalist as it is spiritual. Before his complete metamorphosis, Billy based his beliefs on established monotheistic, Christian doctrine. After the lightning strikes, Billy begins to cultivate the idea of 'spirit', of 'religion based on what religion was before it was religion' (158). Billy's attempt to reach back beyond the Judeo-Christian tradition echoes attempts to reclaim pre-contact spirituality that is often contained in some Native nationalism. As the name 'Kindred' suggests, Billy frames his followers as being united members of the same chosen family, kin. Billy organizes The Kindred on the principle of self-determined community values to consolidate his power. He establishes alternative family structures and forbids the use of identifying markers based on biological ties; thus 'mother' is a forbidden word. What appears to be an equalizing maneuver is really a way for Billy to cement his authority. His core spiritual tenet functions in the same manner, 'Billy believed that a group of minds living together, thinking as one, had the potential to expand further than any individual'(159). The Kindred does think 'as one' but 'that one' is *Billy*. Billy's goal is a kind of native sovereignty but it is defined by his rule over others. What started as a bid to reclaim tribal land and rebuild an inclusive Native community not defined merely by blood becomes a closed order system where a multiplicity of ideas is not permitted. Dissent is not tolerated nor to be thought about in The Kindred. As Marn ominously explains, 'He took his time organizing his strategy and his purpose. He took care smoothing out the rough spots in the Manual of Discipline' (159). Billy develops his own doctrine for The Kindred that is based on nationalist themes, and punishes those who do not adhere to his cause. The Kindred manifests problematic strains in nationalism. There is a direct correlation between the magnitude of Billy's spiritualism and his oppressive control over The Kindred. Marn continues, 'Another year passed and the discipline grew tighter and more intense as the spirit ripped into Billy and wouldn't spare us, either' (161). As The Kindred demonstrates, nationalism, sovereignty and religion often produce oppressive results, especially for women, precisely because these ideologies are ultimately about the use and control of power. Billy uses the talents and skills of The Kindred to authorize his dominance.

Conclusion

Through Louis Riel, Mooshum and Billy Peace, Louise Erdrich traces a genealogy of Native nationalism. Each of these figures displays, to one degree or another, strains found in nationalism, strains that are violent, oppressive and patriarchal. However, Erdrich provides an alternative to masculinist forms of nationalism in Judge Coutts. Like most of the characters in the novel, Judge Coutts is of mixed background. His father was a descendant of one of the original white settlers of Pluto and his mother was Chippewa who lived on the reservation. Judge Coutts is aware of the irony of his position; 'He who goes to law holds a wolf by the ear, said Robert Burton. So there I was, here I am, the clichéd mixed-blood with a wolf by the ear' (114). Judge Coutts may have a mixed racial background but he identifies and aligns himself ideologically and politically with his Native community. This is something he learned, at least partially, from his white father, the only attorney who, as Coutts puts it, 'stood up for us' when 'we traveled to Washington to fight a policy that would have terminated our relationship with the United States Government guaranteed by treaty' (92).

But Judge Coutts understands that nationalism has its limits. 'It is my job to maintain the sovereignty of tribal law on tribal land, but even as I do so, I think of my grandfather's phrase for the land disease, town fever, and how he nearly died of greed, its main symptom' (114). In his narrative, Coutts uses 'us' to show the historical relation of a Native past to Native people in the present. His phrasing grounds his ideology in a historical Native continuum, but also indicates that he figures national-ism differently from US legalistic language. Though, like his father, Judge Coutts supports sovereignty, his nationalism is not based in US legal, diplomatic paradigms. His definition is derived from a recogni-tion of Native nationalism constructed as 'the people', as an 'us' and 'we' and is neither constrained by geographical place nor tied directly to land rights. In fact, Judge Coutts suggests that such thinking leads to pointless failure: 'As I look at the town now, dwindling without grace, I think how strange that lives were lost in its formation. It is the same with all desperate enterprises that involve boundaries we place upon the earth. By drawing a line and defending it, we seem to think we have mastered something. What? The earth swallows and absorbs even those who manage to form a country, a reservation' (114).

Judge Coutts does not dismiss land claims and their importance in Native life, but he situates what Gerald Vizenor calls 'survivance', what others call sovereignty, in people's *relationship* to the land and not possession of land in and of itself. He continues, 'Yet there is something to the love and knowledge of the land and its relationship to dreams – that's what the old people had. That's why as a tribe we exist to the present' (114). Judge Coutts represents a Native nationalism and Native sovereignty that is independent of iconic, patriarchal leadership and is not overdetermined by land claims. Judge Coutts is the summation of Erdrich's critique of nationalism and encapsulates a larger argument that she made about *The Plague of Doves* in an NPR interview, 'I had hope that something like that would resonate today in our hopeless grip that nationalism has on so many of our countries and has on so many of us. It all does come to nothing in the end and that's the truth of history'.[4]

CHAPTER 9

So, a Priest Walks into a Reservation Tragicomedy

Humor in The Plague of Doves

John Gamber

The Plague of Doves begins in the midst of a grisly murder, with a gunman attempting to unjam his rifle so as to kill the sole remaining member of the victim family, an infant in her crib. Indeed, the unveiling of the details of the murder and its horrific aftermath control the course of the narrative. It is about as funny as a novel that begins and ends on such a note can be, I suppose. What is surprising is that a novel that begins in this way *can* be funny at all. And it is funny. Sometimes. However, this pairing of comedy and tragedy is not at all uncommon within Native American literary or storytelling practices. This chapter will examine discussions of humor in Indian stories from the early twentieth century to today, then move to an examination of Erdrich's novel in order to place it within a continuum of Indian humor. This participation in Indian humor traditions takes the form of teasing which generates both inclusion and exclusion, as well as slapstick, punning and language play, and burlesque and bawdy sexual joking. These forms combine to establish a comic mode that simultaneously frames and undercuts the tragedies of the novel – and Native life generally. I will focus on the five major comedic scenes in *The Plague of Doves* as examples of Erdrich's comic mode: those involving the eponymous plague, Mustache Maude Black and three detailing interactions between a reservation priest,

Father Cassidy, and Mooshum (which is his familial title 'Grandfather', not his name; his name is Seraph Milk but he is usually referred to in the text as Mooshum).

Indian Humor

In his 1902 memoir, *Indian Boyhood*, Charles Eastman (Santee Sioux) establishes a pattern of discussing Indian humor with his chapter 'The Laughing Philosopher'. Eastman asserts, 'There is scarcely anything so exasperating to me as the idea that the natives of this country have no sense of humor and no faculty for mirth' (229). Eastman attempts to overcome the stereotype of the stoic, humorless Indian. Indeed, his point is not just that Indians are funny, but that Indian people enjoy humor even more than other people: 'I don't believe I ever heard a real hearty laugh away from the Indians' fireside' (229). Eastman describes 'the recognized wit or story-teller' keeping 'the community in a convulsive state' for an entire evening (229). These stories come from puns and linguistic play, heavily gestural performances and embarrassing anecdotes, especially about men failing in attempts at hunting. For example, one story describes Tamedokah, who once stunned a deer. Thinking it was dead, he set about to dress the animal, at which point 'the animal got up and attempted to run' (230). The man reached for the deer, but 'only succeeded in grasping the tail of the deer' and 'was pulled about all over the meadows and the adjacent woods until the tail came off in his hands' (230). The teasing about this incident continues for pages, with Tamedokah receiving it with grace, humility and good humor, even adding further details to augment the comedy. Nonetheless, Eastman's chapter on humor stands in rather stark contrast to the rest of his text, in which there are very few humorous or even comic moments. Instead, the memoir privileges narratives of grave masculinist training, in many ways reinforcing the aforementioned stone-faced stereotype. Moreover, 'The Laughing Philosopher' represents the penultimate chapter of *Indian Boyhood*, lying buried so late in the text that it is often overlooked. It is uncertain to what degree Eastman shaped this text in anticipation of, or because of, editorial reaction to, and expectations of, an Indian narrative. But the artifact that remains is not terribly funny. Still, the presence of this chapter marks one of the first Native-authored representations of Indian humor in English.

It is striking that, in the face of Eastman's opening exasperation that Indian people are perceived as having no sense of humor, Vine Deloria, Jr. (Standing Rock Sioux) offers such a similar lament in the chapter 'Indian Humor', in his foundational *Custer Died for Your Sins: An Indian Manifesto* (1969). Deloria explains, 'It has always been a great disappointment to Indian people that the humorous side of Indian life has not been mentioned by professed experts on Indian Affairs. Rather the image of the granite-faced grunting redskin has been perpetuated by American mythology' (146). After 67 years, little, it seems, had changed in terms of the stoic Indian stereotype. Deloria's work on the matter is similar in many ways to Eastman's; he begins with a brief description of Indian humor and then gives a series of examples of it. However, Deloria's chapter, rather than a couple of longer comedic anecdotes with the participation of the butt of the jokes, consists of a series of one-liners at the expense of some of the great villains of Indian history, especially Christopher Columbus and George Armstrong Custer. 'Custer's Last Words occupy a revered place in Indian humor', expounds Deloria. Many of these 'concentrate on where those **** Indians are coming from', but Deloria's favorite has Custer turning 'resignedly to his aide and say[ing], "Well, it's better than going back to North Dakota"' (149). However, Deloria gives examples of many jokes that respond to contemporary issues, or deal with specific legal and political events, including the Indian Reorganization Act (1934), the Indian Termination era (1940s –to 1960s), or the 1964 US presidential election. For Deloria, understanding that Indians are funny is important in part because 'People have little sympathy with stolid groups' (146). As such, asserting the humor of Indian people and cultures serves a socio-political purpose, garnering a greater affinity between Native and non-Native people. Mainstream US culture will be more likely to be sympathetic to Indian issues if they recognize Indian humor.

Anishinaabe theorist and author Gerald Vizenor expresses a thought similar to those from Eastman and Deloria. He asserts, 'The tribes have seldom been honored for their trickster stories and rich humor' (*Manifest* 83). Vizenor, who brings in discussions of the trickster – one of the most widely discussed elements of Native stories – goes further in a theoretical frame than Eastman and Deloria: 'The resistance to tribal humor is a tragic flaw. Laughter over that comic touch in tribal stories would not steal the breath of destitute children; rather, children would be healed with humor, and manifest manners would be undermined at the same time' (*Manifest* 83).[1] Rather than embracing the stone-faced Indian image, Native people are better served by recognizing the humor in their own cultural traditions. This humor serves at least the dual purposes of making life in the world better – healing, at least temporarily, the maladies of poverty and disenfranchisement faced by Indian communities – and challenging the hegemonic structures that have created and maintained that disenfranchisement.

Continuing the trend, some 91 years after Eastman and 24 after Deloria, Kenneth Lincoln in *Indi'n Humor: Bicultural Play in Native*

America (1993) notes, 'American Indian humor remains a mystery, if not an oxymoron, to many' (5). By contrast, Lincoln declares, Indian people 'laugh hard and deep among themselves and grimace around whites, exorcising the pain, redirecting their suffering, drawing together against the common enemy – cultural ignorance' (5). For Lincoln, the stone-faced Indian is an adopted grimace performed for an outgroup audience, while laughter and humor are the norm within in-group settings. Like Vizenor, Lincoln demonstrates how humor works to heal and attack, as both shield and weapon. He declares, 'The powers to heal and to hurt, to bond and to exorcise, to renew and to purge remain the contrary powers of Indian humor' (5). Humor defines the community, as jokes demonstrate who is one of 'us' and who is one of 'them'. Being the butt of a joke does not inherently mark a person as one or the other, as all of these critics demonstrate. In Eastman's narrative, the comedic foil is a noted member of the community; in Deloria's, the joke is on the perpetrators of great crimes against indigenous populations. For all, humor is no mere laughing matter, however. It is a cultural practice that demonstrates humility, privileges wit and, perhaps more than anything, demonstrates an ability to adapt, to cope, to overcome and to survive.

Indian Humor in Erdrich's Work

I will return to many of these elements of Indian humor in the pages that follow, but I turn now to a discussion of the critical reception of humor in Erdrich's previous work. Initial reviews of her first novel, *Love Medicine*, emphasized its tragic elements exclusively, eschewing the many humorous moments. Likewise, in her study of 'Indi'n Humor and Trickster Justice in *The Bingo Palace*', one of the most thorough studies of humor in Erdrich's work, Nancy J. Peterson surmises, 'Clearly, cross-cultural misinterpretation might lead to a reading of *Love Medicine* as devastating rather than funny, but the complex nature of tribal humor is another significant factor' (163). It is the 'intermixture of comic laughter and serious matters that has made her vision of Native America so compelling' (163). Such reviews mark the literary vestiges of the stone-faced Indian stereotype. Indians are so associated with tragedy that their humor is illegible and unidentifiable to certain outsiders. Of course Native-authored texts often do portray elements of the crimes committed against Indian people and the indigenous landscape. The fact that these crimes are ongoing, acted out every second of every minute of every day across the continent, makes it close to impossible for a Native author to ignore or not address in some way. But humor is so rarely absent in Native art, from literature to film to plastic and visual art, that to ignore it is to disregard not only the humor of Native

American traditions but the artistic and comedic agency of Indian communities and individuals.

The mere fact that these artists are actively creating combats one of the only stereotypes more pervasive than the stoic warrior: the vanished or extinct Indian. As anyone who studies or teaches Native American studies or literature can attest, the general public finds it incredibly easy to casually discuss American Indian people and communities in the past tense. Since 1890 – with the closing of the frontier under Frederick Turner's hypothesis, and the Wounded Knee Massacre that marks the supposed end of military action against Indian people – Indians and their land have been seen as defeated. And, since indigenous people in the Americas and around the world are so often associated with the binary node of wilderness (seen in contrast to civilization and/or culture), this conquering marks them as no longer 'real' Indians. Any living Indian people, cultures, languages et cetera, are viewed as watered-down or bastardizations, like sad zoo animals removed from their noble wilds. This animalization is not coincidental, but the remnant of the more clearly offensive representations of Indian people as crazed savages as represented in Westerns and captivity narratives. The presence of Indian people and the dissemination of Indian art challenge this past-tense construction of Native America that allows settler colonialism to pretend its crimes against the indigenous population are in the past, rather than an ongoing possessive investment, to borrow from George Lipsitz.[2] As such, Indian humor, rather than a mere defensive coping mechanism, in fact represents a powerful and active method of pointing out and upsetting the whitestream coping mechanism of denial of settler colonial oppression.

To this end, Peterson asserts, 'To understand her laughter, we have to be able to conceive of the almost inconceivable: the possibility of Indian victory. Because of the dismal outcome of the Indian wars of the nineteenth century, any image of Indian victory has come to be charged with irony' (168). The general population seems to expect all stories of Native people to be primarily tragic with reason. For more than half of US history (an extremely brief history compared to Native political organizations), the nation was intent on destroying Indian people and cultures, to the point that any indigenous victory seems impossible. In order to combat this imagined impossibility, Peterson argues that Erdrich's texts provide 'moments of slapstick and humor, [by which] Erdrich insists that readers recognize Indians not as tragic victims but as comic actors and agents' (162). Peterson continues, '*The Bingo Palace* moves toward an unprecedented development – the emergence of a new kind of Indi'n humor rising out of triumphant laughter and (postmodern) trickster justice' (164). Humor, then, is not only a method of entertainment, or, as Deloria asserts, a method by which to forge political coalition or increasing political allegiance. Instead, Indian humor is an assertion of active, vibrant Native presence and a force by which tactical justice can be meted out in the face of anti-Indian sentiment, doctrine and practice.

This tactical agency contrasts with overt (especially violent) confrontation and rebellion. In her analysis, Peterson posits, 'as Indians, used to dealing with ironies and the twisted plots and words of the federal government, Lipsha and Lyman [characters from *The Bingo Palace*] know how to recognize an absurd situation and laugh about it rather than coming to blows (164). Lipsha's and Lyman's approach, opting out of violence, further reflects a comic (as well as humorous) approach to survival. In the comic mode, as discussed by Castor (who draws on Joseph Meeker's *The Comedy of Survival*), survival in Erdrich's work comes from a comic adaptability rather than a tragic confrontation. For Native characters, for whom direct violent action against the settler colonial nation has historically meant overt attempts at military annihilation, the comic mode of survival is also often the only one available.

Kenneth Lincoln also devotes a chapter of his *Indi'n Humor* to *Love Medicine*. According to Lincoln, Erdrich's work emphasizes 'three comic types': the understater, the buffoon and the overstater (224). I will return to Lincoln's analysis later in applying it to *The Plague of Doves*. But these comic types pervade Erdrich's work generally. Other critics draw on common themes in tribal stories. For example, both Gleason and Bowers draw on Lakota Heyoka figures in their commentary on Native humor in Erdrich's work, while Lincoln draws on the Heyoka in his study of Native humor generally. While I am wary of such cross-tribal references, the jokester and clownish figure certainly plays a role in a number of Native cultural productions.[3]

Much has also been made of the humor, or at least the comedy, in Erdrich's narrative form. Her novels make use of multiple narrators giving varying parts of a larger story to create a multi-vocal total narrative. While David Treuer has challenged the categorization of Erdrich's work as multi-vocal, the fact remains that her narratives, with their multiple perspectives and standpoints, challenge assertions of absolute authority or truth (39–48). Instead, narratives unfold, piece by piece, with successive narrators or narrative points of view layering more and more details to the novelistic whole. Such a stylistic approach is important for a number of reasons. First, it emphasizes the communal aspect of storytelling and truth- and mythmaking. Story and history are fashioned out of varying accounts being placed together to form a whole. No single individual does, or, in truth, can, understand – let alone control – the totality of the story. But perhaps more important than this is the fact that many of the narratives subtly differ, or even overtly contradict one another. As such, the reader is left with doubts about many critical details. Erdrich's use of recurring characters and landscapes in many of her novels (reminiscent of Faulkner's work as so many critics have noted), adds to the complexity of such an approach, as the complete story cannot even be bound by a single text, let alone a single narrative perspective within that text. In *The Plague of Doves*, Erdrich continues this multiple narrative formula to involve the reader in the mystery of the murder that begins in the novel's opening paragraph. Until the reader comes to the end of the novel s/he may wonder how some of the narratives relate to that event, though their relationships to characters directly affected by the murder and its aftermath are clear enough.

For the purposes of this chapter, it is important to note the comic and humorous aspects of such a multiple narrator approach to storytelling. In one sense, refusing a single absolute truth or truth-teller denies the tragic mode, in which a hero must be seen as being on the side of right. Erdrich's narratives challenge simplistic absolutes in terms of human actions, most of which are seen as both deeply flawed and at least somewhat laughable. But we must also note that the text itself plays the role of one long joke at the reader's expense. The novel is clowning us, having a bit of fun by yanking us around. We think we have it figured out, and it pulls the rug out from under us. If, as Lincoln argues, one of Erdrich's recurrent comic characters is the buffoon, then the reader becomes one too. We participate in the community of the story, and like all the rest of the community, we do not get to escape being made fun of. But as we have seen in Eastman's and Vizenor's discussions of Indian humor, we should not take this toying personally, but enjoy the play, the tease. We look back on details from earlier in the novel and realize they were clues that we missed, as sloppy detectives who allowed themselves to get lost on the trail of the story. We close the back cover and, ideally anyway, think: good one!

The Plague of Doves

After the ghastly beginning of the novel, with its controlling murder, the novel transitions into the vignette from which the title comes. It is told in a contemporary voice, from Evelina, a mixed-blood Chippewa who matures from childhood to young adulthood over the course of the story, and who occupies the primary narrative position in the novel as a whole. About half the novel is told by her, with another third told by Judge Anton Bazil Coutts, a Chippewa attorney. The remainder is told in two short sections by Marn Wolde and Dr. Cordelia Lochren, a pair of white townspeople in Pluto, North Dakota. Evelina begins, 'In the year 1896, my great-uncle, one of the first Catholic priests of aboriginal blood, put the call out to his parishioners that they should gather at Saint Joseph's wearing scapulars and holding missals' (5). The parishioners gather, toting their Catholic regalia to drive out an enormous piteousness of doves (though the novel does not use this term for the ornithological collectivity; a group of doves can also be called a bevy, a dole, a cote or a flight). They plan on walking through the fields in a long row while praying in an attempt to scare the birds, which are devastating the people's crops. Certainly this seems like a reasonable idea; with a little luck the birds will simply move on from fear or annoyance. But, within this first paragraph, the reader encounters the first joke of the novel.

The opening sentence, as we have seen, represents the adoption of Catholicism by a Native, in this case Chippewa, man. In fact, he has done more than adopt the religion, he has taken Holy Orders, he is a fully-fledged priest. That a Chippewa man would adopt Catholicism rather than Protestantism should not be surprising considering the French influence on the tribe and the region as a whole. Similarly, Evelina notes that the French 'mingled with my ancestors', by which she means not only social, but also procreative, mingling (5). However, the Germans and Norwegians who later arrived 'took little interest in the women native to the land and did not intermarry' (5). She continues, explaining that 'the Norwegians disregarded everybody but themselves and were quite clannish. But the doves ate their crops the same' (5). The joke here, at the end of the first paragraph of the novel, is on a group of people who see themselves apart from those around them. In reality, they share the ecological fate of their neighbors, whether they choose to recognize them or not. The joke is based on mocking those who see themselves as superior. It's not a great joke. But it is pretty funny.

Of course we also identify the irony of doves being seen as a plague. When one thinks, for example, staying within the Judeo-Christian framework established by Evelina's priestly predecessor (who is later described as having saved 'his younger brother ... from excessive freedom') (6), of biblical plagues, one notes a striking contrast. The animal-based plagues that God visits upon Egypt in Exodus are comprised of frogs, lice, flies and locusts (as well as the death of livestock). Most plagues take the form of invading insects, gross creepy-crawlies, any one of which might be enough to induce a fit of the heebie-jeebies. The amphibian frog is another creature of which many people are afraid. But the dove's appearance in the Bible precedes these plagues, as Genesis positions the dove as the harbinger of good tidings and the abatement of the flood. Again, this isn't exactly 'ha-ha' funny, but Erdrich's humor often takes such a subtly ironic form. One does not think of doves as the kind of creatures that would be associated with a plague, but any creature, in excessive numbers, certainly embodies one. We can extend this reading further still, understanding that an excessively large, migrating, white mass of life clamping down on the American land-scape, overusing the land and starving out the indigenous population bears some slight similarities to Native history over the past few 100 years.

Not all of Erdrich's humor, not even as it relates to this vignette, is so sly, however. As the people advance on the doves, the narrator explains:

> there was a sudden agitation among the women, who could not move forward without sweeping birds into their skirts. The birds in panic tangled themselves in the clothes. The line halted sud-denly as, to our Mooshum's eyes, the women erupted in a raging dance, each twirling in her own way, stamping, beating, and flap-ping her skirts. So vehement was their dance that the birds all around them popped into flight, frightening other birds, that in moments the entire field and the woods around it were a storm of birds that roared and blasted down upon the people, who none-theless stood firm with splayed missals on their heads. The women forsook modesty, knotted their skirts up around their thighs, held out their rosaries or scapulars, and moved forward. (8)

Mooshum revels in this scene, enjoying seeing more of women's legs than he is used to being allowed to see. However, 'Instantly he was struck on the forehead by a bird hurtled from the sky with such force that it seemed to have been flung directly by God's hand, to smite and blind him before he carried his sin of appreciation any farther' (8). This moment of slapstick places Mooshum as the butt, but no more so than nineteenth-century Christian modesty, as his sin is one of 'appreciation' of the (divinely created) female body. We will encounter a similar respect for the God-made human body later, but we must note Mooshum's physical comedy, not in the form of a pratfall, but in the form of a story about bodies. However, the narrator also describes Mooshum's storytelling practice, illustrating his comic delivery. She elu-cidates, 'At this point in the story, Mooshum became so agitated that he often acted out the smiting and to our pleasure threw himself upon the floor. He mimed his collapse' (8). We can relate this to what Eastman says of Native storytelling and humor, 'Indian humor consists as much in the gestures and inflections of the voice as in the words, and is really untranslatable' (229). Humor, even Erdrich's written humor, is physical and performative.

A great deal of the humor in *The Plague of Doves* centers on human romantic and/or sexual relationships. Indeed, Evelina's entire family history is comprised of funny, ridiculous and generally over-the-top romances. She explains:

> My uncle Whitey dated the Haskell Indian Princess, who cut her braids off and gave them to him on the night she died of tuberculosis. In her memory he remained a bachelor until his fifties, when he married a small-town stripper. My mother's cousin Agathe, or "Happy," left the convent for a priest and was never heard from again. My brother, Joseph, joined a commune in an act of rash heat. My father's second cousin John kidnapped his own wife and used the ransom to keep his mistress in Fargo. Despondent over a woman, my father's uncle, Octave Harp, managed to drown himself in two feet of water. And so on. As with my father, these tales of extravagant encounter contrasted with the modesty of the subsequent marriages and occupations of my relatives. We are a tribe of office workers, bank tellers, book readers, and bureaucrats. The wildest of us (Whitey) is a short-order cook. . . . (9)

This entire passage represents a combination of the tragic and the comic, all demonstrating the ridiculousness of love and our responses to it, though those responses can nonetheless have profound effects on our lives (like love itself). Moreover, this brief narrative, quite early in the novel, foreshadows almost every meaningful event that will follow.

After the vignette describing the plague of doves, the next sustained comic moment comes as Mooshum leaves the scene with a young woman, Junesse. They eventually come to stay with Mustache Maude Black, a strong and brash but very kind woman for whom 'casual' cattle rustling was 'a kind of sport . . . she never meant any harm by it at all' (17). At first the couple sleeps together in Maude's home, but 'Divining their love, she banished Mooshum to the men's bunkhouse, where he quickly learned all the ways that he could make children in the future with Junesse' (17). This comic irony is plain enough. Maude thinks that separating these two young people will prevent their sexual exploration, but Mooshum merely learns what to do when he and Junesse inevitably find themselves alone.[4] Eventually Mooshum and Junesse are old enough to wed, and Maude plans a great celebration: 'When the day came, she threw a wedding supper that was talked about for years, featuring several delectably roasted animals that seemed the same size and type as many lost to the dinner guests. It caused a stir, but there were only bones left when the wedding was over and Maude had kept the liquor flowing, so most of the surrounding ranchers shrugged it off'

(17). This comic scene is juxtaposed by the line immediately following: 'But what was not shrugged off, and what was in fact resented and what fostered an undercurrent of suspicion, was the fact that Maude had thrown a big and elaborate shindig for a couple of Indians' (17). Erdrich gives the reader a space to laugh, but within a breath takes away the laughter with foreboding within the story and anger (one hopes) at our enduring colonial history. But it is worse, as we learn: 'This was western North Dakota at the turn of the last century. Even years later, when an entire family was murdered outside Pluto, four Indians including a boy called Holy Track were blamed and caught by a mob' (17). This is Erdrich's move throughout this novel, which is not as thoroughly funny as *Love Medicine* or *The Beet Queen*: the tragic and the comic, the humorous and the heartbreaking, are consistently paired in this novel – as they are in our lives. These elements cannot be understood without or outside of one another. And this is not to say that humor works solely as a coping mechanism for pain. In this example, the humor precedes the tragedy, not only in time (the wedding takes place before the murder and lynching) but in the progression of the narrative (we are told about them in the same order). Joy and pain may lie distant from one another on a spectrum of feeling, but both are parts of our feeling. They are not opposites of each other, but elements around which the other is defined. Crying and laughing lie on similarly mutually constitutive locations on a spectrum of emoting. As such, Erdrich's narrative asserts, they cannot be separated from one another, or imagined as mutually exclusive – not for Indians or anyone else.

Within this section, the novel also makes a humorous play of identity. When a mob comes to take Mooshum to lynch him for the murder of a neighboring white woman – who the text suggests was probably killed by her white husband – in a scene that presages the aforementioned white mob assault, they demand that Maude produce 'the goddamn Indian' (18). Maude, however, retorts, 'He ain't no Indian. . . . He's a Jew from the land of Galilee! One of the Lost Tribe of Israel!' (18). The mob does not necessarily believe Maude, of course, but the fact that she suggests an alternative ethnicity points to a certain fluidity of identity, calling into question the mob's collective certainties. Yet Maude and her husband Ott are not done screwing with the mob's mentality. She goes on to claim that Mooshum is Ott's 'trueborn son' (18). As the details of Mooshum's origin multiply and confound, the mob, defeated both by Maude's verbal acrobatics and the fact that they are staring down the barrels of her two pistols, recede into the dark night from which they had emerged. Evelina comments, 'The story could have been true, for as I have said, there really was a Mustache Maude Black with a husband named Ott. Only sometimes Maude was the one to claim Mooshum as her son in the story and sometimes she went on to claim she'd had an affair with Chief Gall. And sometimes Ott Black plugged the man in the gut. But if there was embellishment, it only had to do with facts' (19).[5] The relevant part of the story in this particular case is not the details, which might shift from storyteller to storyteller, or even from telling to telling from the same storier. Evelina's relation of this story emphasizes a comic orality over a tragic transcription.

The next major comedic scene in *The Plague of Doves* comes at the expense of a white reservation priest from Montana, known both teasingly and mockingly as Father Hop Along, for his bouncy stride, cowboy-like persona, and the fact that his last name is Cassidy. The teasing comes largely as Mooshum and Shamengwa sit and drink whiskey with the priest who asks them why they have not been to confession and whether they have sinned. Evelina narrates: ' "old men have no chance to sin much," said Mooshum in a regretful voice. He looked at Shamengwa. "Brother, have you had a chance to sin this year yet?" ' Shamengwa replies, 'you would know it, as I would tell you immediately in order to make you jealous. Hiyn, no, I have been pure' (24). Mooshum couches his lack of sin not as a source of pride and piety, but as 'regretful'. It is not that he eschews sin, but that he has not had the chance, the opportunity, to do so. He asks his brother using the same word, 'chance'. Shamengwa continues the teasing of the priest, telling his brother that he would gladly and proudly boast of any sins he had been able to commit. The 'Hiyn' at the beginning of his sentence, as even a reader with no familiarity with *Anishinaabemowin* might suspect, is an 'exclamation of sympathy and chagrin, meaning "that's too bad" ' (Beidler and Barton 385). The two men are enjoying their playful teasing of the priest, with whom they especially enjoy an afternoon drink. They continue, making the priest uncomfortable by trying to get him to vocalize some carnal sins. 'Dear priest, could you explain to us – exactly what *are* these impure thoughts you mention? As you say, if they are common, we must have experienced them, and yet we haven't noticed somehow' (25). The priest balks, unable to speak of the sexually explicit acts he and the brothers are all quite clearly implying. The brothers feign ignorance, but beg the priest to explain lest they 'sin unknowingly' (25) and 'end up in the bad place without warning' (26). All the while, Evelina's brother Joseph listens in, occasionally inserting snide asides.

Eventually, Father Cassidy blurts out (would it be too on the nose to say, ejaculates?) 'Concupiscence'. He continues, stammering along, 'From the Latin, *concupissery*, I believe, meaning, ah, to dwell upon unclean emissions in one's past or to anticipate such as . . . any act of imaginary or ejaculatory fornication. Bluntly speaking!' (26). The addition of the phrase 'bluntly speaking' to such an obtuse response reeks of irony, of course. Not surprisingly, Father Hop Along's etymology is also incorrect, as concupiscence derives from *concupiscentia*, simply meaning 'to be very desirous of' (OED) although the accurate root does not allow for the bawdy emphasis on *piss* in Father Cassidy's version. But his falling back on Latin, which is meant to mark him as a well-educated authority but merely makes him a buffoon, also allows for Joseph's continuing participation in this mockery. The two brothers respond, 'Ah, fornication!' and tip their glasses, toasting fornication. The priest, discombobulated by his discomfort, does the same. Meanwhile, Joseph chimes in, positing that fornication is 'From the Latin *forn*, as in *foreign*, for relations with foreigners' (26). The priest, flustered and embarrassed, heads outside, stopping by the family's horses. He calls them 'docile scrub ponies' of 'awful conformation, of course, positively knock-kneed and they do need a currycomb something worse' (26). Conformation refers to a horse's skeletal structure; a currycomb is a horse-grooming comb that slides over the hand. One horse, either angry about Father Cassidy's insults, wanting to get in on the action of knocking him down a peg, or just not liking him on sight, strikes 'and crushe[s] his fleshy bicep in her teeth' (26). One might be tempted to read this as just bad luck, or the bad behavior of an ill-trained equine. But Evelina's narrative indicates that after Father Cassidy had besmirched the pony's knees and coiffure, a 'nasty light sparked in the long-necked pinto's eye' (26). Anyone familiar with Native stories can understand that there is nothing unreasonable about an animal understanding human language or when it is being insulted. In the end the Father expresses his gratitude for the anesthetic of the whiskey he has been sharing with the brothers. Joseph again chimes in, 'From the Latin *anesthed*, meaning numskull' (27).

The priest is further and more finally shunned by the family because of the same prudishness and sexual conservatism that disallowed his frank mention of fornication. During Father Cassidy's sermon 'on God's plan for creating babies in the wombs of women' in which he 'preached against interference with this plan', Evelina and Joseph hear their mother muttering. When Evelina asks about the sermon, her mother, cryptically to her child's understanding, explains, 'God's plan was for me to get pregnant again and die. However, the doctor I spoke with did not agree with God's plan and so here I am, alive and kicking' (31–2). In this moment, Erdrich's characters make use of a biting humor that expresses a socio-political statement. Evelina's discussion, in which she recounts her mother's near-fatal childbirth experience and current use of birth control as a health-of-the-mother issue, is both a shot at the priest's facile theology as well as the Church's historic (and ongoing) misogyny that has seen women as little more than vessels to be bred through and (ideally, unsalaried) child-care workers. Her mother's conclusion, 'here I am, alive and kicking', demonstrates not only that resisting such structures of gendered domination is a methodology of survival (alive), but also of resistance (kicking). As such, this moment represents a lesson, handed down from mother to daughter, resisting the masculinist priest (if not necessarily the Church *in toto* – they are, after all, still attending mass) is one of survivance.[6]

The priest's relationship with Mooshum grows worse as the former fails to empathize with historical Indian resistance, especially in the form of movements led by Louis Riel from 1869 to 1885. Riel lobbied for the protection of rights and land for Métis people. His movement culminated in violence, and he was eventually arrested, convicted of high treason and executed. Father Cassidy, Mooshum and Shamengwa are discussing Riel as a hero, as well as the historical crimes against First Nations people in Canada. In response, 'Father Cassidy shrugged' (32). With this simple dismissive body-language statement, the priest shows that he does not relate to the issues most dear to the people of his congregation. He aligns himself with the colonist empire, complete with its military domination. At this point Mooshum's rage bubbles over, but rather than strike violently at the religio-military figurehead of Priest Hop Along, he strikes with mockery. When the priest asks if Mooshum has 'respected Our Lord's wishes this week', Mooshum replies, 'If Our Lord made our bodies down to the male parts, then He also made the male part's wishes. This week, I have respected these wishes, I will tell you that much' (33). Mooshum's aggressive response dumbfounds the priest, changes the subject and reclaims his agency in linguistic, discursive and sexual modes. He demonstrates control of both his mind and his body, denying the priest, the church, the colonialist and the government their prize.

In their final meeting, Mooshum tells a story of his encounter with Liver-Eating Johnson. This grand comic story tells of a day-long battle between the two men in which Mooshum had taken many chunks out of his attacker with his teeth. He shows a relic of his battle, Johnson's supposed nose (though Joseph says it is a 'bit of *Thamnophis radix*', or plains garter snake – a comically unimpressive and common species). Mooshum likens his prize to the 'piece of good Saint Joseph . . . lodged in our church's altar' (39). Father Cassidy is saddened and outraged by this sacrilege, and Mooshum has no intention of letting him off the hook now. He continues, explaining that 'the Eucharist is a cannibal meal' (40). The priest is overwhelmed at this 'heresy' and explains, 'I fear you will be required to make a very special, and grave, confession for us to allow you back into the church' (40). Father Cassidy shows no ability to laugh at himself or his Church. Had he been able to roll with the humorous punches, rather than explaining that a 'grave', serious, dour, tragic confession would be necessary, he might not have alienated and driven away a member of his congregation. Mooshum replies, 'Then back to the blanket I go! . . . The old ways are good enough for me. I've seen enough of your church. For a long time I have had my suspicions. Why is it you priests want to listen to dirty secrets, anyway?' (40). Evelina goes on to explain that this comic teasing will have serious repercussions for the priest:

> Things would be harder, now, for Father Cassidy. As I went back inside to stash the empty bottle and wash out Mama's cups I knew that word would spread – the priest drunk, tripped up by the devil in the form of a mud puppy, cursing an old man to hell, all of these things would be recounted by Mooshum and Shamengwa when talking to their cronies. And Mooshum really did follow through with what had seemed like a drunken threat. He cast his lot in with the traditionals not long afterward and started attending ceremonies. (41)

Mooshum cannot forgive Father Cassidy's lack of humor about his religion when faced with the former's obviously comic story.

Indeed, following his break with the Catholic Church, Mooshum maintains a comic sensibility even in the face of tragic recollections. When Evelina asks him why he left the Church, Mooshum responds, 'Seraph Milk had a full-blood mother who died of sorrow with no help from the priest. I saw that I was the son of that good woman, silent though she was. Also, I was getting nowhere with the Catholic ladies' (42). Mooshum's response combines the very serious and tragic story of Seraph Milk (his given name) with a (mild) sex joke. The Church then is a serious institution but also a social context, a place for our trickster to practice his sexual (or at least romantic) proclivities.

Ultimately, the last and best laugh comes at the priest's expense. After a long gap in the novel's humor – which nearly disappears between Mooshum's leaving the Church and, perhaps surprisingly, a funeral – the narrative rather suddenly announces that Shamengwa dies. Father Cassidy begins his eulogy, '*I come now before you in the holy spirit of forgiveness to bless the soul of Seraph Milk*' (211). The reader might have a moment of confusion, as Mooshum is so rarely referred to by his given name, but rather his family title from Evelina's perspective. But Geraldine hisses, 'he's got the wrong brother!' (211). Father Cassidy goes on to read an entire eulogy on Mooshum, who is sitting in the congregation. Only after several minutes of this service does the priest see 'Seraph/Mooshum waving from the second pew, and his jaw fell slack'

(212). This scene, in which a holy man mistakenly eulogizes a living person while another man's body lies in state, could be heart-wrenching and tragic in another context. But in this case it is mostly just funny. The reader can picture Mooshum, otherwise heartbroken at his brother's passing, waving, grinning at his old adversary, Father Hop Along, who makes himself one more of Erdrich's buffoons.

This event, or perhaps this event combined with the previous events of the novel detailing his relationship to Mooshum, drive the priest from his holy station: 'A year later, he quit the priesthood, went home, grew a beard, and became an entrepreneur. He sold Montana beef, shipped it to Japan and all over the world. We'd see him on billboards and in his TV commercials. His distinctive skipping bound, his calflike and happy energy, became a trademark for the beef industry and made him very rich' (261). The irony of the role of cattle herding in the destruction of the lifeways of Plains peoples mixed with the former Father Cassidy's cartoonish characterization (or caricaturization) generates a combination of humor and anger. Ranchers were major beneficiaries of Indian land when the Great Plains were opened up either to private or non-Indian ownership, which was both cause and effect of the systematic elimination of bison and the enclosure of land.

Humor in *The Plague of Doves* takes the primary forms of bawdy jokes and mockery of Father Cassidy. These jokes continue a long line of Indian humor discussed by Native scholars for at least the past century. Tribal teasing, mockery and humor emphasize Indian continuance and survivance as well as a mental agency and acuity that whitestream colonial discourse attempts to deny them. However, it is critical to remember that indigenous humor pre-dates the arrival of Europeans to the Americas. As such, it is not purely a response to settler colonialism or colonial crimes and injustices. Indian humor is not a defense mechanism – or at least not exclusively. Instead it is an element of many Native cultures that privileges community, wit, entertainment, linguistic mastery, intellect and artistic talent.

CHAPTER 10

Haunted by Birds: An Eco-critical View of Personhood in *The Plague of Doves*

Catherine Rainwater

Western philosophy and psychology have developed increasingly finer distinctions in critical terminology regarding 'self', 'personal identity' and 'personhood'. Circumscribed within Western, humanist master narratives, such distinctions traditionally posit categorical, hierarchical divisions between the 'human' and the 'non-human'. Despite steady erosion of these divisions by contemporary animal studies (Wolfe, 'Introduction'), eco-criticism nevertheless contends with 'tropological enslavement', or language that cages the animal 'in the intellectual zoo' of our conceptions (Bleakley 19, 21). Complete escape from this entrapment seems impossible, but our awareness of our situation marks what Donna Haraway calls a crisis in the 'figuration of the human' (47). Following Derrida, Haraway calls for a 'negative', or disruptive, discourse that might re-conceptualize 'humanity', while avoiding many of the ethnocentric and anthropocentric errors of the past (49). Regarding the human, she writes:

> I want . . . to set aside the Enlightenment figures of coherence and masterful subjectivity, the bearers of rights, holders of property in the self, legitimate sons with access to language and the power to represent, subjects endowed with inner coherence and rational clarity . . . [whom] we have come to know . . . in the death-of-the-subject critiques. . . . Instead, let us attend to another crucial strand of Western humanism thrown into crisis in the late

twentieth century. My focus is the figure of a broken and suffering humanity, signifying – in ambiguity, contradiction, stolen symbolism, and unending chains of noninnocent translation – a possible hope. (48)

Though the title might imply otherwise, precisely this kind of 'hope' inheres in Louise Erdrich's *The Plague of Doves* (2008), a novel that returns with renewed imagination to her past concerns with human and non-human personhood. Throughout her works, Erdrich exposes the inadequacy of Western understanding when confronted with Native ways of knowing that contravene both scientific-materialist and Judeo-Christian frames of reference. *Plague* underscores the Eurocentric propensity for atomization, for making and defending artificial boundaries. This habit of mind alienates Indians, with their holistic worldview distinguished by complex conceptions of relationship, and by malleable ontological demarcations. One of her narrators, Antone Bazil Coutts, contemplates, for example, the 'desperate enterprise' of maintaining the reservation town of Pluto: 'By drawing a line and defending it, we seem to think we have mastered something. What?' (114). A century after its creation, Pluto is 'dwindling without grace' (115). Inhabitants of Pluto and the surrounding region are good examples of Haraway's 'broken and suffering' beings for whom hope lies in the destruction of false boundaries – material, spiritual and ideational.

Restoring hope and an edenic world often seems to be the environmentalist and eco-critical project. Some eco-theorists, however, consider such arguments naive. Among them, Dana Phillips cautions that solutions to environmental crisis lie not in nostalgic retreat to an imagined past, but in the recognition that 'our understanding of the environment has come about through the disruption of nature by agriculture and industrialism and the concomitant rise of science. Without environmental crisis', Phillips argues, 'there might be no "environmental imagination."' . . . Nor might there be ecologists struggling to understand and repair the mechanisms of a damaged natural world. . . . There is considerable irony in the fact that in order to begin to understand nature, we had first to alter it for the worst' (601).

Discussion of eco-critical theory and its relevance to Native American literature, including *The Plague of Doves*, might well begin with a response to Phillips. He correctly implies that 'environmentalism' and 'eco-criticism' are part of a decidedly Western, post-Enlightenment frame of reference. However, when Phillips remarks that to understand nature, 'we' had to despoil it first, he enters into discursive territory that Haraway calls 'dangerous' concerning the 'figuration of the human' (47).

After all, who are the 'we' who claim now to begin to 'understand nature' in the 'damaged natural world'? Indigenous people might argue that Phillips' 'we' refers not to all of humanity, but to such normative Western people as Haraway decries: '*we* – that crucial material and historical construction of politics and history' (49). Indigenous people, after all, usually see themselves as part of the damaged 'natural world' that *they* did not learn to inhabit by destroying it first. In fact, the pan-tribal cosmological principle of 'relationship' purports a radically alternative understanding of the natural world, and ways of living that pre-date by centuries the European, destructive presence in the Americas.[1] Though pre-contact, tribal cultures did not leave completely unscathed natural environments in their wake, their traditions emphasized human interdependence with, rather than dominion over, the rest of the natural world.

Despite their nature-centered worldviews, indigenous people have consistently been excluded from conversations about nature. Indeed, they have more often been represented as objects than subjects in Western fiction and non-fiction, where they have been compared sometimes favorably, sometimes unfavorably, to the 'wildlife' and 'wilderness' that have simultaneously fascinated and terrified Euroamericans (Rainwater). Even as late as the 1980s, anthologies of North American 'nature writing' frequently lacked Native contributors, who did not 'fit' because they share neither the Western view of nature that defines 'nature writing', nor the Western subject-position of the nature writer (Adamson, Murphy).

This absence of Native voices from the universal 'we' is underscored by the exceptions who prove the rule: Grimaldo Rengifo Vasquez, Vandana Shiva and Gregory Cajete number among emergent, non-Western spokespersons, but the question remains of whether or not a more diverse conversation can produce real and enduring change.[2] A good case in point is PRATEC (*Proyecto Andino de Tecnologias Campesinas*). Founded in the mid-1980s by indigenous intellectuals in Peru, PRATEC has designed successful agricultural programs bridging Western scientific and Andean traditional knowledge of the environment. PRATEC's programs do 'not seek to constitute an information base using the formats and protocols of technoscience'. Nevertheless, says PRATEC Coordinator and core member, Jorge Ishizawa, the organization 'admittedly requires much more visibility' to afford 'a more widely shared understanding of the benefits of learning from the ecological wisdom of the indigenous peoples' (Ishizawa, 'Between'). Paradoxically, the European sponsorship and mainstream academic connections that increase PRATEC's visibility also render it, at best, a cross-cultural enterprise emphasizing

Western over indigenous voices and, unfortunately, Western over indigenous ways of knowing and being (Ishizawa 'What Next?').

Like the Peruvian, grassroots environmentalists of PRATEC, eco-feminists worldwide also worry that so long as eco-critical dialogue unfolds within a Eurocentric matrix, no substantive escape from Western conceptual constraints is possible. Australian eco-sophist Freya Mathews warns that radical change cannot result from efforts to repair the Western system of thought, with its fundamental misconceptions of human identity, nature and otherness. Western people 'seeking to shift the values of Western civilization', she writes, must accept that 'what is wrong with our culture is that it offers us an inaccurate conception of the self . . . as existing in competition with and in opposition to nature. . . . [W]e are suffering from a maladaptation in the form of a faulty belief system that misrepresents our identity to us' (126, 132).

Questions about identity, self and personhood are basic to eco-criticism and to understanding the indigenous relationship to the natural world. Extremely different notions of identity, self and personhood derive from Western and indigenous cosmo-visions, and these cosmo-visions are difficult, sometimes impossible, to bridge. Native American literature, in general, affords plentiful challenges to Western views and fosters varieties of cross-cultural understanding. Eco-critical perspectives on Native literature potentially reveal a hopeful strain in post-humanist conversations about the 'refiguration of the human'.

Eco-criticism and Native American Literature

In the late 1990s, Ursula K. Heise defined eco-criticism as an interdisciplinary field that analyzes the role of the natural environment 'in the imagination of a cultural community at a specific historical moment' ('Science and Ecocriticism' n.p.). Eco-criticism focuses on representations of nature, as well as on the underlying assumptions about nature, and the frameworks of values, that representations reveal and conceal. Heise explains that such 'analysis in turn allows eco-criticism to assess how certain historically conditioned concepts of nature and the natural, and particularly literary and artistic constructions of it, have come to shape current perceptions of the environment' ('Science and Ecocriticism'). Over the last decade, some areas of eco-criticism have evolved to include Native voices. Various eco-critical perspectives address ethnicity, gender and species; attempts to reconstruct ideas about 'nature' and the 'natural' develop from deconstruction of ethnocentric, patriarchal and anthropocentric paradigms. Today, consequently, eco-criticism is more difficult to define. It has become 'a highly diverse field encompassing a wide variety of genres and authors in the United States and abroad, as well as the full spectrum of cultural theories and methodologies, from Marxism and poststructuralism and feminism, critical race theory, queer studies, and cognitive science' (Heise 'Greening' 290). Heise adds that this 'diversity has also unfolded in ecocritics' association with various political projects that are usually lumped together under the label of "the environmentalist movement," from conservation and restoration movements mostly focused on the welfare of ecosystems and nonhuman species all the way to the environmental justice movement, whose activism centers on the unequal share of different population groups in ecological resources and risks' (290).

Among the many disciplinary strands composing this field, feminism, critical race theory and Deep Ecology have perhaps most effectively opened the door to eco-critical consideration of Native American literature. All three strands directly confront pertinent issues of identity that Native American literature requires its audience to consider. Feminism and critical race theory have conducted crucial, death-of-the-subject critiques exposing the need, as Haraway suggests, to re-conceive of the 'human'. Going beyond human-centered concerns, Deep Ecology addresses 'self-realization' to be achieved by 'expanding self beyond the boundaries of the narrow ego through the process of caring identification with larger entities such as forests, bioregions, and the planet as a whole' (Drengson xxi–xxii). Proponents of Deep Ecology hope for the development of a 'many-sided maturity' that reflects responsible relationship to all beings, human and nonhuman, together with an attitude of 'aware ignorance' – a sense of the daunting limits of human knowledge. They observe such awareness among indigenous cultures, whose accounts of the phenomenal world belie the fixed boundaries of Western description; this radically different ontology supports the 'indigenous science' that PRATEC, Cajete, Peat, Vasquez, Shiva and others describe.[3]

Heise faults Deep Ecology for what she considers its localist, and thus insufficiently global, preoccupations. Deep Ecology counters this charge by arguing that global initiatives have not sufficiently dealt with the problem of anthropocentrism (McLaughlin 258), and that globalists are human-centered in their primary emphases on Western-style social justice, redistribution of capital and the transformation of industrial society. To seek indigenous wisdom in order to shore up or mend 'industrial society' is not merely another form of appropriation, but a failure to comprehend the grounds of indigenous wisdom. Clinging to human-centered initiatives means failing to understand ourselves as one of many life forms inhabiting the earth. Deep Ecology, by contrast, seeks to de-center the human, and to stress 'our embeddedness in the web of life' (Fleming and Macy 226). Indeed, Deep Ecology resonates with indigenous worldviews precisely because both are 'localist'. As Heise herself understands, the relative absence of Native voices from current strands of 'transnational' and 'global' eco-critical discourse results from the fact that indigenous people have a 'deep-seated suspicion of large-scale social structures such as the nation or modern society, an ambivalent perspective on abstract and intellectual forms of knowledge, and an emphasis on the body and sensory experience, as well as on small-scale communities and economies' ('Eco-criticism' 385).

Mistrust alone, however, does not account for indigenous localism. Indigenous realities arise in terms of specific places, where both human and non-human 'personhood' is inextricable from an intricate web of site-specific interrelationships. Contemporary Native American writers and scholars of Native American literature, alike, emphasize this localist environmental message. Works by celebrated Indian writers including N. Scott Momaday, Leslie Marmon Silko, James Welch, Louise Erdrich, Linda Hogan, Thomas King and others present us with characters whose survival depends on establishing, or re-establishing, *in situ* tribal affiliations. Momaday's Abel in *House Made of Dawn* (1968), Silko's Tayo in *Ceremony* (1977), Welch's Jim Loney in *The Death of Jim Loney* (1979), Erdrich's Nanapush, who appears in several of her novels, Hogan's protagonists in *Solar Storms* (1995) and *Power* (1998) and King's Tecumseh and Lum, in *Truth and Bright Water* (1999), are only a few among many Indian characters inhabiting fictive worlds where physical, mental, emotional and spiritual survival depends on being at home. Sensitive to these concerns, scholars increasingly find some eco-critical approaches well-suited to discussions of Native American literature.

Since 1960, when A. Irving Hallowell produced his ground-breaking study of Ojibwa lifeways, scholars from a variety of fields have addressed conceptions of identity and personhood inherent to tribal worldviews. Hallowell's observations illuminate works by Ojibwa writers such as Erdrich and Vizenor, and Maureen Trudelle Schwarz's studies of the Navajo cosmo-vision illuminate challenging literary works inscribing Navajo worldviews, including Silko's *Ceremony*, Anna Lee Walters' *Ghost Singer* (1988) and A. A. Carr's *Eye Killers* (1995). Moreover, despite obvious differences among tribal groups, common elements of a pan-tribal worldview include a radically non-Western conception of personhood that is inextricably connected to place.[4]

An eco-critical reading of *The Plague of Doves* reveals a skein of Old Testament allusions, Christian symbols, Ojibwa cultural and historical references and animal images sustaining a fictive world that challenges

Western ideas about the boundaries separating humans from one another, as well as from the contiguous, non-human world. *Plague* endorses alternative, relational models of personhood originating in Erdrich's Ojibwan worldview. Re-configuring personhood and the parameters of subjectivity, *Plague* repudiates Western liberal humanism which, as Cary Wolfe observes, 'in its very attempt to recognize the unique difference and specific ethical value of the other . . . reinstates the very normative model of subjectivity that it insists is the problem in the first place' ('Learning' 118). In Erdrich's *Plague*, to be plagued by doves, fed by a dog or 'haunted by birds' (215) is to be shadowed by insistent otherness that resists liberal-humanist, categorical definition.

The Stark Bird that Nests in the Tree

For the Ojibwa, personhood extends beyond humans to animals and spirits; even plants and material objects can sometimes be persons. One of Hallowell's frequently cited anecdotes illustrates the latter point. 'Since stones are grammatically animate, I once asked an old man: Are *all* the stones . . . alive? He reflected a long while and then replied, "No! But *some* are." . . . [T]he allocation of stones to an animate . . . category . . . leaves open a door that [the Western] orientation . . . keeps tight shut. Whereas we should never expect a stone to manifest animate properties of any kind under any circumstances, the Ojibwa recognize, *a priori*, potentialities for animation in certain classes of objects under certain circumstances' (147–8). As Hallowell discovers, a key difference between Western and Ojibwan understanding of 'animate' and 'inanimate' involves relationship. What is 'alive' or has personhood is not fixed; instead, its identity comes into being within a relational matrix. Not all stones are 'persons' at any given time, but a stone displays personhood when it speaks to someone. Some stones might never speak to anyone. Beyond the 'open door' that Hallowell recognizes, there lies a decidedly non-Western world of malleable ontological demarcations.

In *Plague*, Shamengwa's violin is a prime example. The instrument becomes almost a character, seeming incarnated (perhaps even rein-carnated) rather than crafted, kidnapped rather than stolen and mur-dered rather than broken. Indeed, it seems immortal as it finds its way to Shamengwa some 20 years after being lost by Henri and Lafayette Peace; it survives theft by Corwin Peace, and perhaps even Corwin's apparent destruction of it at Shamengwa's funeral, for Corwin turns up later with a violin to play the song that kills Warren Wolde and cures Evelina Harp, and possibly even Corwin himself. Like Antone's grandfather, Joseph, who observed Henri and Lafayette's loving care of their 'fiddle', Antone notes that Shamengwa 'treated this instrument with the reverence we accord our drums, which are considered living beings and require from us food, water, shelter, and love. They have their songs, which are given to their owners in sleep, and they must be dressed up according to their personalities, in beaded aprons and ribbons and careful paints. So with the violin that belonged to Shamengwa. . . . [I]ts sound was certainly human, and exquisite' (197). The music that comes from Shamengwa's 'fiddle', moreover, is power; it can elate or torture, cure or kill an audience. If one were to ask, after the fashion of Hallowell, if all violins and drums are 'alive', Shamengwa, or even Erdrich herself, might reply, 'No! But *some* are.' Where the Western mind sees fixed, impersonal 'laws of nature' governing the material world – laws precluding the personhood of drums and violins – the indigenous mind sees the enfoldment of material and spiritual worlds. As Hallowell insists, the Ojibwa world cannot be separated into 'natural' and 'supernatural' realms, for some phenomena are neither entirely 'natural' nor entirely 'supernatural'. No immutable laws dictate what can or cannot happen within the phenomenal world (151–2).

Erdrich depicts this world in *Plague* not only through the Ojibwan ways of knowing and being that her narrative represents, but also through her creative, trans-cultural management of Old Testament allusions, including the allusion to the dove, a biblical embodiment of the Holy Spirit that accounts for the title of the novel.[5] A look at this Old Testament reference to the dove, and its connections to spirit, through indigenous eyes, puts us in mind of Haraway's remarks concerning the Western habit of 'noninnocent translation' (48). The Western 'translation' of 'holy spirit' is much less 'innocent' than the Ojibwan, for the latter preserves the Old Testament implication of 'spirit' as a force of nature, while the former serves the interests of centuries of Christian political and intellectual history. Indeed, the history of Judeo-Christian thought concerning the Holy Spirit is intriguing. In the Old Testament, references to a holy spirit occur only twice (Psalms 51:11 and Isaiah 63:10–11), and in the New Testament only a few times. Moreover, scripture affords no distinct term for this 'spirit' but merely various metaphors (such as *rûah*) for 'wind' or 'breath'. Biblical commentators on 'breath' described specifically in Genesis (6:17) as the 'wind' that is essential for life, over time begin to equate this 'spiritus' or breath with a holy spirit. Thus, the terms gradually become interchangeable, despite the fact that scriptural references to a holy spirit are not necessarily synonymous with 'breath'.

The scriptural 'holy spirit', unlike the doctrinally defined Holy Spirit in Christian Trinitarian theology, closely resembles indigenous peoples' animating spirit of creation. Old Testament references to spirit show it coming and going, not permanently manifest in any being; indeed, the prophets hope for a permanent bearer of this holy spirit in a messiah – like the Paraclete, or Jesus in his intercessory role, on whom spirit descends in the form of a dove. Spirit, in the Bible as in indigenous foundational stories, is an invisible, unpredictable and uncontrollable force. Moreover, in the Bible, as in indigenous stories including *Plague*, such a spirit is not even consistently benign, but can be evil (1 Samuel 16:14), deceptive (1 Kings 22:22) or ambiguous, inspiring terrifying rapture (1 Samuel 10:6–11 and Num. 11:25) and so forth.

Mixed-blood Catholic characters in *Plague* understand the Holy Spirit less doctrinally than scripturally. The Holy Spirit seems to them the same as the animating force described within the indigenous cosmo-vision as the force that allows some stones, sometimes, to speak. Mooshum and Shamengwa share these and other 'mixed-blood Catholic' (22) perspectives passed down to them through followers of Louis Riel, heroic Ojibwan leader and 'moody prophet'. The heretical brothers enjoy infuriating the local priests. When young Mooshum and Holy Track hide in the church just prior to the 1911 lynching, their conversation is a kind of doctrinal dispute about the powers of the spirit. They call the communion wafers 'spirit bread' but Mooshum says, 'You cannot call it bread. Not even a cracker. You could eat a thousand and not live'. Mooshum, who eventually goes 'back to the blanket' (40), expects the spirit in the bread to help him in the present moment of crisis, to feed his body and his soul. Reminded that 'You're supposed to get everlasting life from it' rather than immediate results, Mooshum maintains his earthly priorities. He complains that the spirit bread 'did not work for Holy Track', who is hanged by Indian-hating white men for a crime he did not commit (66). The pious boy, Holy Track, had 'told Mooshum, it made sense that the bread he had eaten would feed this soul, this spirit, and increase its strength' (66).

Whether or not the communion wafers make Holy Track strong in spirit as he dies remains undisclosed to the reader. Spirit's manifestation at the scene of his execution, however, is unorthodox. The wispy clouds above the hanging tree seem to the Native eye, at least, to 'resolve into wings' while the innocents sing their death songs (79). Local Indians say the tree stays full of doves from that time forward (77). Equally unconventional are other manifestations of the Holy Spirit throughout *The Plague of Doves*. Evelina tells us that when Mooshum first saw his future wife, Junesse, among the 'plague' of thousands of doves, 'the Holy Spirit hovered between them. . . . "We seen into each udder's dept"', says Mooshum (12). Their connection partakes equally, inseparably, of flesh and spirit. Likewise, after Evelina and Corwin Peace take communion on Easter Sunday, they await 'Christ's presence to diffuse' in them (15). Their eyes meet and again, the spirit hovers, the same 'Holy Spirit' that graces the delicate hands of the otherwise grotesque-looking Sister Mary Anita (44, 249); the same spirit that drives the sinister, snake-handling Marn Wolde when she feels 'the stark bird that nests in the tree of the Holy Ghost descend . . . hover,' and spread its wings inside of her (151); the same spirit implied in Shamengwa's name, conferred on him by full-blood children and meaning 'butterfly', sometimes a symbol of the Holy Spirit (204). This indwelling spirit is a single current of energy that runs throughout creation. Recalling the occasionally disturbing visitations of 'spiritus' or 'rûah,' in the Old Testament, the animating force that can inhabit humans, animals and even objects in Erdrich's Ojibwan universe wields its wild power in unpredictable ways. Indeed, this holy spirit is a trickster, a transformer, bearing blessings, wreaking havoc, or both. Spirit is borne by the most unlikely of 'emissaries', who may even be non-human persons – drums or violins, doves or salamanders, horses, wolves or dogs.

A Tribe of Josephs

Missionary era Christians – the sort who persecute Louis Riel in *Plague* – lacked an epistemological frame of reference appropriate for encountering indigenous people and, consequently, for observing indigenous expansive concepts of personhood that would affect their understanding of Christianity. Missionaries working among the Ojibwa saw them as 'absent the influence of the Holy Spirit' (McNally 37). Ironically, Isaac Watt's 'Come Holy Spirit, Heavenly Dove' was one of the first Christian hymns the Ojibwa translated into their own language (39). This hymn appealed to a people for whom music is a primary mediator of spiritual power, and for whom the significance of the biblical dove would have seemed obvious as an animal manifestation of spirit. The Ojibwa warmed to music and song over doctrine. From hymns, Ojibwans acquired an affective experience of Christianity. The 'mixed blood Catholicism' that so offended priests reflected emotive aspects of religion that were (unlike Christian doctrine) easily internalized within the existing Ojibwan cosmo-vision. The people felt the Holy Spirit in *manidoo*, the Algonquian Great Spirit, or 'mystery' comparable to the Old Testament *spiritus*.

Another aesthetic feature of Ojibwan thought that interfered with their orthodox conversion was their delight in polysemy, an important aspect of poetry, song and relational personhood, but anathema to the disambiguating language of theology. The meanings of words such as 'sin', 'salvation' and 'grace', for instance, were subject to uncontrollable permutations of meaning in translation: 'sin' became correctable, inconsequential error; 'salvation' described a good life of abundance in the here and now; 'grace' was understood as pity and compassion shown to one's fellow (not necessarily human) beings (McNally 61). In short, as the Ojibwa transformed Christianity within their own cosmovision, the abstract, systematic language of Christian theology focused on the soul in the hereafter, yielded to freer habits of signification that valued earthly experience and recognized spirit in many forms of nature beyond the human.

This transformational synthesis of Western cultural elements is basic to Erdrich's storytelling strategy in *Plague*, in which an Ojibwan perspective on the Old Testament figures centrally. In key episodes of *Plague* involving Joseph J. Coutts, Erdrich interweaves her eco-critical representation of the Holy Spirit with another Old Testament context, established by the 'Joseph' identity that several of her characters share. In *Plague*, identities and partial identities repeat from character to character in a manner suggestive of biblical typology, according to which, incidentally, Joseph is a 'type' for Jesus or the Paraclete. This same technique of character development achieves an even more significant, and profoundly non-Western end; it suggests how personhood resists containment within Western, individualist categories, for the 'Joseph' identity migrates throughout the human community in a manner reminiscent of the comings and goings of the Old Testament divine spirit of nature.

Joseph's surname, 'Coutts', invokes the Old Testament story of Joseph and the many-colored coat bestowed on him by his father, Jacob. In this story, Jacob's gift deepens a pre-existing rift in a family of conspirators and deceivers – a family resembling the extended, tribal family in *Plague*. The biblical Jacob and his mother, Rebekah, conspire to trick Isaac into mistaking his younger son, Jacob, for his elder son, Esau. Consequently, Isaac unwittingly bestows Esau's rightful blessing onto Jacob. Later, in a variant of Isaac's error, Jacob unfairly favors his own youngest son, Joseph. The coat (signifying a 'coat of arms' or mantle of patriarchal authority) that Jacob gives to Joseph provokes the boy's jealous brothers to try to kill him. He is left to die, sold into slavery and exiled for years in Egypt where his fate runs the gamut of extremes. He is variously a prisoner, an interpreter of dreams and a favorite of the pharaoh, who recognizes in this prophetic dreamer a bearer of the indwelling, trickster-like divine spirit (Genesis 41). Joseph is eventually reunited with his family, but not before they are many times deceived about his true identity. The story of Isaac, Jacob and Joseph is a story rife with ironies and reversals; characters who are tricky and deceptive are usually rewarded rather than punished, and their victims, such as Esau, rarely get revenge or recognizable justice. Nevertheless, the sins of the fathers seem to be visited upon the sons, for Joseph suffers for Jacob's misdeed just as Jacob, thinking his favorite son is dead, perhaps pays for the sins of his father, Isaac, along with his own.

Erdrich's spin on this Old Testament scheme of oddly distributed rewards and punishments defines family and tribal relations in *Plague*, relations characterized by visitations of an Old –Testament–style spirit of nature. In the latter part of the nineteenth century, young Joseph J. Coutts joins a group of land speculators, who venture 'out past the Dakota–Minnesota border to survey and establish claims by occupancy on several huge pieces of land' (97). Like his biblical prototype, Erdrich's Joseph acquires an 'overcoat' just before leaving home (99), and he also has prophetic dreams; he sees the future, with towns and cities sprung up around the railroad. Perilous and terrifying, Joseph's travels, recalling his namesake's, afford him valuable time among cultural Others, most significantly, Henri and Lafayette Peace. Besides playing soul-wrenching songs on their violin (eventually Shamengwa's), the Peace brothers can summon beneficent spirits. After the fashion of the Old Testament Joseph in Egypt, Joseph J. Coutts on the frontier acquires new ways of knowing the world that prepare him for future leadership. Joseph's trials teach him that 'there was something powerful in store for him' (103).

Similar to his Old Testament counterpart, he (and later his son and his grandson) eventually becomes a wise counselor in his dysfunctional, extended tribal family. This family includes those who would cheat, deceive and betray one another, as when Edward Harp and his sister, Neve Harp, vie for possession of a million-dollar stamp collection (83); as when John Wildstrand conspires with Billy Peace to kidnap John's wife, Neve; and as when Mooshum betrays the innocent Holy Track, Cuthbert Peace and Asiginak, and lives on as a storyteller to lie about it.

Recalling the biblical Jacob, who accuses a wolf of killing Joseph but then sets it free when God allows the wolf to speak in its own defense, Joseph J. Coutts also makes profound connections with animal Others that revise his Judeo-Christian conceptions of reality and justice. Beleaguered first by ice and snow, and next by rising water, the starving men have resorted to eating stewed boots and moccasins when Joseph encounters a Christ-like otter. The animal 'regarded him with the curious and trusting gaze of a young child' (108). As soon as he shoots it, he begins 'weeping helplessly. . . . For he'd had the instant horror that he had committed a murder. . . . The creature was an emissary of some sort. He'd known that as they held that human stare. Joseph himself was part of all that was sustained and destroyed by a mysterious power. He had killed its messenger. And the otter wasn't even edible' (108–9). This mysterious power is the holy spirit that makes 'relations' of all things animate and inanimate; within Erdrich's fictive universe, 'spirit' connects the human and the non-human, for the term has not succumbed to 'noninnocent translation' in line with Judeo-Christian tradition.

English Bill's little dog finds the otter's flesh palatable; she stuffs herself, then begins to find abundant food for the men – snow buntings, catfish, a squirrel and a snapping turtle. Later, back at home, Joseph ponders 'the mystery of his survival and the meaning of the otter' who is, like Jesus, 'an innocent saint' (113) whom he had sinned against but who, nevertheless, had died and empowered the dog who, in turn, had saved his life. Joseph's broadened frame of reference affords insight into justice – local, tribal and universal. At this moment, Joseph decides to go home and become a lawyer.

The incident of the otter and the dog illustrates the species of justice that defines the world of Erdrich's novel and that underscores the text's decidedly non-Western conception of personhood. Erdrich suggests that our lives are marked by punishments and blessings, deprivations and gifts that point to a greater reality, to mystifying evidence of a trickster-like 'holy spirit' of creation that animates all of creation. All of us are both sinned against and sinner, both rescuer and rescued; our misdeeds might be recompensed by others who owe us nothing, or by creatures we have wronged; we might ourselves inexplicably pay the price for another person's evil deeds. Joseph 'murders' an otter, and Corwin Peace destroys a 'living' violin. Christ-like, the otter preserves the life of Joseph, and a violin rehabilitates Corwin. Cordelia Lochren, whose family is murdered by Warren Wolde when she is an infant, ends up years later saving the killer's life without knowing his identity. Meanwhile, based on her own sense of eye-for-an-eye justice, she has for years sinned against others; as the local physician, she has refused medical care to Indians because she has always mistakenly believed that Indians killed her family when, in fact, four Indians had saved her life.

Plague implies that justice exists in the universe. However, the Judeo-Christian idea of justice proves inadequate to account for phenomenal experience. Justice in the world of *Plague* resists Western codification within constructed, intellectual (and human) boundaries. The world we inhabit is wild. To be sure, Judge Antone Basil Coutts, Joseph J. Coutts's grandson, declares that 'He who goes to law holds a wolf by the ear' (114). 'Justice', he maintains, 'is prey to unknown dreams' (117), such dreams as came to Joseph, son of Jacob, and to Joseph J. Coutts, who 'dreamed a banquet' (105) and enjoyed one, courtesy of an otter and a dog.

Besides Joseph J. Coutts, other Josephs appear in *Plague*. Some literally bear the name, while others are types, exhibiting 'Joseph' traits or
reflecting parts of the 'Joseph' family story. This technique of character
development implies that personal identity, like the protean 'holy spirit',
is unbounded, spread in baffling ways across time and space. The other
Josephs include Joseph Milk, father of Severine, Seraph (Mooshum)
and Shamengwa; and Joseph Harp, Evelina's brother. Joseph Milk and
his family live in Old Testament–style exile south of the Canadian border as a result of their loyalty to the martyred, mixed-blood Catholic
'prophet', Louis Riel. Joseph Harp, like Esau, loses his inheritance, the
million-dollar stamp collection, owing to his father's and aunt's com-
petitive greed.

Not literally named Joseph, but nevertheless displaying some 'Joseph'
traits in comic relief, is Father 'Hop Along' Cassidy. A ridiculous figure,
he resembles the Joseph of Hebrew myth; he is vain, disagreeable and
effeminate (often adorning his eyes with kohl). Unlike the heroic Joseph
of Christian tradition, the Hebrews' Joseph is a gossip who (also similar
to Mooshum) alienates his brothers by spreading stories. Father Hop
Along, with his 'unfortunate tendency to hop a bit too daintily along on
his pointed feet' (23), is such a Joseph-like buffoon, continually infuri-
ated by the Milk brothers' arguments about matters of Catholic doctrine. Tipsy and in a fit of pique one afternoon, the priest storms out of
their house only to offend their horse, who bites him and seems to laugh
about it (27); at the end of another failed visit, the drunken priest slips
on a salamander, one of the creatures the nuns have called 'emissaries of
the unholy dead' (29). Unlike Joseph J. Coutts, this Joseph cannot count
on the good will of animals.

Two other 'Josephs' not literally bearing the name are Judge Antone
Basil Coutts (Joseph J.'s grandson) and Billy Peace, the brother of Maggie Peace with whom John Wildstrand (Neve Harp's husband) has an
extramarital affair (producing Corwin Peace). Like his father and
grandfather before him, Antone is a lawyer, serving his people as wise
counsel (in the tradition of the Spirit-filled Paraclete, a Greek word
meaning 'legal advocate' and 'comforter'). Antone inherits from his
grandfather his surname, Coutts, signifying the 'coat' of tribal authority.
Erdrich develops an interesting variation on Antone's 'Joseph' qualities,
for, unlike the biblical Joseph, adept at concealing his own identity from
his brothers, Antone is himself deceived about an aspect of his own
identity. Throughout the years of his youthful, secret affair with the
much older Cordelia Lochren, he never knows that she is using him to
assuage her guilt. She refuses medical care to all Indians, except Antone.
Only long after the affair ends does he understand: 'I'd always be her
one exception. Or worse, her absolution. Every time I touched her, she

was forgiven' (292). Cordelia and Antone are like Joseph J. and the otter, or like Warren Wolde and Cordelia – integral parts of an existential tangle of transgression and grace beyond rational comprehension.

Other fragments of the Old Testament Joseph's life appear in Billy Peace's story. Young Billy is incensed when he learns that his sister, Maggie, is pregnant by the married John Wildstrand (offspring of the Wildstrand who helped lynch Billy's ancestor, Cuthbert Peace). Billy comes to Wildstrand's door with a gun and demands ten thousand dollars. Instead of handing over the money, John talks Billy into kidnapping his wife, Neve; this way, the transfer of funds looks like ransom money and, therefore, makes John seem a hero rather than an adulterer. Similar to the Old Testament Joseph who is sold to the Ishmaelites by his brothers, Neve becomes barter in a kidnapping. When eventually Neve discovers Billy's identity, he flees, but returns, Joseph-like, from exile to become head of a tribe, a large following of cultish 'kindred'.

A Wide Lake Haunted by Birds

The Plague of Doves is a delicately nuanced assault on Western conceptions of personhood, and on the idea of human superiority over the rest of creation. Interlacing references to the Old Testament, Judeo-Christian tradition and Ojibwan cosmology, Erdrich commands our attention to the local, immediate, phenomenal manifestations of the sacred in the varied forms of 'persons' who are human, non-human and even inanimate. The holy spirit may descend in the form of a fiddle, an otter, a dog or a dove. It may appear as a blessing or a plague, like the thousands of doves that descend on the Pluto of Mooshum's youth. The holy spirit might play the trickster in many guises. 'Ours is a wide lake . . . haunted by birds who utter sarcastic or sorrowing human cries', says Henri Peace, describing the place where he lives (215). Henri's words also describe the spirit-haunted earth in general, home to all manner of beings that spirit animates. Erdrich's narrative invites readers to consider the earthly common ground we all inhabit, a place where 'spirit' is viscerally known in elemental forms to all beings – Western and non-Western, human and non-human – and where we are all connected like numerous 'Josephs' in our spirit-haunted, earthly embodiment. Erdrich's critique of Western culture draws attention to 'broken and suffering humanity' and implies that through 'noninnocent translation' (Haraway) of terms such as the Old Testament 'spirit' into the doctrinal 'Holy Spirit", the Western mind has distanced itself from elemental experience in the phenomenal world, experience that indigenous people value and preserve. *The Plague of Doves* shows us a world in which the Western mind has created its own unique misery – and inflicted it on numberless others – by insisting on imagined boundaries between material and spiritual being, boundaries the indigenous mind does not acknowledge. Erdrich's assault on Western mind–forged manacles amounts also to an eco-critical 'refiguration of the human' in profound relationship with the non-human world that Haraway and many post-humanists equate with 'possible hope' (48).

Notes on Chapters

Chapter 1

1. This overview of US–Native American history originally appeared in Connie Jacobs' chapter but for reasons of space has been moved to this Introduction. I am grateful to her for the historical outline of these events.

Chapter 3

1. See Piero Scaruffi's list of the worst genocides of the twentieth century under '1900–2000: A Century of Genocides'. Web. 25 March 2010.
2. For more information on the structure of her workshops and Brave Heart's model of intervention and healing, visit the Takini website.
3. See Friedman's article for a fuller discussion of Roman and medieval saints, whom Pauline aspires to emulate. One of the more interesting saints Pauline does not name is Saint Catherine of Sienna, whose actions bear a striking resemblance to those of Pauline (121–3).

Chapter 4

1. Three trials presided over by Justice John Marshall: *Johnson versus M'Intosh* (1823), which 'dealt with the issue of whether title to land could be conveyed by a Native American', the foundational *Cherokee Nation versus Georgia* (1831) from which comes the phrase 'domestic dependent nations'; and *Worcester versus Georgia* (1832), which limited Georgia's power to impose its laws on Cherokee land (Seibert, 393).
2. Under Minnesota congressman Knute Nelson, the Act initiated allotment in Minnesota firstly by attempting to relocate all Ojibwe in the State to White Earth at the relinquishment of their lands, contrary to all prior treaties with the Ojibwe. It was fiercely resisted.
3. While 'Anishinaabe' is the name by which the people refer to themselves, 'Chippewa' is the term used in US legal terminology.
4. The term 'mixed-blood' referred more or less generally to those open to market capitalism, and the term 'full-blood' to those opposed to its perceived threat to traditional lifeways.

5. The Steenerson Act and Clapp Rider were named after congressman Halvor Steenerson and Minnesota senator Moses Clapp.
6. In 1997 Joy Harjo and Gloria Bird published a voluminous and hugely significant compendium of Native American women's writing titled *Reinventing the Enemy's Language*.
7. A grass-roots organization, Anishinaabe Akiing was formed by heirs of allottees in 1984, taking the fight over land claims back to their various non-Native opponents and even challenging the Tribal Council when they endorsed the controversial White Earth Land Settlement Act (1986). The Act compensated the tribe for 10,000 acres of original White Earth land to the tune of $17 million – 'the 1910 value of their titles, without interest or damages' (LaDuke 124).

Chapter 5

1. In *Towards a Native American Critical Theory* Elvira Pulitano writes that 'Native American literature operates within the context of what Krupat . . . has termed "anti-imperialist translation" (*The Turn to the Native* 35), presenting an English powerfully affected by a foreign tongue, and adopting Western literary forms to convey, in writing, the rhythms and patterns of the oral tradition' (129).
2. In 'Keepers of the Earth' Jeannette Armstrong writes 'I have always felt that my Okanagan view is perhaps closer in experience to that of an eyewitness and refugee surrounded by holocaust' (317). In the Preface to *I Am Woman* Lee Maracle writes 'It . . . remains my attempt to present a Native woman's sociological perspective on the impacts of colonialism on us, as women, and on myself personally' (vii).
3. Following Erdrich's own procedure in *Last Report* I shall use 'he' when referring to Father Damien and 'she' when discussing the perceptions and character of Sister Cecilia and Agnes DeWitt.
4. The *windigo* (also commonly spelled *wendigo*) is a malevolent cannibal spirit, and is part of the traditional belief systems of the Algonquin people, among them the Ojibwe and the Cree. Kate McCafferty sees Pauline as an evil shaman driven insane, or *windigo*, through communion with skeletal cannibal forces.

Chapter 6

1. Maori scholar Linda Tuhiwai Smith outlines these strategies in *Decolonizing Methodologies: Research and Indigenous Peoples*.
2. The musical transformations in Ojibwe were explained in a discussion with Margaret Noori at the Native American Literature Symposium, Mt. Pleasant, Michigan, 2007.
3. Erdrich also uses the idea of 'pulling' across in *The Master Butchers Singing Club* (2003) to describe the relationship between characters Delphine Watzka and Eva Waldvogel when Eva is dying: 'There flowed between them an odd and surprising electricity. Their gaze was a power – comforting, frightening. Delphine was pulled somewhere fast, yanked right out of her skin. With their eyes locked, they rushed through the air, ecstatic, hearts lurching' (137).

Chapter 8

1. For thoroughgoing critiques of the masculinism of cultural nationalism in the Asian American, African American and Chicana/o contexts, see Kim, Dubey and Perez.
2. For an excellent account of the Silko-Erdrich debate see Castillo.
3. See Vizenor's account of the 'paracolonial' in *Manifest Manners: Postindian Warriors of Survival* (1994) and Weaver's discussion of 'pericolonialisms' in chapter 1 of *American Indian Literary Nationalism*.
4. NPR, '"Plague of Doves": Multigenerational Murder Mystery'. www.npr.org/templates/story/story.php?storyId=90167624. 6 November 2010.

Chapter 9

1. See for example, Babcock, Jahner, Velie, and Vizenor, 'Trickster Discourse'.
2. George Lipsitz, *The Possessive Investment in Whiteness: How White People Profit from Identity Politics*. Philadelphia: Temple University Press, 2006.
3. The Lakota Heyoka and Pueblo clown are two often cited examples.
4. We might also relate this passage to that of the Norwegians in the novel's opening paragraph. The attempt to divide people from one another in this novel seems to lead to the exact opposite of the intended purpose, or to illustrate how such isolations and divisions are seldom more than cosmetic.
5. Chief Gall was a prominent Hunkpapa Lakota military leader who led forces in the Battle at Little Big Horn, and as such, was an agent in Custer's 'last stand'.
6. 'Survivance' is Vizenor's term combining survival with resistance: see his introduction to *Survivance: Narratives of Native Presence*.

Chapter 10

1. The deceptively simple phrase, 'all my relations' that most tribal people recite in various ways sums up their complex cosmologies. Vine Deloria provides a detailed, extensive discussion of this pan-tribal relational model.
2. Grimaldo Rengifo Vasquez was a prominent director of Peruvian development projects, but in 1987 he and two colleagues formed PRATEC. Vandana Shiva is a physicist, ecofeminist, environmentalist, and a prolific writer. Gregory Cajete (Santa Clara Pueblo) is a well-known educator in Native studies and, in particular, ethno-botany.
3. A group of indigenous intellectuals in Peru formed an NGO called PRATEC (*Proyecto Andino de Tecnologías Campesinas*). One of PRATEC's aims is to deconstruct Western epistemology with its various claims to universality.
4. On the importance of place to identity, see especially Deloria, Schwartz, and Peat.
5. In this chapter, 'Holy Spirit' capitalized refers to the Christian Trinitarian conception. Written in lower case, 'holy spirit' refers to the Old Testament conception and to the Ojibwan idea of spirit.

Works Cited

Primary Sources

Erdrich's Works

The Antelope Wife: A Novel. New York: HarperCollins, 1998.

Baptism of Desire: Poems. New York: Harper Perennial, 1989.

The Beet Queen: A Novel. 1986, rpt. New York: HarperFlamingo, 1998.

The Bingo Palace. New York: HarperCollins, 1994.

The Birchbark House. New York: Hyperion, 1999.

The Blue Jay's Dance: A Birth Year. New York: HarperCollins, 1995.

Books and Islands in Ojibwe Country. Washington: National Geographic, 2003.

Commemorative. Northfield, MN: Red Dragonfly Press, 2008.

The Crown of Columbus, with Michael Dorris. 1991, rpt. New York: Harper, 1999.

'Dartmouth Commencement Address'. www.dartmouth.edu/~news/releases/2009/06/14a.html.

'Foreword', in Michael Dorris, *The Broken Cord.* New York: Harper and Row, 1989.

Four Souls: A Novel. New York: HarperCollins, 2004.

The Game of Silence. New York: HarperCollins, 2005.

Grandmother's Pigeon. New York: Hyperion, 1996.

Imagination. Columbus, OH: Merrill, 1981.

Jacklight: Poems. London: Little, Brown /Abacus, 1984.

The Last Report on the Miracles at Little No Horse. New York: HarperCollins, 2001.

'The Leap'. *Harper's Magazine,* March 1990. 65–8.

Love Medicine. Columbus, OH: McGraw-Hill, 1984.

Love Medicine: New and Revised. New York: HarperCollins, 1993.

The Master Butchers Singing Club. New York: HarperCollins, 2002.

Original Fire: Selected and New Poems. New York: Harper, 2003.

The Painted Drum. New York: HarperCollins, 2005.

The Plague of Doves. New York: HarperCollins, 2008.

The Porcupine Year. New York: HarperCollins, 2008.

The Range Eternal. New York: Hyperion, 2002.

The Red Convertible: Selected and New Stories, 1978–2008. New York: Harper, 2009.

Route Two, with Michael Dorris. Northridge, CA: Lord John P, 1991.

Shadow Tag. New York: Harper, 2010.

Tales of Burning Love. New York: HarperCollins, 1996.

Tracks: A Novel. New York: HarperCollins, 1988.

'Two Languages in Mind, But Just One in the Heart', *New York Times,* 22 May 2000. www.nytimes.com/library/books/052200erdrich-writing.html.

'Where I Ought to Be: A Writer's Sense of Place', in Hertha D. Wong, ed., *Louise Erdrich's Love Medicine: A Casebook.* New York: Oxford University Press, 2000, 43–50.

Winter Reader 2003–2004. Minneapolis: Minnesota Center for Book Arts, 2003.

Erdrich's Interviews

'A Conversation with Louise Erdrich.' 2006. *Book Browse,* 1997–2007. 28 November. www.bookbrowse.com/author_interviews/full/index.cfm?author_number=613.

Bacon, Katy. 2001. 'An Emissary of the Between-World: A Conversation with Louise Erdrich', *Atlantic Unbound,* January. www.theatlantic.com/past/docs/unbound/interviews/int2001-01-17.htm.

Bruchac, Joseph. 1987. 'Whatever is Really Yours: An Interview with Louise Erdrich' in Joseph Bruchac, ed., *Survival This Way: Interviews with American Indian Poets.* Tucson: University of Arizona Press. 73–86.

Chavkin, Allan, and Nancy Feyl Chavkin, eds. 1994. *Conversations with Louise Erdrich and Michael Dorris.* Jackson, MS: University Press of Mississippi.

Coltelli, Laura, and Joseph Bruchac. 2000. 'Interviews with Louise Erdrich and Michael Dorris', in Hertha Sweet Wong, ed., *Louise Erdrich's Love Medicine: A Casebook.* New York, Oxford University Press, 155–60.

Erdrich, Louise. n.d. 'Birchbark Blog'. http://birchbarkbooks.com/_blog/Birchbark_Blog.

Gee, Leslie. 2005. 'Lunch with Louise Erdrich: An Interview'. www.iaiachronicle.org/archives/LunchwithLouise2005.htm.

George, Jan. 1985. 'Interview with Louise Erdrich', *North Dakota Quarterly,* 53(2) (Spring), 240–6.

'Interview'. www.bookbrowse.com/author_interviews/full/index.cfm/author_number/613/Louise-Erdrich. Accessed 1 August 2010.

Jordan, Courtney. 2006. 'A Writer's Beginnings', *Smithsonian Magazine,* August. www.smithsonianmag.com/people-places/erdrich.html.

Moyers, Bill. 2010. 'Louise Erdrich', *Bill Moyers Journal,* 9 April. www.pbs.org/moyers/journal/04092010/profile.html.

Rawson, Josie. 2001. 'Cross-dressing the Divine', *Mother Jones,* May/June. motherjones.com/media/2001/05/cross-dressing-divine.

Rolo, Mark Anthony. 2002. 'Louise Erdrich: The *Progressive* Interview', *The Progressive,* April. www.highbeam.com/doc/1G1-84866888.html.

Spillman, Robert. 1996. 'Louise Erdrich: The *Salon* Interview', www.salon.com/weekly/interview960506.html

Wong, Hertha Sweet, Nancy Feyl Chavkin and Allan Chavkin. 2000. 'Interview with Louise Erdrich and Michael Dorris', in Hertha Sweet Wong, ed., *Louise*

Erdrich's Love Medicine: A Casebook. New York: Oxford University Press, 107–14.

—. 1987. 'An Interview with Louise Erdrich and Michael Dorris', *North Dakota Quarterly*, 55 (1) (Winter), 196–218.

Secondary Sources

Adamson Clarke, Joni. 1998. 'Toward an Ecology of Justice: Transformative Ecological Theory and Practice', in Michael P. Branch and Rochelle Johnson, et al., eds, *Reading the Earth: New Directions in the Study of Literature and Environment*. Moscow, ID: University of Idaho Press, 9–18.

Albers, Patricia, and Beatrice Medicine, eds. 1983. *The Hidden Half: Studies of Plains Indian Women*. Lanham, MD: University Press of America.

Alfred, Taiaiake. 2009. *Peace, Power, Righteousness: An Indigenous Manifesto*. New York and Oxford: Oxford University Press.

Allen, Chadwick. 2000. 'Postcolonial Theory and the Discourse of Treaties', *American Quarterly*, 52(1), 59–89.

Allen, Paula Gunn. 1992. *The Sacred Hoop: Recovering the Feminine in American Indian Traditions*. Boston: Beacon Press.

American Psychiatric Association. 2000. *Diagnostic and Statistical Manual of Mental Disorders*. 4th ed. Washington, DC: American Psychiatric Association.

Angel, Michael. 2002. *Preserving the Sacred: Historical Perspectives on the Ojibwa Midewiwin*. Winnipeg, MB: University of Manitoba Press.

Armstrong, Jeannette. 1995. 'Keepers of the Earth', in Theodore Roszak, Mary E. Gomes and Allen D. Kramer, eds, *Ecopsychology: Restoring the Earth, Healing the Mind*. San Francisco: Sierra Club Books, 316–24.

Babcock, Barbara. 1985. '"A Tolerated Margin of Mess": The Trickster and His Tales Reconsidered', in Andrew Wiget, ed., *Critical Essays on Native American Literature*. Boston: G. K. Hall and Co. 153–85.

Balev, Michelle. 2008. 'Trends in Literary Trauma Theory', *Mosaic*, 41(2), 149–66.

Barak, Julie. 1996. 'Blurs, Blends, Berdaches: Gender Mixing in the Novels of Louise Erdrich', *Studies in American Indian Literatures*, 8(3) (Fall), 49–62.

Barker, Debra K. S. 2008. '"The Divine in Mary Kashpaw": A Tribute to Moral Beauty' in Brajesh Sawhney, ed., *Studies in the Literary Achievement of Louise Erdrich, Native American Writer: Fifteen Critical Essays*. Lewiston, NY: Edwin Mellen Press, 265–9.

Becvar, Dorothy Stroh, and Robert J. Becvar. 2009. *Family Therapy: A Systemic Integration*. 7th ed. Boston: Pearson.

Beidler, Peter G., and Gay Barton. 2006. *A Reader's Guide to the Novels of Louise Erdrich: Revised and Expanded Edition*. Columbia, MO: University of Missouri Press.

Berger, James. 1997. 'Trauma and Literary Theory', *Contemporary Literature*, 38(3), n. p. *Academic Search Premier*. Accessed 1 February 2010.

Berninghausen, Tom. 1998. '"This Ain't Real Estate": Land and Culture in Louise Erdrich's Chippewa Tetralogy', in Susan L. Roberson, ed., *Women, America, and Movement: Narratives of Relocation*. Columbia, MO: University of Missouri Press, 190–210.

Bevis, William. 1987. 'Native American Novels: Homing In', in Arnold Krupat and Brian Swann, eds, *Recovering the Word: Essays on Native American Literature*. Berkeley, CA: University of California Press, 580–620.

Bird, Gloria. 1992. 'Searching for Evidence of Colonialism at Work: A Reading of Louise Erdrich's *Tracks*', *Wičazo Ša Review*, 8. 2, 40–7.

Blaeser, Kimberly M. 1997. 'On Mapping and Urban Shamans', in William S. Penn, ed., *As We Are Now: Mixedblood Essays on Race and Identity*. Berkeley, CA: University of California Press, 115–25.

Bleakley, Alan. 2000. *The Animalizing Imagination: Totemism, Textuality, and Eco-criticism*. New York: St. Martin's.

Bornstein, Kate. 2009. Lecture. University of Nevada, Las Vegas. Fall Semester.

Bowen, Murray. 1978. *Family Therapy in Clinical Practice*. New York: Jason Aronson.

Bowers, C. A., and Frédérique Apffel-Marglin, eds. 2005. *Rethinking Freire: Globalization and the Environmental Crisis*. Mahwah, NJ: Lawrence Erlbaum.

Bowers, Sharon Manybeads. 1992. 'Louise Erdrich as Nanapush', in Regina Barreca, ed., *New Perspectives on Women and Comedy*. Philadelphia: Gordon and Breach, 135–42.

Branch, Michael P., and Rochelle Johnson, et al., eds. 1998. *Reading the Earth: New Directions in the Study of Literature and Environment*. Moscow, ID: University of Idaho Press.

Brave Heart, Maria Yellow Horse. 2007. 'American Indian and Alaska Natives in Health Careers', www.aianhealthcareers.org. Accessed 20 February 2010.

—. 2005. 'From Intergenerational Trauma to Intergenerational Healing', Wellbriety Conference. Keynote Speaker. April 22. www.whitebison.org/magazine/2005/volume6/no6.htm. Accessed 20 February 2010.

—. 19 December 2010. 'Welcome to Takini's Historical Trauma', www.historicaltrauma.com. Accessed 20 February 2010.

Brown, Laura. 1995. 'Not Outside the Range: One Feminist Perspective on Psychic Trauma', in Cathy Caruth, *Trauma: Explorations in Memory*. Baltimore: Johns Hopkins University Press, 100–12.

Butler, Judith. 2003. 'Performative Acts and Gender Constitution: An Essay in Phenomenology and Feminist Theory', in Carole R. McCann and Seung-Kyung Kim, eds, *Feminist Theory Reader: Local and Global Perspectives*. New York: Routledge, 415–27.

Cajete, Gregory. 1999. *Native Science: Natural Laws of Interdependence*. Santa Fe: Clear Light.

—, ed. 1999. *A People's Ecology: Explorations in Sustainable Living*. Santa Fe: Clear Light.

Carpenter, Kristen A. 2006. 'Contextualizing the Losses of Allotment through Literature', *North Dakota Law Review*, 82, 605–26.

Caruth, Cathy. 1995. 'Recapturing the Past', in Cathy Caruth, *Trauma: Explorations in Memory*. Baltimore: Johns Hopkins University Press, 151–7.

—. ed. 1995. *Trauma: Explorations in Memory*. Baltimore: Johns Hopkins University Press.

—. 1996. *Unclaimed Experience: Trauma, Narrative, and History.* Baltimore: Johns Hopkins University Press.

Castillo, Susan Pérez. 1991. 'Postmodernism, Native American Literature and the Real: The Silko-Erdrich Controversy', *The Massachusetts Review*, 32(2), 285–94.

—. 1994. 'The Construction of Gender and Ethnicity in the Texts of Leslie Silko and Louise Erdrich', *The Yearbook of English Studies: Ethnicity and Representation in American Literature*, 24, 228–36.

Castor, Laura. 2004. 'Ecological Politics and Comic Redemption in Louise Erdrich's *The Antelope Wife*', *Nordlit: Arbeidstidsskrist I litteratur*, 15, 121–34.

Chapman, Allison A. 2007. 'Rewriting the Saints' Lives: Louise Erdrich's *The Last Report on the Miracles at Little No Horse*', *Critique*, 48(2), 149–67.

Chavkin, Allan, ed. 1999. *The Chippewa Landscape of Louise Erdrich*. Tuscaloosa, AL and London: University of Alabama Press.

Chavkin, Allan, and Nancy Feyl Chavkin. 1994. 'An Interview with Louise Erdrich' in Allan Chavkin and Nancy Feyl Chavkin, eds, *Conversations with Louise Erdrich and Michael Dorris*. Jackson, MS: University Press of Mississippi, 220–53.

Cheung, King-Kok. 1990. 'The Woman Warrior versus the Chinaman Pacific: Must a Chinese American Critic Choose Between Feminism and Heroism?' in Marianne Hirsch and Evelyn Fox Keller, eds, *Conflicts in Feminism*. New York: Routledge, 234–51.

Cobell versus Salazar. www.CobellSettlement.com. www.cobellsettlement.com/press/faq.php#settlement_1. Accessed 25 March 2010.

Cook-Lynn, Elizabeth. 1993. 'The American Indian Fiction Writer: "Cosmopolitanism, Nationalism, the Third World, and First Nation Sovereignty"', *Wičazo Ša Review*, 9(2), 26–36.

—. 1996. *Why I Can't Read Wallace Stegner and Other Essays: A Tribal Voice.* Madison, WI: University of Wisconsin Press.

Daly, Mathew. 2010. 'Senate looks at suicide on Indian reservations', *Native American Times*. www.nativetimes.com/index.php?option=com_content&view=article&id=3297:us-senate-looks-at-suicide-on-indian-reservations&catid=51&Itemid=27. Accessed 29 March 2010.

Debo, Angie. 1995 [1970]. *A History of the Indians of the United States*. London: Pimlico.

Deloria, Vine, Jr. 1969. *Custer Died for Your Sins: An Indian Manifesto.* New York: Macmillan.

—. 1999. 'Relativity, Relatedness and Reality', in Deloria et al., *Spirits and Reason: The Vine Deloria, Jr., Reader*. Golden, CO: Fulcrum.

Denham, Aaron. 2008. 'Rethinking Historical Trauma: Narrative of Resilience', *Transcultural Psychiatry*, 45(3), 391–414.

Deschenie, Tina. 2006. 'Historical Trauma: An Interview with Maria Yellow Horse Brave Heart', *Tribal College Journal*, 17(3), n. p. *Academic Search Premier*. Accessed 19 January 2010.

Di Prete, Laura. 2005. *Foreign Bodies: Trauma, Corporeality, and Textuality in Contemporary American Culture*. New York: Routledge.

Drengson, Alan, and Yuichi Inoue, eds. 1995. *The Deep Ecology Movement: An Introductory Anthology*. Berkeley, CA: North Atlantic.

Driskill, Qwo-Li. 2001. *Gender Talk*. Web Radio: Program #315. June 18. www.gendertalk.com/radio/programs/300/gt315.shtml. Accessed 25 October 2003.

Dubey, Madhu. 1994. *Black Women Novelists and the Nationalist Aesthetic*. Bloomington, IN: Indiana University Press.

Duran, Bonnie, Eduardo Duran and Maria Yellow Horse Brave Heart. 1998. 'Native Americans and the Trauma of History', in Russell Thorton, ed., *Studying Native America: Problems and Prospects*. Madison, WI: University of Wisconsin, 60–76.

Duthu, Bruce N. 2000. 'Incorporating Discourse in Federal Indian Law: Negotiating Tribal Sovereignty through the Lens of Native American Literature', *Harvard Human Rights Journal*, 13, 141–90.

Eastman, Charles. 1971. *Indian Boyhood*. New York: Dover.

Englebert, Omer. 1994. *The Lives of the Saints*. Trans. Christopher and Anne Fremantle. New York: Barnes and Noble Books.

Erickson, Kai. 1995. 'Notes on Trauma and Community', in Cathy Caruth, *Trauma: Explorations in Memory*. Baltimore: Johns Hopkins University Press, 183–99.

Essed, Philomena, and David Theo Goldberg, eds. 2002. *Race Critical Theories: Text and Context*. Malden, MA: Blackwell Publishers.

Fanon, Franz. 1967 [1952]. *Black Skin, White Masks*. Trans. Charles Lam Markmann. New York: Grove.

Flavin, Louise. 1995. 'Gender Construction amid Family Dissolution in Louise Erdrich's *The Beet Queen*', *Studies in American Indian Literatures*, 7(2), 17– 24.

Fleming, Pat, and Joanna Macy. 1995. 'The Council of All Beings' in Alan Drengson and Yuichi Inoue, eds, *The Deep Ecology Movement: An Introductory Anthology*. Berkeley, CA: North Atlantic, 226–36.

Foucault, Michel. 1986. 'Of Other Spaces', *Diacritics*, 16 (Spring), 22–7.

—. 1987. 'The Order of Discourse' in Robert Young, ed., *Untying the Text: A Post-Structuralist Reader*. London: Routledge and Kegan Paul, 48–78.

—. 1982. 'The Subject and Power' in Herbert L. Dreyfus and Paul Rabinow, eds, *Michel Foucault: Beyond Structuralism and Hermeneutics*. Brighton: Harvester Press, 208–6.

Friedman, Susan Stanford. 1994. 'Identity Politics, Syncretism, Catholicism, and Anishinabe Religion in Louise Erdrich's *Tracks*', *Religion and Literature*, 26(1), 107–33.

Gilbert, Roberta M. 2006. *The Eight Concepts of Bowen Theory*. Falls Church, VA: Leading Systems Press.

Gilmore, Leigh. 2008. 'What Do We Teach When We Teach Trauma?' in Miriam Fuchs and Craig Howes, eds, *Teaching Life, Writing Texts*. New York: MLA. 367–73.

Gleason, William. 2000. ' "Her Laugh an Ace": The Function of Humor in Louise Erdrich's *Love Medicine*', in Hertha D. Sweet Wong, ed., *Louise Erdrich's Love Medicine: A Casebook*. Oxford: Oxford University Press, 115–35.

Gould, L. Scott. 1996. 'The Consent Paradigm: Tribal Sovereignty at the Millennium', *Columbia Law Review*, 96(4), 809–902.

Grant, Herb. 2008. 'American Indians and Historical Trauma', *Illness, Crisis and Loss*, 16(2), 125–36.

Gross, Lawrence W. 2005. 'The Trickster and World Maintenance: An Anishinaabe Reading of Louise Erdrich's *Tracks*', *Studies in American Indian Literatures*, 17(3), 48–66.

Gulig, Anthony G., and Sidney L. Harring. 2002. '"An Indian Cannot Get a Morsel of Pork . . . ": A Retrospective on *Crow Dog, Lone Wolf, Blackbird*, Tribal Sovereignty, Indian Land, and Writing Indian Legal History', *Tulsa Law Review*, 38, 86–111.

Hafen, Clark. 2007. 'They Do Not Consider Themselves as Such', Seminar Paper for Dr. Tyler's ENG 277, University of California, Riverside. 15 December.

Hallowell, A. Irving. 1975. 'Ojibwa Ontology, Behavior, and World View', in Dennis Tedlock and Barbara Tedlock, eds, *Teachings from the American Earth: Indian Religion and Philosophy*. New York: Liveright, 141–78.

Hanafin, Patrick, Adam Gearey and Joseph Brooker. 2004. 'Introduction: On Writing: Law and Literature' in Hanafin et al. *Law and Literature*. Oxford and Malden, MA: Blackwell, 1–2.

Haraway, Donna. 2004. *The Haraway Reader*. New York: Routledge.

Hartman, Geoffrey. 1995. 'On Traumatic Knowledge and Literary Studies', *New Literary History*, 26, 537–63.

Heise, Ursula K. 2008. 'Eco-criticism and the Transnational Turn in American Studies', *American Literary History*, 20 (Spring/Summer), 381–404.

—. 2006. 'Greening English: Recent Introductions to Ecocriticism', *Contemporary Literature*, 47(2), 289–98.

—. 1997. 'Science and Ecocriticism', *The American Book Review*, 18(5). www. asle.org/site/resources/ecocritical-library/intro/science/. Accessed 12 June 2010.

Herdt, Gilbert. 1997. 'The Dilemmas of Desire: From Berdache to Two Spirit', in Sue-Ellen Jacobs, Wesley Thomas and Sabine Lang. *Two-Spirit People: Native American Gender Identity, Sexuality, and Spirituality*. Urbana, IL: University of Illinois Press, 276–83.

Hobson, Geary, ed. 1987 [1979]. *The Remembered Earth: An Anthology of Contemporary Native American Literature*. Albuquerque: University of New Mexico Press.

Horne, Dee. 2008. '"I Meant to Have but Modest Needs": Louise Erdrich's *The Last Report on the Miracles at Little No Horse*', in Brajesh Sawhney, ed., *Studies in the Literary Achievement of Louise Erdrich, Native American Writer: Fifteen Critical Essays*. Lewiston, NY: Edwin Mellen Press, 275–92.

Howe, LeAnne. 2002. 'The Story of America: A Tribalography', in Nancy Shoemaker, ed., *Clearing a Path: Theorizing the Past in Native American Studies*. New York: Routledge, 29–48.

Hughes, Sheila Hassell. 2004. 'Conversions and Incorporations: Crossing Genders and Religions with Louise Erdrich's Father Damien', in Cyriac K. Pullapilly, et al., eds, *Christianity and Native Cultures: Perspectives from Different Regions of the World*. Notre Dame, IN: Cross Cultural, 597–626.

Huhndorf, Shari M. 2009. *Mapping the Americas: The Transnational Politics of Contemporary Native Culture.* Ithaca, NY: Cornell University Press.

Hynes, William J. 1993. 'Mapping the Characteristics of Mythic Tricksters: A Heuristic Guide', in William J. Hynes and William G. Doty, eds, *Mythical Trickster Figures: Contours, Contexts, and Criticisms.* Tuscaloosa, AL and London: University of Alabama Press, 33–45.

Iovannone, J. James. 2009. '"Mix-Ups, Messes, Confinements, and Double-Dealings": Transgendered Performances in Three Novels by Louise Erdrich', *Studies in American Indian Literatures,* 21(1) (Spring), 38–68.

Ishizawa, Jorge. n.d. 'Between Scylla and Charybdis: The Vicissitudes of a Postgraduate Curriculum Based on Andean Campesino Agriculture', *The EcoJustice Review.* www.ecojusticeeducation.org/index.php?option=com_content&task=view&id=28&Itemid=49. Accessed 23 June 2009.

—. 2006. 'What Next? From Andean Cultural Affirmation to Andean Affirmation of Cultural Diversity – Learning with the Communities in the Central Andes', Draft Thematic Paper for What Next Forum, 1 September Dag Hammarskjöld Foundation. *www.dhf.uu.se/whatnext/papers_public/Ishizawa-Draft-01Sep2006.pdf.* Accessed 25 June 2009.

Jacobs, Connie A. 2001. *The Novels of Louise Erdrich: Stories of Her People.* New York: Peter Lang.

Jacobs, Sue-Ellen, Wesley Thomas and Sabine Lang. 1997. *Two-Spirit People: Native American Gender Identity, Sexuality, and Spirituality.* Urbana, IL: University of Illinois Press.

—. Message to Cynthia Bailin. 12 December 2009. E-mail.

'Jewish Museum, Berlin, Daniel Libeskind 1998'. *Galinsky.* www.galinsky.com/buildings/jewishmuseum. Accessed 26 March 2010.

Jahner, Elaine A. 2000. 'Trickster Discourse and Postmodern Strategies', in A. Robert Lee, ed., *Loosening the Seams: Interpretations of Gerald Vizenor.* Bowling Green, OH: Bowling Green State University Popular Press, 38–58.

Keenan, Deirdre. 2006. 'Unrestricted Territory: Gender, Two Spirits, and Louise Erdrich's *The Last Report on the Miracles at Little No Horse*', *American Indian Culture and Research Journal,* 30(2), 1–15.

Kerr, Michael E., and Murray Bowen. 1988. *Family Evaluation: An Approach Based on Bowen Theory.* New York: Norton.

Kidwell, Clara Sue. 2009. 'American Indian Studies: Intellectual Navel Gazing or Academic Discipline?' *The American Indian Quarterly,* 33(1) (Winter), 1–17.

Kim, Daniel Y. 2005. *Writing Manhood in Black and Yellow: Ralph Ellison, Frank Chin, and the Literary Politics of Identity.* Stanford, CA: Stanford University Press.

King, Thomas. 1990. 'Godzilla vs. Post-Colonial', *World Literature Written in English,* 30(2), 10–16.

Kinsey, Alfred C., Wardell B. Pomeroy, and Clyde E. Martin. 1948. Chapter 21. *Sexual Behavior in the Human Male.* Philadelphia: W. B. Saunders. Rpt. in Ron Schow, Wayne Schow, and Marybeth Raynes, eds., Appendix I. *Peculiar People: Mormons and Same-Sex Orientation.* Salt Lake City, UT: Signature, 1991, 341–58.

Knapp, John V., and Kenneth Womack. 2003. *Reading the Family Dance: Family Systems Therapy and Literary Study*. Newark, NJ: University of Delaware Press.

Krogseng, Kari. 2000. 'Minnesota v. Mille Lacs Band of Chippewa Indians', *Ecology Law Quarterly*, 27, 771–97.

Krupat, Arnold. 2002. *Red Matters: Native American Studies*. Philadelphia: U of Pennsylvania P.

—. 1996. *The Turn to the Native: Studies in Criticism and Culture*. Lincoln, NE: University of Nebraska Press.

Krystal, Henry. 1995. 'Trauma and Aging: A Thirty-Year Follow-Up', in Cathy Caruth, *Trauma: Explorations in Memory*. Baltimore: Johns Hopkins University Press, 76–99.

LaCapra, Dominick. 1994. *Representing the Holocaust: History, Theory, Trauma*. Ithaca, NY: Cornell University Press.

—. 2001. *Writing History, Writing Trauma*. Baltimore: Johns Hopkins University Press.

LaDuke, Winona. 1999. *All Our Relations: Native Struggles for Land and Life*. Cambridge, MA: South End Press.

Larson, Sidner. 1993. 'The Fragmentation of a Tribal People in Louise Erdrich's *Tracks*', *American Indian Culture and Research Journal*, 17(2), 1–13.

—. 1997. 'Fear and Contempt: A European Concept of Property', *American Indian Quarterly*, 21(4), 567–77.

Ledwon, Lenora. 1997. 'Native American Life Stories and "Authorship": Legal and Ethical Issues', *American Indian Quarterly*, 21(4), 579–93.

Lincoln, Kenneth. 1993. *Indi'n Humor: Bicultural Play in Native America*. Oxford: Oxford University Press.

Lipsitz, George. 1998. *The Possessive Investment in Whiteness: How White People Profit from Identity Politics*. Philadelphia: Temple University Press.

Lister, Rachel. 2008. ' "Power from the In-Between": Dialogic Encounters in *The Antelope Wife* and *The Last Report on the Miracles at Little No Horse*', in Brajesh Sawhney, ed., *Studies in the Literary Achievement of Louise Erdrich, Native American Writer: Fifteen Critical Essays*. Lewiston, NY: Edwin Mellen Press, 213–31.

Lone Wolf versus Hitchcock. 1903. 187 U.S. 553. *http://caselaw.lp.findlaw.com/scripts/getcase.pl?court=US&vol=187&invol=553*. Accessed 25 March 2010.

Maracle, Lee. 1996. *I Am Woman: A Native Perspective on Sociology and Feminism*. Vancouver, BC: Press Gang Publishers.

Marshall, Leni. 2007. 'Kiss of the Spider Woman: Native American Storytellers and Cultural Transmission', *Journal of Aging, Humanities, and the Arts*, 1(1—2), 35–52.

Matchie, Thomas. 2003. 'Miracles at Little No Horse: Louise Erdrich's Answer to Sherman Alexie's *Reservation Blues*', *North Dakota Quarterly*, 70(2), 151–62.

Mathews, Freya. 1995. 'Conservation and Self-Realization: A Deep Ecology Perspective' in Alan Drengson and Yuichi Inoue, eds, *The Deep Ecology Movement: An Introductory Anthology*. Berkeley, CA: North Atlantic, 124–35.

Maxmen, Jerrold S., Nicholas G. Ward and Mark Kilgus. 2009. *Essential Psychopathology and Its Treatment*. 3rd ed. New York: Norton.

McCafferty, Kate. 1997. 'Generative Adversity: Shapeshifting Pauline/Leopolda in *Tracks* and *Love Medicine*', *American Indian Quarterly*, 21(4) (Autumn), 729–51.

McLaughlin, Andrew. 1995. 'For a Radical Ecocentrism', in Alan Drengson and Yuichi Inoue, eds, *The Deep Ecology Movement: An Introductory Anthology*. Berkeley, CA: North Atlantic, 257–80.

McNally, Michael. 2000. *Ojibwe Singers: Hymns, Grief, and a Native Culture in Motion*. New York: Oxford University Press.

Medicine, Beatrice. 1983. ' "Warrior Women" – Sex Role Alternatives for Plains Indian Women' in Patricia Albers, and Beatrice Medicine, eds., *The Hidden Half: Studies of Plains Indian Women*. Lanham, MD: University Press of America., 267–80.

Meeker, Joseph W. 1997. *The Comedy of Survival: Literary Ecology and a Play Ethic*. Tucson, AZ: University of Arizona Press.

Meisenhelder, Susan. 1994. 'Race and Gender in Louise Erdrich's *The Beet Queen*', *ARIEL: A Review of International English Literature*, 25(1) (January), 45–57.

Meyer, Melissa L. 1994. *The White Earth Tragedy: Ethnicity and Dispossession at a Minnesota Anishinaabe Reservation, 1889–1920*. Lincoln, NE and London: University of Nebraska Press.

Miller, Susan A. 2008. 'Native America Writes Back: The Origin of the Indigenous Paradigm in Historiography', *Wičazo Ša Review*, 23(2) (Fall), 9–28.

—. 2009. 'Native Historians Write Back: The Indigenous Paradigm in American Indian Historiography', *Wičazo Ša Review*, 24(1) (Spring), 25–45.

Minnesota versus Mille Lacs Band of Chippewa Indians. 1999. No. 97–1337. www.law.cornell.edu/supct/html/97-1337.ZS.html. Accessed 25 March 2010.

Miranda, Deborah. 2003. E-mail to Patrice Hollrah. Accessed 25 October.

Morace, Robert A. 1999. 'From Sacred Hoops to Bingo Palaces: Louise Erdrich's Carnivalesque Fiction', in Allan Chavkin ed., *The Chippewa Landscape of Louise Erdrich*. Tuscaloosa, AL and London: University of Alabama Press, 36–66.

Murphy, Patrick D. 1995. *Literature, Nature, and Other: Ecofeminist Critiques*. New York: SUNY Press.

Nichols, Michael P. 2007. *The Essentials of Family Therapy*. 3rd ed. Boston: Pearson.

NIV Study Bible, rev. ed. 2002. Kenneth L. Barker, gen. ed. Grand Rapids, MI: Zondervan.

Noori, Margaret. 2010. 'Review of *Shadow Tag* by Louise Erdrich', *Studies in American Indian Literatures*, 22(2) (Summer), 89–96.

Nuclear Information and Resource Service, 'Environmental Racism, Tribal Sovereignty, and Nuclear Waste'. www.nirs.org/factsheets/pfsejfactsheet.htm. Accessed 14 April 2010.

Orban, Maria and Alan Velie. 2003. 'Religion and Gender in *The Last Report on the Miracles at Little No Horse*', *European Review of Native American Studies*, 17(2), 27–34.

Ortiz, Simon J. 1981. 'Towards a National Indian Literature: Cultural Authenticity in Nationalism', *MELUS*, 8(2) (Summer), 7–12.

—. 2002. 'History's Midst', *Out There Somewhere*. Tucson, AZ: University of Arizona, 16.

Owens, Louis. 2001. 'As If an Indian Were Really an Indian: Native American Voices and Postcolonial Theory' in Gretchen M. Bataille, ed., *Native American Representations: First Encounters, Distorted Images, and Literary Appropriations*. Lincoln, NE: University of Nebraska Press, 11–24.

—. 1994. *Other Destinies: Understanding the American Indian Novel*. Norman, OK: University of Oklahoma Press.

Palacios, Janelle F., and Carmen J. Portillo. 2009. 'Understanding Native Women's Health: Historical Legacies', *Journal of Transcultural Nursing*, 20(1), 15–27.

PARR. *Protect Americans' Rights and Resources*. http://www.parr1.com/. Accessed 30 March 2010.

Peat, F. David. 2002. *Blackfoot Physics: A Journey into the Native American Universe*. Grand Rapids, MI: Phanes.

Pérez, Emma. 1999. *The Decolonial Imaginary: Writing Chicanas into History*. Bloomington, IN: Indiana University Press.

Peterson, Nancy J. 1999. 'Indi'n Humor and Trickster Justice in *The Bingo Palace*', in Allan Chavkin, ed., *The Chippewa Landscape of Louise Erdrich*. Tuscaloosa, AL and London: University of Alabama Press, 161–81.

Phillips, Dana. 1999. 'Eco-criticism, Literary Theory, and the Truth of Ecology', *New Literary History*, 30(3) (Summer), 577–602.

Pollock, Mary S., and Catherine Rainwater, eds. 2005. *Figuring Animals: Essays on Animal Images in Art, Literature, Philosophy, and Popular Culture*. New York: Palgrave/Macmillan and St. Martin's Press.

Prince-Hughes, Tara. 2000. 'Worlds in and out of Balance: Alternative Genders and Gayness in the *Almanac of the Dead* and *The Beet Queen*', in Michael J. Meyer, ed., *Literature and Homosexuality*. Amsterdam: Rodopi, 1–21.

Prochaska, James O., and John C. Norcross. 2007. *Systems of Psychotherapy: A Transtheoretical Analysis*. 6th ed. Belmont, CA: Thomson Brooks/Cole.

Pulitano, Elvira. 2003. *Toward a Native American Critical Theory*. Lincoln, NE: University of Nebraska Press.

Purdy, John. 1999. 'Against All Odds: Games of Chance in the Novels of Louise Erdrich', in Allan Chavkin ed., *The Chippewa Landscape of Louise Erdrich*. Tuscaloosa, AL and London: University of Alabama Press, 8–35.

Rader, Pamela. 2007. 'Dis-robing the Priest: Gender and Spiritual Conversions in Louise Erdrich's *The Last Report on the Miracles at Little No Horse*', in Jeana DelRosso, Leigh Eicke, and Ana Kothe, eds, *The Catholic Church and Unruly Women Writers*. New York: Palgrave Macmillan, 221–35.

Rainwater, Catherine. 1990. 'Reading between Worlds: Narrativity in the Fiction of Louise Erdrich', *American Literature*, 62(3), 405–22.

—. 2005. 'Who May Speak for the Animals? Deep Ecology in Linda Hogan's *Power* and A. A. Carr's *Eye Killers*', in Mary S. Pollock and Catherine Rainwater, eds, *Figuring Animals: Essays on Animal Images in Art, Literature, Philosophy, and Popular Culture*. New York: Palgrave/Macmillan and St. Martin's Press, 261–80.

Rapaport, Herman. 1968. *Between the Sign and the Gaze*. Ithaca, NY: Cornell University Press.

Ruoff, A. LaVonne. 1999. 'Afterword', in Allan Chavkin ed., *The Chippewa Landscape of Louise Erdrich*. Tuscaloosa, AL and London: University of Alabama Press, 182–8.

Said, Edward W. 1993. *Culture and Imperialism*. New York: Knopf.

Sawhney, Brajesh, ed. 2008. *Studies in the Literary Achievement of Louise Erdrich, Native American Writer: Fifteen Critical Essays*. Lewiston, NY: Edwin Mellen Press.

Scarberry-García, Susan. 2004. 'Beneath Creaking Oaks: Spirits and Animals in *Tracks*', in Greg Sarris, Connie A. Jacobs and James R. Giles, eds, *Approaches to Teaching the Works of Louise Erdrich*. New York: MLA, 42–50.

Schwarz, Maureen Trudelle. 2001. *Navajo Lifeways: Contemporary Issues, Ancient Knowledge*. Norman, OK: University of Oklahoma Press.

Seibert, April L. 2003. 'Who Defines Tribal Sovereignty? An Analysis of *United States v. Lara*', *American Indian Law Review*, 28(2), 393–412.

Shiva, Vandana. 1999. *Biopiracy: The Plunder of Nature and Knowledge*. Cambridge, MA: South End.

—. 2005. *Earth Democracy: Justice, Sustainability, and Peace*. Cambridge, MA: South End.

Silko, Leslie Marmon. 1986. 'Here's an odd artifact for the fairy tale shelf', *Studies in American Indian Literatures*, 10(4), 178–84.

Singel, Wenona T., and Matthew L. M. Fletcher. 2006. 'Indian Treaties and the Survival of the Great Lakes', *Michigan State Law Review*, 5, 1285–97.

Smith, Linda Tuhiwai. 1999. *Decolonizing Methodologies: Research and Indigenous Peoples*. New York: St. Martin's.

Soliz, Cristine, and Harold Joseph. 2009. 'Native American Literature, Ceremony, and Law', in Austin Sarat, Catherine Frank and Matthew Anderson, eds, *Options for Teaching Literature and Law*. New York: MLA. http://ssrn.com/abstract=1320322. Accessed 1 January 2011.

Stannard, David E. 1993. *American Holocaust: The Conquest of the New World*. Oxford and New York: Oxford University Press.

Stirrup, David. 2010. *Louise Erdrich*. Manchester: Manchester Union Press.

Stoler, Ann Laura. 2002. *Carnal Knowledge and Imperial Power*. Berkeley, CA: University of California Press.

Tal, Kalí. 1996. *Worlds of Hurt: Reading the Literatures of Trauma*. New York: Cambridge University Press.

Tatonetti, Lisa. 2009. 'The Both/And of American Indian Literary Studies', *Western American Literature*, 44(3) (Fall), 276–88.

Tedlock, Dennis, and Barbara Tedlock, eds. 1975. *Teachings from the American Earth: Indian Religion and Philosophy*. New York: Liveright.

Thomas, Brook. 1987. *Cross Examination of Law and Literature: Cooper, Hawthorne, Stowe, and Melville*. NY and Cambridge. Cambridge University Press.

Titelman, Peter, ed. 2003. *Emotional Cutoff: Bowen Family Systems Theory Perspectives*. New York: Haworth.

—. 2008. *Triangles: Bowen Family Systems Theory Perspectives*. New York: Haworth.

Treuer, David. 2006. *Native American Fiction: A User's Manual.* St. Paul, MN: Graywolf Press.

Trigger, Bruce G., and Wilcomb E. Washburn. 1996. *The Cambridge History of the Native Peoples of the Americas.* North America. Vol. 2. New York: Cambridge University Press.

Turner, Victor. 1969. *The Ritual Process: Structure and Anti-Structure.* Chicago: Aldine Publishing. Excerpted in Michael Lembek, ed. 2002. *A Reader in the Anthropology of Religion.* Malden, MA: Blackwell, 358–73.

Utter, Jack. 1993. *American Indians: Answers to Today's Questions.* Lake Ann, MI: National Woodlands Publishing Company.

Van Der Kolk, Bessel A., and Onno Van Der Hart. 1995. 'The Intrusive Past: The Flexibility of Memory and the Engraving of Trauma', in Cathy Caruth, *Trauma: Explorations in Memory,* Baltimore: Johns Hopkins University Press, 158–82.

Van Dyke, Annette. 2008. 'A Hope for Miracles: Shifting Perspectives in Louise Erdrich's *The Last Report on the Miracles at Little No Horse*', in Brajesh Sawhney, ed., *Studies in the Literary Achievement of Louise Erdrich, Native American Writer: Fifteen Critical Essays.* Lewiston, NY: Edwin Mellen Press, 63–74.

Van Styvendale, Nancy. 2008. 'The Trans/Historicity of Trauma in Jeannette Armstrong's *Slash* and Sherman Alexie's *Indian Killer*', *Studies in the Novel,* 40(1/2), 203–23.

Vasquez, Grimaldo Rengifo. 2005. 'Nurturance in the Andes', in C. A. Bowers and Frédérique Apffel-Marglin, eds, *Rethinking Freire: Globalization and the Environmental Crisis.* Mahwah, NJ: Lawrence Erlbaum, 31–48.

Velie, Alan. 1989. 'The Trickster Novel', in Gerald Vizenor, ed., *Narrative Chance: Postmodern Discourse on Native American Indian Literatures.* Norman, OK: University of Oklahoma, 121–39.

Vizenor, Gerald. 1994. *Manifest Manners: Postindian Warriors of Survivance.* Hanover, NH: Wesleyan University Press.

—. 1999. *Manifest Manners: Narrative on Postindian Survivance.* Lincoln, NE: University of Nebraska Press.

—. 1989. 'Minnesota Chippewa: Woodland Treaties to Tribal Bingo', *American Indian Quarterly,* 13(1), 30–57.

—. 1989. 'Trickster Discourse: Comic Holotropes and Language Games', in Gerald Vizenor, *Narrative Chance: Postmodern Discourse on Native American Indian Literatures.* Albuquerque, NM: University of New Mexico, 187–211.

—. 2008. 'Aesthetics of Survivance: Literary Theory and Practice', in Gerald Vizenor, ed., *Survivance: Narratives of Native Presence.* Lincoln, NE: University of Nebraska Press, 1–23.

Vizenor, Gerald, and A. Robert Lee. 1999. *Postindian Conversations.* Lincoln, NE: University of Nebraska Press.

Ward, Ian. 1995. *Law and Literature: Possibilities and Perspectives.* New York and Cambridge: Cambridge University Press.

Warrior, Robert, Jace Weaver, and Craig Womack. 2006. *American Indian Literary Nationalism.* Albuquerque, NM: University of New Mexico Press.

Weaver, Jace. 2001. *Other Words: American Indian Literature, Law, and Culture.* Norman, OK: University of Oklahoma Press.

Whitbeck, Les B., and Gary W. Adams, Dan R. Hoyt, and Xiaojin Chen. 2004. 'Conceptualizing and Measuring Historical Trauma Among American Indian People', *American Journal of Community Psychology*, 33(3/4), 119–29.

White, James Boyd. 1985 [1973]. *The Legal Imagination.* Rpt. Chicago and London: University of Chicago Press.

—. 2000 [1999]. *From Expectation to Experience: Essays on Law and Legal Education.* Rpt. Ann Arbor, MI. University of Michigan Press.

Wilson, Robert Rawdon. 1989. 'SLIP PAGE: Angela Carter, In/Out/In the Postmodern Nexus', *Ariel*, 20(4), 96–114.

Wolfe, Cary. 2003. 'Introduction', in Cary Wolfe, ed., *Zoontologies: The Question of the Animal.* Minneapolis, MN: University of Minnesota Press, ix–xxiii.

—. 2008. 'Learning from Temple Grandin, Or, Animal Studies, Disability Studies, and Who Comes After the Subject', *New Formations*, 64 (Spring), 110–23.

Womack, Craig S. 2008. 'A Single Decade: Book-Length Native Literary Criticism between 1986 and 1997', in Janice Acoose, et al., *Reasoning Together: The Native Critics Collective*, Craig S. Womack, et al., eds. Norman, OK: University of Oklahoma Press, 3–104.

—. 1999. *Red on Red: Native American Literary Separatism.* Minneapolis, MN: University of Minnesota Press.

Woodward, Kenneth L. 1996. *Making Saints: How the Catholic Church Determines Who Becomes a Saint, Who Doesn't, and Why.* New York: Touchstone.

Young, Robert J. C. 1995. *Colonial Desire: Hybridity in Theory, Culture and Race.* London and New York: Routledge.

Further Reading

Louise Erdrich is among the most written-about of Native American writers and her work has been studied from very diverse perspectives. The chapters included in this book present some of the more dominant approaches (tribal, environmental, gender and sexuality, postcolonial and critical race theory, psychoanalytic, and the like) to highlight the importance of such issues as law, religion, humour, narrative technique and literary language in her novels. Many of the important book-length studies about Erdrich have also already been cited. However, it is worth describing some of the features of these books that are of general interest to the reader of Erdrich. An indispensable reference for the reader coming to Erdrich's writing for the first time is *A Reader's Guide to the Novels of Louise Erdrich*, edited by Peter G. Beidler and Gay Barton (2nd ed. 2006). The editors are concerned to explain the details of Erdrich's work that might escape an uninitiated reader such as the geography or cartography of her fictional settings, the Ojibwe words and expressions she uses, and the tribal/family genealogies of her characters. Other helpful resources for the uninitiated reader are Lorena Stookey's bio-bibliographical guide, *Louise Erdrich: A Critical Companion* (1999), *which appears* in Greenwood Press's Critical Companions to Popular Contemporary Writers series, and Jennifer Fleischner's *A Reader's Guide to the Fiction of Louise Erdrich* (1994). A further useful book that comprises primary rather than critical material, and so offers valuable contextual and biographical information, is the collection of interviews with Erdrich and her first husband, Michael Dorris, edited by Allan Chavkin and Nancy Feyl Chavkin (1994).

Approaches to Teaching the Works of Louise Erdrich, edited by Greg Sarris, Connie A. Jacobs and James Richard Giles (2005), takes a pedagogical approach to Erdrich's writing and consequently is addressed primarily to teachers of Erdrich's writing; however, the essays collected in this volume offer helpful insights into individual texts as well as points of interconnection among Erdrich's works. *The Chippewa Landscape of*

Louise Erdrich, edited by Allan Chavkin (1999), also takes a closely defined approach to Erdrich's work, focusing upon her literary use of her Ojibwe heritage. There is no thematic focus to the collection of essays edited by Brajesh Sawhney, *Studies in the Literary Achievement of Louise Erdrich, Native American Writer* (2008), which results in a wide-ranging selection of critical essays that address both the entire Erdrich oeuvre and the diversity of issues her work engages. In contrast, the essays included in the collection *Louise Erdrich's Love Medicine: A Casebook*, edited by Hertha D. Sweet Wong (1999), discuss only her first novel; however, there is much to be learned from the critical perspectives employed that is applicable to her later fiction. The same is true of P. Jane Hafen's short study, *Reading Louise Erdrich's Love Medicine* (2003), which appears in the Boise State University Western Writers Series.

Connie A. Jacobs' study, *The Novels of Louise Erdrich: Stories of Her People* (2001), focuses on Erdrich's techniques as a storyteller and offers insights into the narrative dimensions of her early novels. Fabienne C. Quennet, in *Where 'Indians' Fear to Tread?: A Postmodern Reading of Louise Erdrich's North Dakota Quartet* (2001) discusses *Love Medicine*, *The Beet Queen*, *Tracks* and *The Bingo Palace* within the context of postmodern and Native/mainstream narrative aesthetics. The most recent book-length treatment of Erdrich's entire oeuvre is David Stirrup's highly readable, though challenging, *Louise Erdrich* (2010). Stirrup engages with Erdrich's achievements in all genres – fiction, poetry, memoir and children's literature – as a dialogue between her Ojibway and American heritages, focussing on issues of ethics and aesthetics.

Special journal issues on Erdrich have appeared in *Studies in American Indian Literatures* (https://facultystaff.richmond.edu/~rnelson/asail/): 9(1) (Winter 1985), which is a special issue on *Love Medicine*; the linked special issues on her writing more generally are 3(4) (Winter 1991) and 4(1) (Spring 1992); and 12(2) (Summer 2000). Among sources of tribal cultural and historical information that is relevant to Erdrich's work, Anton Treuer's *Ojibwe in Minnesota* (2010) is both readable and informative.

Online sources include 'Louise Erdrich: The Online Guide', maintained by Joe Buenker at Arizona State University (www.west.asu.edu/jbuenke/erdrich/index.html), which is particularly useful for bibliographical information. Buenker's alphabetized list of the 584 instances where a short story by Erdrich has appeared in an anthology (which are not listed in the primary bibliography above) is a valuable resource for readers who wish to locate the original stories that have been incorporated into Erdrich's novels. The 'Voices from the Gaps' (voices.cla.umn.edu/ artistpages/erdrichLouise.php) page devoted to Erdrich provides,

in addition to bio-bibliographical information, a short critical introduction to her work. A fascinating 2010 interview with Henry Louis
Gates, Jr. in the 'Faces of America' series is available on video at: www.
pbs.org/wnet/ facesofamerica/profiles/louise-erdrich/10/.

Readers who want to pursue further some of the theoretical contexts
explored in the chapters of this book may find the following readings
useful. In the field of Trauma Studies, the work of Sigmund Freud is
indispensable and his collected works are required reading: *The Standard Edition of the Complete Psychological Works of Sigmund Freud*, trans.
James Strachey. 24 vols. (1920, rpt. 1955). Among recent theories of
historical trauma, Robert Jay Lifton's *The Broken Connection: On Death
and the Continuity of Life* (1979) is usefully read in conjunction with the
essays collected by Cathy Caruth in *Trauma: Explorations in Memory*.
On the issue of textual testimony and literature as a medium in which
trauma can be effectively communicated, Shoshana Felman and Dori
Laub's co-authored book, *Testimony: Crises of Witnessing in Literature,
Psychoanalysis, and History* (1992), is required reading. Foundational to
critical approaches to Native American Literature using Critical Race
Theory are Richard Delgado and Jean Stefancic's *Critical Race Theory:
An Introduction* (2001), David Theo Goldberg's *Racist Culture: Philoso-
phy and the Politics of Meaning* (1994) and *Crossroads, Directions, and a
New Critical Race Theory* (2002), edited by Francisco Valdes, Jerome
McCristal Culp and Angela P. Harris. As Mark Shackleton remarks in
his chapter above, the theorist whose work informs this area is Michel
Foucault, whose *The History of Sexuality* Vol.1. trans. Robert Hurley
(1978, rpt. 1984) is a useful starting-point. Important work in the field
of ecocriticism and environmental justice that is relevant to Native literatures generally and the work of Louise Erdrich in particular include:
Joni Adamson's *American Indian Literature, Environmental Justice, and
Ecocriticism: The Middle Place* (2001) as well as the edited volume by
Michael P. Branch, et al., *Reading the Earth: New Directions in the Study
of Literature and Environment* (1998) and Donelle N. Dreese's *Ecocriticism: Creating Self and Place in Environmental and American Indian Literatures* (2002). Both Diane P. Freedman's 'Maternal Memoir as
Eco-Memoir', *ISLE: Interdisciplinary Studies in Literature and Environment*, 15(2) (Summer 2008), 47–58 and Lee Schweninger's *Listening to
the Land: Native American Literary Responses to the Landscape* (2008)
discuss Erdrich's *The Blue Jay's Dance* (1995) in the context of environmentalism. The essay by Peter G. Beidler – ' "The Earth Itself Was Sob-
bing": Madness and the Environment in Novels by Leslie Marmon Silko
and Louise Erdrich', *American Indian Culture and Research Journal*,
26(3) (2002), 113–24 – is a helpful complement to Catherine Rainwater's chapter in the present volume.

Notes on Contributors

Volume Editor

Deborah L. Madsen is Professor of American Literature and Culture at the University of Geneva and life member of Clare Hall, University of Cambridge. Her research focuses on issues of settler-nationalism, indigeneity, and migration, exemplified by her work on American Exceptionalism and the ideology of Manifest Destiny. Publications include *Allegory in America: From Puritanism to Postmodernism* (1996), *American Exceptionalism* (1998), *Beyond the Borders: American Literature and Post-Colonial Theory* (ed. 2003), *Understanding Gerald Vizenor* (2009), *Native Authenticity: Transatlantic Approaches to Native American Literature* (ed. 2010), and *Gerald Vizenor: Texts and Contexts* (co-ed. 2011). She is co-editor of two book series: 'Companions to Native Literatures' (University of Nebraska Press) and 'Native Traces' (State University of New York Press). Currently she serves as President of the Swiss Association for North American Studies (SANAS), on the International Committee of the American Studies Association (ASA), and on the Editorial Advisory Committee of PMLA.

Contributors

Allan Chavkin is Professor of English at Texas State University–San Marcos, where he teaches courses on American literature. He has published numerous articles on American writers in such journals as *Philological Quarterly, Comparative Literature Studies, Papers on Language and Literature*, and *Studies in the Novel*. His books include *The Chippewa Landscape of Louise Erdrich* (1999); *Conversations with Louise Erdrich and Michael Dorris* (1994); *Leslie Marmon Silko's Ceremony: A Casebook* (2002); *Conversations with John Gardner* (1990); and *English Romanticism and Modern Fiction: A Collection of Critical Essays* (1992). His book *Saul Bellow* is forthcoming from

Salem Press. His research has been supported by grants from the National Endowment for the Humanities, the American Council for Learned Societies, and the American Philosophical Association. He is the recipient of Texas State's Presidential Award for Excellence in Scholarship.

Nancy Feyl Chavkin is Regents' Professor of Social Work and Director of the Center for Children and Families at Texas State University–San Marcos, where she specializes in interdisciplinary research and community partnerships. She has published articles on family systems theory and social issues in literature, family-school-community partnerships, and child welfare. Her books include *Conversations with Louise Erdrich and Michael Dorris* (1994), *Families and Schools in a Pluralistic Society* (1993) and *The Use of Research in Social Work Practice* (1993). Her research has been supported by grants from the US Department of Education, US Department of Health and Human Services and others. She is the recipient of Texas State's Presidential Award for Excellence in Scholarship and the Minnie Stevens Piper Teaching Award for Excellence in Teaching.

John Gamber, an Assistant Professor of English and Ethnic Studies at Columbia University, received his BA from University of California, Davis, his MA from California State University, Fullerton (both in Comparative Literature), and his PhD in English from University of California, Santa Barbara. He co-edited *Transnational Asian American Literature: Sites and Transits* (2006), and has published articles about the novels of Gerald Vizenor (Anishinaabe), Louis Owens (Choctaw/Cherokee), and Craig Womack (Creek), among others, in several edited collections and journals including PMLA and MELUS. His monograph, entitled *Positive Pollutions and Cultural Toxins*, examines the role of waste and contamination in late-twentieth century US ethnic literatures and is forthcoming from the University of Nebraska Press.

P. Jane Hafen (Taos Pueblo) is a Professor of English at the University of Nevada, Las Vegas. She serves as an advisory editor of *Great Plains Quarterly*, on the Western Writers Series editorial board, the editorial board of Michigan State University Press, American Indian Series, on the board of the Charles Redd Center for Western Studies, and is an Associate Fellow at the Center for Great Plains Studies. She is a Frances C. Allen Fellow, D'Arcy McNickle Center for the History of the American

Indian, The Newberry Library and is a Clan Mother of the Native American Literature Symposium. She edited *Dreams and Thunder: Stories, Poems and The Sun Dance Opera by Zitkala-Ša* (2005), co-edited *The Great Plains Reader* (2003), and is author of *Reading Louise Erdrich's Love Medicine* (2003) and articles and book chapters about American Indian Literatures.

Patrice Hollrah is Director of the Writing Center and Instructor in the Department of English at the University of Nevada, Las Vegas. She is the author of *'The Old Lady Trill, the Victory Yell': The Power of Women in Native American Literature* (2003) and essays on such Native American authors as LeAnne Howe, Sherman Alexie, Louise Erdrich and Leslie Marmon Silko. Her research focuses upon Native American Literature, as well as Rhetoric and Composition, and she has interests in the fields of Women's Literature and the Novel.

Connie A. Jacobs is Professor Emerita from San Juan College in Farmington, NM, where she taught for 15 years. She is the author of *The Novels of Louise Erdrich: Stories of Her People* (2001) and *Teaching the Novels of Louise Erdrich* (2004), edited with Greg Sarris and James Giles. She and Debra Barker are currently working on an edited volume of essays that highlight under-represented American Indian writers. The purpose of the volume is to heighten awareness of the many voices of Native authors that deserve space in our classrooms. Jacobs presents regularly at MLA and NALS (Native American Literature Symposium) on Erdrich and Diné poets, Esther Belin and Luci Tapahonso. She served on MLA's Committee on Community Colleges 2007–2010. She is a member of the National Association of Ethnic Studies (NAES) where she is Vice President. Locally she is president of the Durango Adult Education Center.

Catherine Rainwater is a Professor of Literature at St. Edward's University in Austin, Texas. She is the author of numerous literary critical essays in books and in journals including *American Literature*, *Modern Fiction Studies*, *Mississippi Quarterly*, *Philological Quarterly*, and others. Her books include *Dreams of Fiery Stars: The Transformations of Native American Fiction* (1999), and *Figuring Animals: Essays on Animal Images in Art, Literature, Philosophy, and Popular Culture* (co-ed. 2005). She is a contributor to the *Cambridge Companion to Native American Literature* (2005), and the recipient of literary awards including the Norman

Foerster Prize for an essay on Louise Erdrich, and the Penelope Niven Creative Nonfiction Award. Her current work-in-progress includes an eco-critical study of contemporary Native American writing.

Mark Shackleton lectures at the Department of English, University of Helsinki, Finland and is Director of the University of Helsinki project 'Cross-Cultural Contacts: Diaspora Writing in English'. He has published on postcolonial writing as well as Native North American writing, including articles on Tomson Highway, Thomas King, Monique Mojica, Gerald Vizenor, Louise Erdrich, and Simon J. Ortiz.

David Stirrup is Director of the Centre for American Studies at the University of Kent at Canterbury, where he lectures in American Literature. His research currently focuses on twentieth-century Native American fiction, drawing on a wide range of contexts including Native American scholarship, politics, history, ethnography and some aspects of postcolonial theory. He is the author of *Louise Erdrich* (2010) and is currently working on a monograph on the representation of art in contemporary Native American literatures. Further research interests include cultural intersections at the Canada–US border; border studies; postcolonial and indigenist theory; and contemporary American and Canadian Literature. He is a committee member of the Native Studies Research Network, UK.

Gina Valentino is Assistant Professor at the University of Rhode Island. Her research interests in contemporary comparative ethnic and literary studies include class mobility, globalization and neoliberalism, gambling and US culture, American Indian, Asian American, African American and Chicana/o literatures. She is co-editor of *Transnational Asian American Literature: Sites and Transits* (2006). Her current book project, *Hustling: Work, Survival, and US Literature in the New Economy,* analyzes race and working-class identities in late-twentieth century US ethnic literatures.

Index